FROISSART: HISTORIAN

Froissart: Historian

Edited by J. J. N. Palmer

THE BOYDELL PRESS · ROWMAN & LITTLEFIELD

© Contributors 1981

Published by
The Boydell Press, an imprint of
Boydell & Brewer Ltd, PO Box 9, Woodbridge, Suffolk IP12 3DF
and
Rowman & Littlefield, 81 Adams Drive, Totowa, N.J. 07512, U.S.A

ISBN 0 85115 146 9
U.S. ISBN 0 8476 7029 5

British Library Cataloguing in Publication Data

Froissart.
 1. Froissart, Jean. Chroniques
 2. Hundred Years' War, 1339-1453
 3. France — History — House of Valois, 1328-1589
 4. Great Britain — History — 14th century
 5. Europe — History — 476-1492
 I. Palmer, J. J. N.
 944'.025   D113

ISBN 0 85115 146 9

Library of Congress
Catalog Card No.: 81-51602

Palmer, J.J.N., ed.

Froissart

Totowa, NJ: Rowman and Littlefield

256 p.

8106   810423

Printed in Great Britain by
St Edmundsbury Press, Bury St Edmunds, Suffolk

CONTENTS

LIST OF MAPS AND TABLES

Maps

Tables

LIST OF ABBREVIATIONS

AD	Archives départementales
AN	Archives nationales
BEC	*Bibliothèque de l'École des Chartes*
Berners	Froissart, *Chronicles*, trans. Lord Berners, ed. W. P. Ker. 6 vols. 1901-3
BM	Bibliothèque municipale
BN	Bibliothèque nationale
BIHR	*Bulletin of the Institute of Historical Research*
BJRL	*Bulletin of the John Rylands Library*
BL	British Library
CCR	*Calendar of Close Rolls*
CPR	*Calendar of Patent Rolls*
Cronyke	*Jehan Froissart's cronyke van Vlaenderen*, ed. N. de Pauw. Ghent, 1898
Diller	Froissart, *Chroniques*, ed. G. T. Diller. Geneva, 1972
Diverres	Froissart, *Voyage en Béarn*, ed. A. H. Diverres. Manchester, 1953
DNB	*Dictionary of National Biography*
EETS	Early English Text Society
EHR	*English Historical Review*
HMSO	Her Majesty's Stationery Office
Johnes	Froissart, *Chronicles*, trans. T. Johnes. 2 vols. 1839
KL	Froissart, *Oeuvres*, ed. Kervyn de Lettenhove. Brussels 1867-77
Le Bel	Jean le Bel, *Chronique*, ed. J. Viard and E. Déprez. 2 vols. 1904-5. SHF
Ord.	*Ordonnances des rois de France de la troisième race*, ed. D. F. Secousse *et al.* 23 vols. 1723-1849
Poésies	Froissart, *Poésies*, ed. A. Scheler. 3 vols. 1870-2
PRO	Public Record Office
RC	Record Commission
RH	*Revue historique*
RHS	Royal Historical Society
RP	*Rotuli Parliamentorum*, ed. J. Strachey *et al.* 7 vols. 1783-1832
RS	Rolls Series
SHF	Froissart, *Chroniques*, ed. S. Luce *et al.* Société de l'Histoire de France. 15 vols. 1869- (in progress)
TRHS	*Transactions of the Royal Historical Society*

Preface

THERE have been many biographical and literary studies of Jean Froissart but no previous full-length treatment of his work as an historian, an omission all the more to be regretted in view of the fact that he was the most prolific of all medieval historians and has always been one of the most widely read and loved. The immense scope of his *Chronicles* — covering as they do most of western Europe during the greater part of one of the most violent and eventful centuries of its history — is perhaps responsible for this neglect; and, certainly, the scholar who undertook to supply this omission single-handed must devote a lifetime to acquire the range of expertise required for the task. By pooling the talents of a team of English, French, Dutch and American historians, the present volume aims to examine the major areas treated by the *Chronicles* at a level which would be beyond the capacity of a single individual. In order to minimise the lack of coherence which often attends such cooperative enterprises, the essays have been commissioned on specified topics; and although the final form of the volume is not quite that originally envisaged, it is hoped that a reasonable balance has been struck between the different periods spanned by the *Chronicles* and the principal areas and themes with which Froissart was concerned. An effort has been made throughout to place the work of Froissart in the context of the best of modern historical scholarship, in the hope that the volume will be of equal value to those interested in Froissart as an historian, those wishing to use him as a source, and those concerned with the history of the first phase of the Hundred Years War.

I would like to thank all the contributors for their cooperation in the production of this volume. A particular debt is due to Mr Richard Barber, of the Boydell Press, at whose suggestion the project was originally undertaken and who throughout lent it his warm support. Finally, my friend, Dr J. L. Price, not only translated Dr van Herwaarden's contribution but, at even greater expense of his time and patience, offered much useful advice and criticism on several drafts of my own essay.

INTRODUCTION *

J. J. N. Palmer

AT the height of his career, Froissart expressed the hope that when he was 'dead and rotten' his 'noble history' would survive to immortalise him (XII, 2). Although the greater part of his historical output had yet to be produced when these words were penned (1388), his hopes of immortality already appeared to be well-founded, for by the 1380s he had established himself as an historian of European stature and as *the* historian of the epic struggle between the dynasties of Plantagenet and Valois for hegemony in western Europe. As early as 1381, the international significance of his work had been marked by the seizure by the French authorities of certain portions of the *Chronicles* destined for the king of England (Moranvillé 1887: 7); while towards the end of the decade the count of Foix observed that the *Chronicles* were destined to be 'more famous' than any other history he knew of, an observation recorded by Froissart himself with a justifiable complaisance (XII, 3). The roll-call of his noble patrons and of those members of the higher nobility known to have possessed copies of the *Chronicles*, serves to highlight their fame during Froissart's lifetime, as does the evident alacrity with which many of his contemporaries sought to ensure their personal immortality by regaling their author with accounts of events and feats of arms in which they had participated. As Froissart wryly remarked of one such encounter, his would-be informant seemed prepared to recount his entire life history and would no doubt have done so had he not been inopportunely summoned to the dinner table of the count of Foix, a summons which cheated him of immortality by half-an-hour.

The fame enjoyed by the *Chronicles* during their author's lifetime was, if anything, surpassed during the century after his death. The very large number of fifteenth-century manuscripts of this vast and highly expensive work are testimony to the regard in which it continued to be held, as are the care and expense lavished upon the illumination of many of these manuscripts, which represent some of the finest work of the miniaturists of the period. Linguistic difficulties and the dominance of the St Albans school of historical writing may — temporarily — have inhibited Froissart's influence in England, but on the continent it was more widespread than ever. Monstrelet, who paid him the supreme compliment of continuing and imitating his work, predicted that his 'renown on account of his excellent reputation will be of long duration' (Johnes 1849: 2); and the *Chronicles* were freely plundered by Waurin, by Zanfliet, by Jean de St Paul, and by the anonymous authors of the *Chronographia regum Francorum* and of

* All references to the *Chronicles* are to volume and page of the SHF edition unless otherwise stated.

Cotton MS Julius E VI, while other writers revealed both their appreciation and their indebtedness by interpolating Froissart's work, by epitomising it, or by 'correcting' it.[1]

The sheer bulk of the *Chronicles* and the linguistic problems they increasingly presented must have rendered them inaccessible to many sixteenth-century readers; but both obstacles to their continued influence were overcome with the advent of printing. No medieval author benefited more than did Froissart from this invention. In the quarter-century after 1495, the *Chronicles* went through at least ten editions; and the appearance of Sleidan's Latin abridgement — which was itself republished a dozen times and translated into English, French and Dutch — in 1537, made the work available to scholars and gentlemen throughout Europe. A Flemish translation had appeared as early as 1430, and the highly influential English translation of Lord Berners — which became 'common in mens hands' according to the Tudor antiquary John Stow (1574: viii) — was first published in 1523, to be shortly followed by a Spanish abridgement made by a secretary of the Emperor Charles V, by a modern French rendering, and, in 1559-61 and 1574, by the 'critical' editions of Denis Sauvage.

The greatly increased availability of the *Chronicles* is amply reflected in the humanist historical writing of the period. The temporary eclipse of Froissart's influence in England was ended for good. 'Read Froissart,' Caxton urged the gentlemen of England, and his advice was certainly heeded by English historians (Byles 1926: 123). Although Fabyan (d.1513) made somewhat sparing use of the *Chronicles*, his successors gave an increasingly larger part to this source in their accounts of the fourteenth century (Smith 1915: 43-59). The trend was set by Polydore Vergil's influential *Anglica Historia* (1534), and was followed in the histories of Edward Hall (1548), Grafton (1569) and Holinshed (1577). John Stow, indeed, accused Grafton of having plagiarised his entire history from Froissart and modern authors (McKisack 1971: 111-12), while Hall seems to have believed that Froissart was one of only two authors (the other being the *Brut*) worth consulting for the whole of the fourteenth and fifteenth centuries (ibid.: 106-7). As for Holinshed, his dependence upon Froissart for his lengthy account of the fourteenth century is almost total and extends not merely to his narrative of the foreign wars of Edward III and Richard II but even to the domestic histories of the reigns of those two kings.

A similar trend may be observed in French historical writing in the same period. The early humanist historians — Robert Gaguin (d.1501), Nicholas Gilles (d.1503), and Paulus Emilius (d.1529) — made frequent but selective use of Froissart; but by the second half of the sixteenth century, the *Chronicles* had come to dominate all narratives of the first part of the Hundred Years War. Alain Bouchart had, indeed, already shown the way in his popular *Grandes Cronicques de Bretaigne* (1514), and was followed in this respect by the equally popular history of D'Argentré (1582). The new trend was perhaps most clearly evidenced by a new edition of Gilles' influential *Chroniques et Annales* produced by Belleforest in 1573. Gilles' use of Froissart was not nearly as extensive as Belleforest thought to be appropriate, and he made dozens of corrections to Gilles' text in the light of information supplied by Froissart while noting that an even more thoroughgoing revision of Gilles' work could well be undertaken using the *Chronicles* as the main source.

2

The trends established in the sixteenth century set the basic pattern for the next century and a half. Although the historians of the seventeenth and early eighteenth centuries showed some discrimination in their use of the *Chronicles*, Froissart's narrative nevertheless dominated virtually all accounts of the fourteenth century. Only the most individual authors — such as Robert Brady — managed to escape this dominance; and such standard histories as those of Eudes de Mézeray (1643), De Choisy (1688), Daniel (1720) and Rapin (1724) in France, and of Sir Richard Baker (1643), Joshua Barnes (1688) and Lawrence Echard (1707) in England, took the *Chronicles* as their main source for both the foreign and domestic history of England and France in the fourteenth century, relegating all other chronicle and record sources for that period to the status of supplementary materials.

Even these modest restrictions to the influence of the *Chronicles* were markedly attenuated in the century or so after 1750. All of the popular and influential histories of the ages of Enlightenment and Romanticism took Froissart as their main, and often their only guide to the history of the fourteenth century. This was true of the histories of Tobias Smollett (1757), David Hume (1761), Oliver Goldsmith (1764), John Lingard (1819), James MacKintosh (1830) and Charles Dickens (1852) in England, and of D'Anquetil (1805), Barante (1820), Sismondi (1821) and of Jules Michelet (1837) in France, to name only the most widely read and most frequently republished of the general histories of the period. Dependence upon the *Chronicles* was carried to quite ludicrous extremes. Michelet, for instance, dismissed Froissart as 'this Walter Scott of the Middle Ages' (1879: 168) and then proceeded to base his very substantial narrative of the first half of the Hundred Years War almost exclusively upon the *Chronicles*, from which he quoted copiously, with barely a reference to other contemporary sources. Similarly, the philosophic Hume, while declaring that 'the numberless mistakes of Froissart, proceeding either from negligence, credulity or love of the marvellous, invalidate very much his testimony' (1825: 386), nevertheless went on to construct his entire narrative around the *Chronicles*, quoting them extensively and dissenting only over one or two details which had offended his patriotic (rather than his critical) sensibilities. His almost total dependence upon Froissart, however, did not preserve him from some somewhat agitated criticism from the pen of the greatest of eighteenth century French medievalists, La Curne de Saint-Palaye, to whom any criticism at all of Froissart was tantamount to *lèse-majesté*. La Curne's own 'excessive and unquestioning reliance upon the testimony of Froissart' (Gossman 1968: 245), so characteristic of his age, was — thanks to the success of his *Mémoires sur l'ancienne chevalerie* (1759) — responsible for providing generations of readers with a distorted and unbalanced view of medieval chivalry, a view derived in all its essentials from Froissart's *Chronicles*, thereby contributing in no small measure to the Romantic vogue for that work.

By this date Froissart had been elevated to the status of a classic, and no gentleman's library was complete without its copy of the *Chronicles* alongside the familiar historians of Greece and Rome. Men of letters such as Dickens and Thackeray, who showed no interest in other medieval writers, possessed one or more copies, and Froissart was the only medieval chronicler whom Hazlitt thought fit to recommend to his readers.[2] To the poet, Thomas Gray, he was 'the Herotodus of a Barbaric Age', who would have earned immortality had he only had the good fortune to write in Greek (Tovey 1912: 299); while the poet laureate Robert Southey prescribed a reading of the *Chronicles* as a recipe for writing good poetry in the modern age (Curry 1965: 148), advice followed half a century later by William Morris, in the *Defence of Guinevere* (1858).

Morris even projected an edition of the *Chronicles* by the Kelmscott Press, unfortunately never published.[3] This was only one of a number of similar projects by gentlemen and men of letters in this period. Lady Pomfret worked for two decades on a translation, still unfinished when she died in 1761 (Lewis 1962: 60), and Sir Walter Scott planned another,[4] declaring Froissart to be 'the most entertaining, and perhaps the most valuable historian of the Middle Ages' (1804-5: 347). Scott's remark was prompted by the appearance of the translation of Thomas Johnes (1803), which was to go through many reprints and editions in the next forty years, rivalling in popularity that of Lord Berners — reissued several times in this period — and making the *Chronicles* available to those men of letters to whom fourteenth-century French, or even sixteenth-century English and Latin, were increasingly inaccessible.

In France, too, at this time new editions and translations made the *Chronicles* available to a wider audience. Dacier (1742-1833) received the support of the government of Louis XVI for his projected edition (killed by the Revolution), while the editions of J. A. C. Buchon (1824-6, 1835) made the *Chronicles* available to his compatriots in a modernised French, and Leon Lacabane laboured for more than thirty years between the 1830s and 1860s to produce a critical edition, without result. Like their English counterparts, French savants and men of letters also showed an easy familiarity with Froissart, from the days of Montaigne onwards. Voltaire, indeed, appears to have been alone in having the temerity to discourse on the Middle Ages without first having read his Froissart, though even he sought to make use of the *Chronicles*, though at second-hand.[5] But Chateaubriand was more characteristic of his age in the extensive use he made of the *Chronicles* in his writings on manners, morals, Christianity and history. Like the poet Gray before him, and like Merimée, Taine and Wallon after him, Chateaubriand declared Froissart to be the Herodotus of the fourteenth century.[6]

The vogue for Froissart reached its peak in the decades around the middle of the nineteenth century, when a statue to him was erected in Valenciennes, his *Chronicles* were debated in the Belgian parliament, and Sainte-Beuve could declare that the reading of Froissart 'est désormais devenu vulgaire', a declaration supported by the steady stream of editions, translations, epitomes and 'stories rendered from' Froissart which issued from the presses of Europe and the United States from this time forward until well into the present century.[7]

But at a time when Froissart's popularity appeared to have reached its peak, his reputation received its first really serious setback for almost six centuries, at the hands of a new scientific school of historians. He had, of course, not been entirely immune from criticism in the intervening half millenium; but hitherto all such criticism had been casual and erratic, and had had no cumulative effect. By contrast, the attack of the scientific school of the late nineteenth century has been thorough, inexorable and, above all, systematic. Its inception can be dated with some precision to the latter part of the 1860s. It was heralded in 1868 by the work of Bertrandy on the war in Gascony between 1345 and 1346,[8] continued by the critical works of Plaine on the Breton wars from 1871 onwards, and crowned by the first truly critical editions of the *Chronicles*, the monumental editions of Kervyn de Lettenhove (1867-77) and of the Société de l'histoire de France (from 1869), whose copious scholarly annotation provides an almost line-by-line critique of the *Chronicles*.

Thereafter, attacks upon their accuracy and veracity have become legion and are scattered in scores of periodicals and hundreds of books on dozens of different subjects. One of the objects of the present volume is to synthesise some of this mass of material and to assess the value of the *Chronicles* in the light of the best of modern historical scholarship. But it is hoped that these essays will also do something to redeem Froissart's reputation. For the relentless exposure of his every mistake by several generations of historians, the rescue work done on other chronicle sources, and the intensive exploitation of the archives of western Europe in the past century have all contributed — despite the sympathetic biographies of Darmesteter (1895) and Shears (1930) — to diminish the apparent value of the *Chronicles* to an unacceptable degree, to a point, indeed, where the immortality that Froissart hoped for his work might appear to be seriously in jeopardy for the first time in over half a millenium.

Yet it would be more than premature to consign the *Chronicles* to a dusty oblivion. As readers in all ages have observed, they are as much a work of literature as of history and will continue to be read for pleasure long after much of the destructive criticism lavished upon them has been forgotten. Much of this criticism, moreover, can now be seen to have been misplaced, or at least exaggerated. Even where Froissart is at his most fallible, a 'blanket condemnation' is inappropriate (below, p.82), and even the least historically valuable of the four books of his *Chronicles* is rich in interest of other kinds, as the first and last essays in this volume illustrate.

But the greatest weakness of the scientific school of criticism of the past century has been its narrow focus. It has been almost entirely concerned with the errors and defects of Froissart's treatment of institutional history and of 'l'histoire événementielle'. The defects here are, it is true, grave enough and must be acknowledged; but even these undoubted defects are, when properly appreciated, valuable reflections of the mentality of the author and of his audience and their age, as many of the contributors to this volume have observed in different contexts. More significantly, the narrow focus of much of the criticism of the *Chronicles* has tended to obscure their true value. 'Froissart', it has been observed, 'is a world' (SHF I, i); and no single author has more to offer the historian in his efforts to recreate the mental and social dimensions of this world than has Froissart, whether it be the mental world of the historian himself, or of his patrons and audience; or whether it be contemporary attitudes towards political society, aristocratic *mores*, social divisions, the social dimensions of warfare, or the nature and techniques of war itself. On these, and a host of other topics, the *Chronicles* — as this collection of essays tries to reveal — communicate to us 'directly ... the voices and emotions of the' fourteenth century (below, p.153), thereby ensuring their immortality for as long as 'we prefer a knowledge of mankind to a mere acquaintance with their actions' (Scott 1804-5: 347).

I BOOK I (1325-78) AND ITS SOURCES *

J. J. N. Palmer

FEW, if any, of the literary sources of the fourteenth century have attracted such sustained and destructive criticism as Book I of Froissart's *Chronicles*. Volumes have been devoted to analysing the mistakes it contains,[1] and practically the only serious works of modern historical scholarship which have failed to add to its list of errors of chronology, geography and genealogy are those which have elected to ignore it as worthless (Russell 1955: ix). Even the most judicious and sympathetic of its critics have been prone to praise it for its literary rather than its historical value, and the most indulgent of commentators recognise that it is necessary to sift mountains of dross in order to recover the occasional nugget of historical truth.[2] As a source for its period, Book I is undoubtedly much inferior to Books II, III and IV and ranks very low indeed among the surviving literary sources of the age.

But Froissart's *Chronicles* are much more than a quarry of facts, and from one particular point of view Book I is the most interesting and valuable of the four books of the *Chronicles*. For the historiographer, it is a potential goldmine. No other part of Froissart's historical *oeuvre* enables us to see so clearly his working habits, his techniques, his method of composition. And no other work remotely approaches the value of Book I for the opportunities it affords to trace Froissart's development as an historian. It is with this aspect of Book I that this essay will concern itself.

The historiographical value of Book I is a reflection of the time and labour that Froissart himself lavished upon this particular work. While the composition of Books II, III and IV may have occupied him in all for rather less than two decades, he was concerned with Book I throughout the whole of his working life. In a famous passage (I, 210), Froissart tells us that he began his historical researches as a young man — probably of about twenty — on the morrow of the battle of Poitiers. That these early researches were of a serious nature is evident from a number of references in Book I to information and documents supplied to him by a lord of St Venant who died in 1360.[3] It seems probable, though impossible to prove, that the famous 'lost chronicle' presented to Queen Philippa in 1361 embodied some of these early researches and represented Froissart's first effort to chronicle the early stages of the Hundred Years War; and it has been suggested with some degree of probability that portions at least of this lost chronicle are embedded in the early recensions of Book I, though it is impossible to identify them with any degree of confidence (Cartier 1961: 424-34).

* All references to the *Chronicles* are to volume and page of the SHF edition unless otherwise stated.

Although this is unavoidably somewhat speculative, the later stages of the evolution of Book I are rather better documented. There can be no doubt that Froissart was at work on his material in the latter half of the 1360s[4] and throughout the 1370s (I, xiiff); and evidence will shortly be introduced to show that he continued to revise and polish the work in the 1380s and early 1390s. As is well known, the final recension of Book I — the famous Rome manuscript — was only begun after 1399;[5] and since it contains something like a quarter of a million words, its composition must have occupied much of the last decade of its author's life. In short, Froissart was preoccupied with Book I from the outset of his career in 1356 until shortly before his death, traditionally fixed at about 1410; and at no time in that half century did he apparently lay it aside for more than a few years at a time.

The historiographical interest of Book I is further enhanced by its dependence upon written sources. In no other work did Froissart make very much use of written sources, and indeed he often appears to have made no use of them at all. In Book I, however, where he was writing about events which lay some way in the past, he was almost entirely dependent upon the work of two earlier historians, some two-thirds of his narrative being derived from them, often verbatim. As is well known, for his narrative for the years 1325 to 1361, Froissart drew very heavily indeed upon the *Chronicle* of Jean le Bel, while for the events of the mid-1360s, he made extensive use of the poem on the *Life of the Black Prince* by Chandos Herald. Since both these sources have survived we have, in Book I, a unique opportunity to observe the manner in which Froissart shaped and manipulated his materials — copying and cutting, expanding and compressing, altering and rearranging his sources from chapter to chapter throughout the greater part of the half a million or so words of Book I.

But the feature which above all others enhances the historiographical value of Book I is its author's persistent dissatisfaction with what he had written and his equally persistent compulsion to rewrite it. As Shears has observed (1930: 82):

> ... the surest proof of Froissart's superiority lies in his critical attitude to his own work, and to the fact that he never long remained satisfied with his writings, and least of all with his first redaction, of which so much had been borrowed from Jehan le Bel. No sooner was it finished than he started to re-write it, and he was constantly revising it till the end of his life, confirming or correcting his earlier statements, adding fresh matter and remodelling the expression. Few writers have ever been more scrupulous and indefatigable in this respect ...

No other work of his went through more than two editions, and in none of them could the changes from one edition to another be described as of fundamental importance. Yet Froissart has been credited with no less than five editions of Book I, and three of them are by any standards major works. Whatever the reasons for this lifelong compulsion to revise Book I may have been, the results from our point of view could scarcely have been bettered. For the existence of a series of major revisions, spread over a lifetime, of a work whose sources can be identified, enables us to trace Froissart's development as an historian in a way that is rarely, if ever, possible for a medieval author.

Or rather, we *would be able* to follow this development but for one critical

8

technical problem, a problem which has to be resolved before any serious discussion of the broader question of Froissart's development is possible. It is this technical problem with which I shall be concerned in the remainder of this paper though I hope, in discussing this technicality, to throw some light on the broader theme which was the original object of this research.

The technical problem concerned is the order of the various editions of Book I or, to be more precise, the problem of the order of composition of one particular version, that generally known as the Amiens MS. Like most other historical problems, however, this one cannot be entirely isolated from a number of related difficulties; and in the course of the discussion it will be necessary to examine the evidence for the dating of the major editions of Book I and also to inquire into certain aspects of Froissart's relationship to his written sources.

With five different versions of Book I to compare, the relative order of composition of just one of them might not appear to be all that serious a problem. But it is, for reasons which must be briefly explained before examining the particular difficulties posed by the Amiens MS.

Although it is accurate to say that there are five versions of Book I, it is also misleading to say so, for the five versions are of unequal scope and importance. In the conventionally accepted order of composition, the five versions are:[6]

1. First edition:　A MSS
2. Revised first:　B MSS
3. Second edition: Amiens MS[7]
4. Epitome:　　　MS B6
5. Third edition:　Rome MS

For present purposes, the epitome, MS B6, may be dismissed. It reduces Book I to something like one-sixth of its original length; and since it is the analytical passages which have been pruned most ruthlessly, B6 is of very little value for the purpose of observing Froissart's development as an historian.[8]

Nor are the changes from the A to the B MSS all that significant. There are good reasons why these two versions have not been designated separate editions. For something like three-quarters of their narratives, the two are identical. In particular, the narrative for the years 1325 to 1350, and for 1356 to 1372, in the A MSS is reproduced without alteration in the B MSS. It is true that the revisions which were made were substantial enough and totalled something like a fifth of the whole work:

(a)　paras. 1-11　(I, 1-26)
(b)　1350-1356　(IV, 84-198)
(c)　1372-1378　(VII, 60-252)[9]

After all, even a fifth of Book I is a substantial amount of rewriting, since the complete narrative exceeds a half a million words. However, the length of these revised sections is misleading, for two reasons. In the first place, although it is incorporated into his *Chronicles*, the narrative in the A MSS for the years 1350-6 is not by Froissart at all! It has been copied into this version of Book I in order to fill a gap in his own composition, and had been taken virtually word for word from the *Grandes chroniques de France*.[10] Although there is an entirely new narrative for the years 1350-6 in the B MSS, therefore, there is nothing by

Froissart in the A MSS with which to compare it. Finally, although the two versions of the years 1372-8 in the A and B MSS are different and are both by Froissart, they offer relatively little opportunity to observe his development since the changes from one to the other are changes of detail rather than of interpretation. Froissart was here writing about events which had occurred during his own adult lifetime, and not so very long after they had happened. There were consequently only limited possibilities of changing perspectives or new interpretations. Despite their differences, therefore, the two versions of Book I represented by the A and B MSS afford very restricted opportunities for observing significant development in either the style or the content of Froissart's *Chronicles*.

The Rome edition is another matter entirely. Substantially rewritten throughout — something like ninety per cent or more of the text is new — it also incorporates a very considerable amount of new detail and quite fundamental revisions of interpretation. Since it is undoubtedly the final edition of Book I, we here possess the work of a mature historian with which to compare his stumbling first efforts. The developments which may be seen between the version represented by the A and B MSS on the one hand and the Rome edition on the other, are undoubtedly very considerable and could provide the basis for an analysis of the changing style, technique and philosophy of its author over the span of his career.

However, if we had only these editions to compare, our analysis would undoubtedly lack much in the way of nuance or sophistication. There are two reasons for this. In the first place, the Rome edition extends only to the year 1350, covering rather less than half the ground surveyed by the A and B MSS. And secondly, much of the narrative in the A and B MSS down to the year 1350 is not, in fact, an original composition by Froissart at all but is culled by him — with revisions and additions, it is true — from the *Chronicle* of Jean le Bel.

These points indicate the importance of the Amiens MS which is the only complete version of Book I other than that in the A and B MSS which covers the entire period from 1325 to 1378 and which offers substantially revised, or at least different, versions of the majority of events described in Book I. Unfortunately, it is precisely this edition whose place in the sequence of editions is uncertain. The Rome version is undoubtedly the final edition; but the relative order of the A and B MSS on the one hand, and of the Amiens version on the other hand, is open to question.

The rival claims to priority of these two MSS traditions divided scholars in the nineteenth century into two often hostile camps. One, headed by Simon Luce, claimed precedence for the A/B version and used a B MS for the base text of the SHF edition of the *Chronicles*. Kervyn de Lettenhove, however, in his own edition of Book I which appeared almost simultaneously with that of the SHF, printed the Amiens MS and devoted part of his introductory volume to arguing that it represented Froissart's first edition of Book I. But Luce stated his case with such Gallic lucidity, and with such an array of scholarly expertise (I, vi ff), that he virtually annihilated the opposition, whose views have scarcely been heard for the past century.

The case has recently been reopened, however,[11] and Luce's arguments are not as overwhelming as they have appeared to be. Some, indeed, are clearly makeweights. He argued, for instance, that the style of the A and B MSS was that of a young man — more spontaneous and lively, less grave and ponderous. Apart from the fact that this was a subjective impression, and one whose basic assumption is perhaps open to challenge, it can be shown — as I shall attempt to do shortly — that all the versions of Book I were completed when Froissart was already well advanced in years. Luce also argued that the Amiens MS must be the second edition because many of its episodes were much more highly developed than the corresponding versions in the A and B MSS. This is undoubtedly true, but the point is nevertheless disingenuous; for, as Lettenhove had pointed out in his own edition (I, i, 38-9), there are also many episodes in the A and B MSS which are more highly developed than the corresponding accounts in Amiens.

However, the main thrust of Luce's argument depended upon two quite different points: internal evidence of their dates of composition on the one hand, and the structural relationship of the main editions to each other on the other hand. These two arguments must be considered in more detail.

Luce himself gave precedence to the first of these points. He argued that the Amiens MS contained an unambiguous reference to the death of the Black Prince quite early in its narrative and must therefore have been *begun* later than 1376. The A and B MSS, on the other hand, must have been completed before this date. Luce reached this last conclusion by two routes. To begin with, several of these MSS end in either 1369 or in 1372, some in mid-sentence. This, Luce argued, indicated that the first version of Book I had evolved in two or more stages, originally ending perhaps in 1369, then progressing to various dates in 1372, and only at a later date reaching its eventual termination in 1378. And since the narrative of the A and B MSS prior to 1372 contained no reference to events later than that year, this indicated that this version of Book I was certainly in progress before 1372 and very likely completed within a year or two of that date, some time before work on the Amiens MS had even been begun. Amiens was therefore the second edition.

The argument appears plausible but contains a major weakness which, in my view, negates it. In essence, it is a dangerous version of the argument from silence: since the narrative in the A and B MSS prior to 1372 contains no reference to later events, therefore it had been completed by that date or very shortly afterwards. This would be a reasonable point if Froissart habitually referred to subsequent events in his narrative. But, in fact, he did so very sparingly. In the entire seven volumes of the text of Book I down to 1372, Luce could detect only one such allusion, the reference to the death of the Black Prince in the Amiens MS. A single date is clearly an insecure basis for so bold a generalisation.

The dangers of using internal references as a means of determining the order of the various editions of Book I are further highlighted by the fact that Luce missed three further such references which date all the MSS at least a decade, and very probably two decades later than the latest date for which he argued.

The first of these occurs under the year 1367 and alludes to the accession of Richard II to the English throne in 1377. This detail occurs in the MSS of all three editions — A, B, and Amiens — and in all of the many families of MSS of these groups.[12] There can be no question, therefore, of a scribal insertion. Clearly, none of the MSS of any version of Book I were complete in the form in which we have them before the year 1377 at the very earliest. The allusion to the death of the Black Prince in the Amiens MS is therefore of no significance at all. Indeed, it is apparent from this reference to the accession of Richard II that even the earliest version of the basic narrative of Book I — whichever that might be — cannot have been drafted before c.1380, since by mid-1377 the narrative had only reached the year 1367.

Two other internal allusions occur in one or other of the different editions. The Amiens MS contains, under the year 1358, an unmistakable reference to an event in the mid-1380s (V, 335-6) which is also reported in Book II of the *Chronicles* (XII, 124). The earliest date which this permits for the Amiens MS is mid- to late 1380s. But this by no means proves that it is later than the A and B MSS, for they contain a mention of the death of the *condottiere*, Bernard de la Salle, which occurred in the year 1391 (Durrieu 1885: 107-71). This reference, too, is to be found in all the many families of the A and B MSS and so must be considered an original part of the text of those editions.[13]

These very late dates for the completion of all the manuscripts of Book I of the *Chronicles* are, at first sight, very difficult to credit and are contrary to the basic chronology of Froissart's career as accepted for the past two centuries. If confirmed, they would call for the reconsideration of many apparently established facts such as, for instance, the relationship between Books I and II. Difficult though they are to credit, however, they are warranted in a general manner by one further consideration. It has long been accepted that Froissart borrowed his version of the events of the years 1366-7 from the poem on the *Life of the Black Prince* by Chandos Herald. Now since all editiors of the poem are agreed in dating its composition to c.1385, it follows that neither of the main versions of Book I could have been completed until some years after that date.

Indeed, it is possible to take this particular line of argument one step further. Although Froissart borrowed from Chandos Herald in all three versions of Book I — A, B and Amiens — his dependence upon this source was much greater in the Amiens MS than in the other two editions and there can be no doubt that it is the first of his versions of the events of 1366-7 (below). Now the Amiens MS has another peculiarity. Unlike the A and B MSS, its borrowings from Chandos Herald are not confined to his account of the Spanish campaign of the Black Prince but include some details taken from elsewhere in the poem, notably from its account of the early stages of the Crécy campaign. This being the case, we must conclude that by c.1385 — at the very earliest — Froissart's narrative in the Amiens MS had not yet reached the year 1346. However soon after its composition the poem came into his hands, this will not allow us to date the completion of the Amiens MS before about 1390; and since the version of the events of 1366-7 in the A and B MSS must be subsequent to that of the Amiens text, they too cannot have been completed before the opening decade of the fourteenth century, and probably some years later. It follows of course that all three versions of Book I only achieved their present shape in the 1390s.[14]

However, I have drifted from my main point. Whatever the merits of these arguments for dating the various versions of Book I by the internal references which they contain, the fact that there are so very few of these references makes them highly unsatisfactory as a means of establishing the relative order of composition of the different editions. To establish this, we must consider Luce's final point.

His final argument, and his most convincing one, concerns the structural relationship of the Amiens edition to the A and B MSS and, in particular, the structural relationship of the Amiens MS to those parts of the A and B MSS which diverge from each other. As we have already seen, the A and B MSS have identical narratives for something like three-quarters of their length, diverging only at three points: their opening paragraphs and their accounts of the years 1350-6 and 1372-8. In the B MSS all three of these sections are more elaborate and are undoubtedly later than the version of the A MSS.[15] Now the Amiens MS has precisely the same text as the B MSS for the years 1372-8, the final section of Book I; and although its account of the years 1350-6 is not identical to that in the B MSS, it is clearly based upon a version of events recognisably similar to those related there and very different indeed from that in the A MSS, which is a dry-as-dust annal copied from the *Grandes chroniques de France*. This being the case, the Amiens edition must be later than the A MSS; and if it is later than the A MSS, it must also be later than B. For it is inconceivable that an author would labour for years to rewrite an immense narrative of some half a million words and then subsequently ignore this new version and use his first effort as a basis for a later edition. Amiens cannot, therefore, lie *between* the A and B editions. It must either precede both or be later than both.

This argument appears fairly conclusive and can be made even more so by an extension of the same line of argument which — rather astonishingly — does not appear to have been considered. Luce's argument depends upon the structural relationship of the Amiens MS to the A and B editions of Book I. Why not extend this argument to include all three of these versions in their relationship with Froissart's sources on the one hand and the Rome MS on the other? The clear advantage here is that the points of reference are fixed. There is no doubt that Le Bel and Chandos Herald were Froissart's sources, and there is equally no doubt that the Rome MS is the final edition of Book I. If, therefore, any of the three early versions of Book I has a closer relationship to Le Bel or Chandos Herald than the others, it must presumably be the first edition. Conversely, if any of these three early versions are more closely related to the Rome edition, it must be a later and therefore second edition of Book I.

Do either of these tests supply confirmation that the Amiens MS is, as argued by Luce, the second edition of Book I? The answer is an emphatic 'yes'. There are, for instance, literally scores of chapters in both the A and B MSS where the entire chapter, or very substantial sections of it, are copied word-for-word from Le Bel but where the Amiens version is largely or even entirely rewritten. There are, as I have said, literally scores of chapters of which this is true, so citing individual instances is perhaps superfluous. But let me cite one or two examples just by way of illustration. Froissart's account of the battle of Cassel (1328) is fairly typical.[16] The version to be found in the A and B texts (here identical) is copied word-for-word from Le Bel. Not so that in the Amiens MS. Here a few odd phrases have survived from Le Bel but the bulk of the account is not only rewritten but is expanded by the addition of much extra detail. The same is true of Froissart's narrative of the French capture of Vannes and Auray in 1343. Once again, the story in the A/B MSS is taken very nearly verbatim from Le Bel, some ninety per cent of the text being copied from that source. In the Amiens MS a few passages have again survived from Le Bel; but only a few. Much of the text is rewritten and the story is expanded by the addition of new detail.[17] Similar

13

examples could be multiplied. The accounts of the opening shots in the Hundred Years War and of Edward III's search for allies; of the rise of van Artevelde; of English intervention in Brittany in 1341; of Philip VI's relations with John of Montfort; of many of the exploits of Sir Walter Mauny; of the beginnings of Edward III's notorious passion for the countess of Salisbury — all these[18] and many more are substantially copied by Froissart from Le Bel in the A and B versions of Book I of the *Chronicles* whereas these episodes are all either rewritten or expanded — and usually both — in the Amiens edition.

In all these examples the priority of the A and B MSS would seem to be firmly established by their almost total dependence upon Le Bel. The Amiens edition, being rewritten, must be subsequent to that of A and B. We can also establish that the Amiens MS is the second edition of Book I by demonstrating that it is more closely related to the Rome MS than are the A and B versions. Here again, numerous examples could be cited but one or two illustrations must suffice. A fairly typical example from the early chapters of Book I is provided by Froissart's account of the death of Charles IV and the succession of Philip VI of Valois. Here the A, B and Amiens MSS all copy Le Bel's account word-for-word; but whereas A and B only copy Le Bel, Amiens inserts into the text copied from Le Bel a description of Philip VI's coronation, an episode which reappears in the Rome edition.[19] A second example is provided by Froissart's sketch of the career of Robert of Artois, the man he blames for fomenting the Hundred Years War. Once again, the story in the A and B MSS is simply plagiarised from Le Bel. In Amiens, however, the story is rewritten in parts and incorporates several new episodes, in particular a lengthy description of Robert's escape from France to Hainault and the subsequent intervention of the count of Hainault on his behalf at the French court. This addition, not so much as hinted at in Le Bel or the A and B editions, reappears in the Rome version of Book I.[20] One final example among many which could be cited must suffice. This concerns the sieges of Conq, Dinan and Guérande during the early stages of the Breton civil war. In describing these, the A and B MSS once again copy Le Bel, with only minor verbal variations, whereas the Amiens account is both rewritten and expanded, notably in relation to the description of the siege of Dinan. The Amiens version also differs from Le Bel and the A and B MSS in that it suppresses the story found in these three of a sortie made by the garrison of Hennebont in an effort to force the French to raise one of their sieges. In both these respects, the structure of the Rome account is the same as that of Amiens, enlarging the story of the siege of Dinan and omitting that of the sortie made by the garrison of Hennebont.[21]

There would thus appear to be overwhelming evidence that the Amiens MS is indeed the second edition of Book I of the *Chronicles*. Only by challenging the methodology can the conclusion be disputed. Yet the methodology would seem to be unexceptionable: the A and B MSS represent the first edition because they are much closer to Froissart's source, Le Bel; while the Amiens MS, in addition to being further removed from that source, is structurally much closer to the Rome MS, the final version of Book I of the *Chronicles*. Both lines of argument converge on the conclusion that the Amiens MS is the second edition.

Yet unexceptionable though it would seem to be, this methodology may well appear open to challenge when it is demonstrated that it can produce diametrically opposed conclusions. For the same line of argument can, in fact, be used to prove that the Amiens MS is the first, not the second, edition of Book I.

Let me begin to illustrate this with a completely trivial but nevertheless revealing incident from Book I. At an early stage in his narrative, Froissart tells the story of Edward II's efforts to escape from Bristol castle, then besieged by the army of Queen Isabella. Edward, accompanied by his favourite Despenser, attempted to reach south Wales in a small boat; but despite the assistance of a kindly mist which obscured his efforts from the watchers on the shores of the Bristol Channel, he was inexorably driven back towards the English side of the channel by winds and tide. Finally, after eleven days of unremitting effort which left them more or less where they began, the unfortunate king and his companions were spotted by the besiegers, who sent out a boat to bring them in.[22]

Now this story is copied by Froissart from Le Bel and appears in substantially the same form in all versions of Book I. 'Substantially the same form' because there is one significant variation of detail between Le Bel, Amiens and the A MSS on the one hand, and the Rome and B MSS on the other. According to the first three sources, the actual capture of Edward II was effected by a boatload of Dutchmen; whereas according to Rome and the B MSS, the king was taken by Sir Henry of Beaumont. Now on the conventional view that the Amiens MS is the second edition of Book I, we are obliged to accept that Froissart changed his mind no less than three times over this detail. He first accepted Le Bel's Dutchmen in the A MSS, then rejected them in favour of Sir Henry of Beaumont in the B MSS, then rejected Sir Henry once again in favour of the Dutchmen when he wrote the Amiens text; and finally, in the Rome version, rejected the Dutchmen all over again and restored the honour of this deed to the twice rejected Sir Henry of Beaumont. Such indecision, even frivolity, seems scarcely credible. Yet we are driven to it if we believe that the Amiens text is the second edition of Book I. If, on the other hand, we accept for the moment that in this episode at least the Amiens edition is the earliest, then all difficulties disappear. In that case, Froissart accepted the story he found in Le Bel in his first two editions (Amiens and the A MSS respectively); discovered an error of detail and corrected it in his next edition (the B MSS), and reproduced this correction in his final version of Book I (Rome):

Amiens as First Edition		Amiens as Second Edition	
Le Bel	Dutchmen	Le Bel	Dutchmen
Amiens	Dutchmen	A MSS	Dutchmen
A MSS	Dutchmen	B MSS	Beaumont
B MSS	Beaumont	Amiens	Dutchmen
Rome	Beaumont	Rome	Beaumont

Instead of three changes of mind, we have one correction of error by an historian in search of the truth.

It is just conceivable that this particular illustration represents no more than an aberration on the part of the author or of some of his scribes. This objection cannot, however, be raised against the conclusions forced upon us by Froissart's handling of many of the major episodes in Book I. Take, for instance, his justly famous description of the battle of Crécy. This is a substantial piece of analysis, of some 5,000 or more words, and cannot therefore be dismissed as a trivial matter of detail. Yet there is no doubt that here, as in the incident of Sir Henry of Beaumont, the Amiens version is derived in all essentials from Le Bel whereas the A and B MSS (here identical) are substantially rewritten and closely related to the Rome edition. In stating the size of the contending armies, for instance, the Amiens text follows Le Bel verbatim while the A, B and Rome versions all omit this item. More significantly, the A, B and Rome editions contain accounts of no less than twelve separate incidents in the battle — in all, more than a quarter of their entire narrative — which do not appear at all in either Le Bel or the Amiens MS. These incidents include a French reverse early in the battle; the participation of the French rabble; Philip VI's command to commence battle, the reluctance of the Genoese crossbowmen to fight, the reaction of Aumâle to their cowardice, and the king's order to cut them down; the augury of a flight of crows above the battlefield; Philip VI's efforts to join forces with the counts of Alençon and Flanders during the course of the battle; the feat of arms of Thomas de Sancelles; the deaths of various French nobles; and, finally, Edward III's congratulations to his son after victory had been won.[23]

In addition to all this, much of what is common to all versions of the battle in so far as their substance is concerned, is nevertheless derived by the Amiens text verbatim from Le Bel whereas the narratives in the A, B and Rome MSS are substantially rewritten. Only a very small fraction of the A and B texts, and none of the Rome version, is copied from Le Bel; but much more than half of the Amiens version of the battle is taken word-for-word from that source.[24] And finally, throughout its narrative, the Rome MS copies many odd phrases and sentences from the A and B MSS but nothing at all from Amiens.[25] It is therefore overwhelmingly clear that the Amiens account of the battle of Crécy is directly derived from Le Bel and is Froissart's first attempt to compose a narrative of the battle. The A and B MSS are restructured, rewritten and substantially expanded accounts which are intimately related to the Rome MS, the final edition of Book I. They therefore represent Froissart's second attempt to narrate Edward III's triumph at Crécy.

Froissart's narrative of the battle of Crécy is justly famous and it has not escaped notice that the Amiens version is heavily dependent upon Le Bel while the A and B MSS are much closer to Rome. How, then, has this observation been squared with the conventional belief that the Amiens text is the second edition of Book I? In fact, it has not. The problem has simply been ignored. The nearest approach to an attempt to explain this paradox is tucked away in a brief footnote to the SHF edition of the *Chronicles* (III, li), where Luce stated his belief that Froissart first composed his own, largely original, account of the battle when writing the A and B MSS, but then 'reverted' to Le Bel's version when composing his second edition because Le Bel's story was more favourable to the French and at the time of producing the Amiens edition Froissart was becoming increasingly sympathetic to the French viewpoint. But having abandoned his own original composition in favour of copying that of Le Bel in his second (Amiens) edition, Froissart subsequently 'reverted' back to his own first edition account when he came to produce the Rome version, because he wrote this last version in order to free himself from his excessive dependence upon Le Bel!

One can see here the contortions forced upon anyone who wishes to maintain that no part of the Amiens text was composed prior to that of the A and B MSS. No scholar would now hold that Froissart's partisanship was at any time as blatant as this hypothesis demands, and Luce's argument to this effect has been vigorously rejected by Shears (1930: 98-102). Moreover, the major premise of Luce's argument is demonstrably untenable. For Le Bel's version of the battle of Crécy is in no way favourable to the French. It is difficult to see how the idea that it is could ever have arisen. Throughout his *Chronicle*, Le Bel showed the greatest admiration for Edward III and considerable contempt for Philip VI. His partisanship is, in fact, so marked that Froissart has omitted from all versions of Book I Le Bel's denunciation of the rule of Philip VI and his several eulogies of Edward III, just as he has dropped Le Bel's habit of referring to Edward as 'the noble King Edward' while denying any such epithet to Philip VI. Furthermore, in so far as the A, B and Rome versions of Crécy are more favourable to the English than is Amiens, this is not primarily due to the additional material they incorporate. Although one or two of these additional episodes might be interpreted in this light, the majority are either neutral and simply fill out the story, or they positively represent the French in a flattering manner, as for instance the stories of the feats of Thomas de Sancelles, of Philip VI's efforts to join forces with Alençon and Flanders and of the deaths of some of the French nobles. The pro-French slant of the Amiens MS is very largely peculiar to itself and is due neither to its dependence upon Le Bel nor to its exclusion of material which appears in the other versions of Book I of the *Chronicles*.

But the most convincing reason for rejecting any attempt to explain away the fact that the narrative of Crécy in the Amiens MS appears to be Froissart's first attempt to describe that battle, is that there are numerous other episodes in this version of Book I which also bear the hallmarks of being the first efforts of a fledgling historian who had not yet managed to free himself from excessive dependence upon his source.

Let me cite a few but representative examples. There are, to begin with, numerous passages scattered througout the Amiens text which are word-for-word reproductions of the text of Jean le Bel, passages which are not reproduced in any of the other versions of Book I. Such passages occur, for example, in Froissart's account of Queen Isabella's flight to France in 1326; in his account of the end of Edward III's first campaign against the Scots in 1327; in his story of the aftermath of the battle of Sluys; of Edward's invasion of Normandy in 1346; of his narrative of the Poitiers campaign of 1356; and of his lengthy analysis of the great chevauchée of 1359.[26] It is somewhat pointless, in fact, to cite individual instances since they are so numerous. 'Numerous' indeed is something of an understatement. At a very rough calculation, something like half of Le Bel's text is incorporated verbatim or very nearly so into the Amiens MS, and only a fraction of this resurfaces in the A, B and Rome MSS, which are usually rewritten and often expanded as well.

Precisely the same relationship may be observed between the Amiens MS and the poem on the *Life of the Black Prince* by Chandos Herald.[27] Approximately half of this poem — the half which deals with the Black Prince's invasion of Castile and the battle of Nájera in 1367 — has been absorbed into the narratives of the A, B and Amiens versions of the *Chronicles*; but whereas the A and B MSS (here identical) follow the outline of the poem, rewriting, adding and subtracting material fairly freely, the Amiens MS throughout follows the poem much more closely, often indeed word-for-word. Impressed by this feature of the Amiens MS but obliged to accept the conventional view that Amiens is the second edition of Book I, the editors of the poem felt themselves compelled to assume that the A and B version must have been written from the Herald's notes rather than from his finished work. But there is no shred of evidence to support this speculation, which is not only inherently implausible but which is rendered virtually impossible by the faithfulness with which the A/B version follows the precise sequence of events in the poem. One may admire the ingenuity of the hypothesis but it is made unnecessary by accepting the much more obvious conclusion that the Amiens version is closer to the poem simply because it is Froissart's first effort to describe these events and therefore the one most dependent upon his source.

In addition to the close textual relationship between the Amiens MS and Froissart's written sources, the view that the Amiens MS is the first edition is also supported by the strong textual relationship between the A and B MSS on the one hand and Rome edition on the other, which indicates that the A and B versions are second editions. Examples of this have already been noted in analysing the different accounts of the battle of Crécy. Other examples may easily be multiplied: the description of Edward III's homage to Philip VI, of the earl of Derby's campaigns in Gascony in 1345, of the death of van Artevelde, of the siege of Aiguillon in 1346.[28] But again, it is somewhat pointless to multiply individual examples since this characteristic is pervasive, reappearing in scores, indeed hundreds of instances.

Finally, in addition to the close textual relationship between Le Bel and Amiens on the one hand, and between the A and B MSS and Rome on the other, it is also possible to point to many passages where a textual transition may be observed from Le Bel through Amiens to the A and B MSS and finally to Rome,[29] and also to many scores of episodes whose structure in the Amiens MS is closer to that of Le Bel than to any other version of Book I.[30]

Thus a comparison of the structure and text of the Amiens MS with Le Bel, Chandos Herald, and the other versions of Book I of the *Chronicles* affords ample proof that the Amiens MS is indeed Froissart's first edition of Book I, as argued by Lettenhove. But since it has already been demonstrated that the Amiens MS is equally undoubtedly the second edition, as Luce believed, it follows that *both* Lettenhove and Luce were right or, to be more exact, both were wrong. The Amiens MS is neither first nor second edition but both simultaneously. It also follows, of course, that the A and B MSS are also both first and second editions simultaneously. And it naturally follows from these two conclusions that there is no first or second edition of Book I at all in any meaningful sense of those terms, only a large number of MSS which combine elements of the two editions in different manners and different proportions.[31]

One further conclusion would also seem to follow, though this must be offered rather more tentatively. If we consider the enormous length of Book I in the light of the conclusions reached above and of the argument at the beginning of this essay that no version of this book was complete before the 1390s, it would appear highly probable that the A, B and Amiens MSS were compiled simultaneously (or very nearly so), not successively. In this sense, too, we must deny that they are different 'editions' in any modern sense of that word.

The light which these conclusions throw upon Froissart's working methods and practices as an historian is almost too awful to contemplate. No admirer of Froissart – the present writer included – will readily accept such conclusions. It should therefore be emphasised that no semantic quibble is involved. Even if it were possible to demonstrate that the A and B MSS were in circulation before the Amiens MS (or vice versa), this would not alter the fact that the A and B MSS contain many scores of chapters, amounting to tens of thousands of words, which are clearly of later composition than the corresponding chapters in the Amiens version, while that version itself is a similar mishmash of 'first' and 'second' edition elements. How any author could allow this situation to arise is beyond comprehension. But the facts of the case are plain, and it would seem that Froissart was guilty of an almost incredible levity in his attitude to his materials, an attitude which amounts to an almost total disregard of his basic duties as an historian. Set beside these conclusions, his frequent protestations of his labours to establish the truth of the events he records have a very hollow ring indeed.

Or so it would appear. There is, however, just one other possible explanation of the confusion to be found among the various manuscript editions of Book I, an explanation which would exculpate Froissart from some of the more serious features of the charges laid above. And that explanation is that the Amiens version of Book I is not, in fact, the work of Froissart at all.

On the face of it, this is a most improbable suggestion; for of all the editions of Book I, or indeed of Books II, III and IV for that matter, the Amiens MS would appear to be the one whose attribution to Froissart is most securely established. Froissart had the engaging habit of referring from time to time to his own travels and experiences to authenticate certain events described in his *Chronicles*. Now of all versions of the *Chronicles*, the Amiens MS is the most liberally supplied with such references. On two occasions, for instance, Froissart refers there to a journey he made to Scotland in 1365. He also describes visits to Berkeley castle, to Sandwich and to Dover, as well as a journey from Rome to Aquitaine. Only one of these references appears in any other version of Book I. In addition, he several times refers to his labours in gathering materials for his work, and to the use he has made of the *Chronicle* of Jean le Bel; to his service at the court of Queen Philippa; and to the sources from whom he has gathered some of the material he has added to Le Bel's account. Again, only one of these references reappears in any other version of Book I.[32]

In addition to these personal allusions in the Amiens MS, there are major textual and structural features of the work which might seem to confirm that it is indeed that of Froissart himself. Whoever composed the Amiens MS clearly had access to the *Chronicle* of Jean le Bel, copied at times from both the A and B MSS of Book I and, as we have seen, anticipated some of the features which were later to appear in the Rome version.[33] Finally, and perhaps most persuasively, the author of the epitome of Book I (MS B6) drew indiscriminately on both the A/B MSS and the Amiens MS in compiling his abbreviated account of the years 1325-78.[34] All this would seem to place Froissart's authorship of the Amiens text beyond reasonable doubt.

However, none of these points prove conclusively that Froissart was responsible for the Amiens text in the form in which it has come down to us. To prove this with any certainty, we should need to possess either a holograph or multiple

19

copies which would enable us to reconstruct a standard text. In the absence of either of these, we cannot preclude the possibility that the Amiens MS, though based upon an edition of Book I by Froissart, has nevertheless been worked over by another author. We know this to have been the case with some of the A MSS, after all.

What are the grounds for thinking that another hand has been at work on the Amiens MS? There are a variety of reasons. The first is the almost total absence of any textual relationship between the Amiens version and that of Rome. As will by now be all too evident, Froissart was a considerable plagiarist. Of all the versions of Book I of his *Chronicles*, the Rome MS is the most extensively rewritten and the one which contains the least material taken word-for-word from earlier editions. Even so, rather more than five per cent of the text of the Rome edition — which means many thousands of words — is copied from the A and B MSS. Yet except where the texts of these versions are identical with that in the Amiens MS, the Rome MS does not similarly copy from the Amiens text, not even from those portions of the Amiens MS which I have designated 'second' edition elements. In the entire quarter of a million words of the Rome edition, I have been able to identify only one very brief passage which appears to be derived from the Amiens text;[35] and in view of the fact the A text of Book I has not been published in full, we cannot rule out the possibility that even this one passage is a variant which occurs in MSS of the A family. This is an extremely puzzling feature of the Amiens MS for which I can suggest no explanation other than that Froissart's text has been rewritten by someone other than Froissart himself.

There is another aspect of the textual relationship of the various editions of Book I which is equally curious. As has already been noted, many passages in the Rome MS are textually derived from the A and B MSS which in their turn derive from Le Bel. In these instances, therefore, we may observe an unbroken textual transmission from Le Bel via the A and B MSS to Rome, the final edition. Unbroken, that is, if we exclude the Amiens MS, for in many of the instances which could be cited, the text found in all other versions, from source to final edition, is inexplicably rewritten in Amiens.[36]

Another peculiarity of the Amiens MS is the truly vast amount of new detail — added either to Le Bel or to the A and B MSS — which makes its appearance in the Amiens MS and does not reappear in the Rome version.[37] This must be related to another feature of this MS: not only is much of the new detail it provides ignored in the Rome edition, but much of that detail is flatly contradicted by the other versions (or contradicts them).[38] Of course, all versions of Book I omit or alter points of detail to be found in the other versions; but the scale on which the Amiens MS does so is peculiar to itself. Again, no obvious reason for this peculiarity presents itself other than the suggestion that the MS is the work of someone other than Froissart himself.

Yet another feature of the Amiens text which distinguishes it from all other versions of Book I (and its sources) is its pronounced pro-French bias. Attention has already been drawn to this aspect in relation to its account of the battle of Crécy; but it is very far from being confined to this episode. Its narrative of the battle of Poitiers, for instance, has been even more drastically edited to produce a version favourable to the French, with the disparity between the size of the two armies considerably reduced and almost all the stories of English feats of arms or acts of chivalry expunged, leaving a narrative in which French feats of arms dominate the story despite the fact that they lost the battle.[39] Similar episodes are scattered thoughout the Amiens text. One might instance, for example, its account of French subtlety in the making of the treaty of Calais, of French valour at Cocherel, of their invasion of Castile, of the activities of the duke of Anjou.[40] In all these, and many more that could be cited, the Amiens text is markedly more favourable, and often unreasonably so, to the French point of view or hostile to the English as, for example, in its treatment of the sack of Limoges.[41] Such partisanship is apparent in no other version of the *Chronicles*. Froissart prided himself on his lack of partisanship and proclaimed that he was not unduly influenced by his patrons. The tendency of recent studies has been to uphold his testimony on this point. Is the Amiens text an exception, or should we detect the hand of another author at work to produce this unaccustomed bias?

Finally, there are major structural differences between the Amiens MS and all other versions of Book I. This reveals itself in several different ways. There are, for instance, a number of chapters which appear in all other versions in one form or another but which do not appear in any form at all in the Amiens MS.[42] There are also some chapters in the Amiens MS which are not to be found in any of the other versions of Book I.[43] Even more striking are the block of chapters in Amiens covering the years 1347 to 1356, a very large block, well over ten per cent of Book I (KL V, 108-338). Almost every one of these chapters is highly abbreviated — so highly abbreviated, in fact, that many of them are considerably briefer than their source, Le Bel's *Chronicle* (and Froissart was not given to abbreviation!). All of these features are peculiar to this manuscript.

But perhaps the most striking discrepancy between the structure of the Amiens MS and that of the other editions of Book I is the many instances where the overall interpretation of an entire story differs in the Amiens MS from all other versions when they — and the source from which the story derives — agree among themselves.

Take, for example, the account given by Le Bel, the A, B and Rome MSS of Edward III's first invasion of Scotland in 1333, the invasion which led to his first great military triumph, at Halidon Hill.[44] Although the Rome version of this campaign is considerably more detailed than the others, all nevertheless tell essentially the same story. According to this story, Edward III bypassed Berwick when he invaded, in search of the Scottish army. In an effort to provoke the Scots to battle, he devastated Lowland Scotland from one end to the other. Taking Edinburgh, he crossed the Forth and led his armies as far east as Aberdeen and as far west as Dumbarton, still looting and burning. All this failing to provoke the Scots, who had retired to Selkirk forest, Edward returned towards the border and sat down to besiege Berwick. The garrison of the town called upon King David to relieve them; and when he refused to do so, the town capitulated and Edward returned to England.

This is the version originally sketched by Le Bel, followed by the A and B MSS and elaborated by Rome. The Amiens story differs in almost every major respect. According to Amiens, Edward III made straight for Berwick after crossing the Scottish border, and immediately settled down to besiege the town. Far from

21

refusing to relieve Berwick, King David marched towards the English king with a large army at his back, an army which confronted the English before the town, skirmished with them, and withdrew only after the hopelessness of the situation had been appreciated. Only after the fall of the town did Edward pursue his campaign elsewhere in Scotland; but even then he did not march directly towards the Forth, but first went westwards, to attack Roxburgh. His campaign was concluded — not begun, as in the other versions — with the devastation of Lowland Scotland.

An equally striking instance is offered by the Amiens account of the opening shots in the Hundred Years War and Edward III's efforts to recruit allies in the Low Countries. Once again, Le Bel, the A and B MSS and the Rome edition are all in substantial agreement, despite some minor differences of detail.[45] All four sources recount two English embassies to Valenciennes, both led by the bishop of Lincoln, the first sent to seek the advice of the count of Hainault, the second to conclude alliances with the duke of Brabant and the counts of Guelders and Juliers and some lesser figures. According to all four sources, only the second of these embassies travelled outside Valenciennes, and then only to visit the duke of Brabant, singled out for this honour because of his particular importance. The remaining would-be allies all had to travel to Valenciennes to meet the English ambassadors there.

The Amiens version of these events is different both in structure and in most of its details. There were three embassies (not two) according to this version, and neither of the first two were led by the bishop of Lincoln. Far from basing themselves almost entirely in Valenciennes, the first embassy visited Brabant and Guelders and the second was sent to consult with the emperor, Louis of Bavaria, in Coblenz. The third embassy described in the Amiens account did, it is true, base itself in Valenciennes and conduct negotiations with potential allies; but it did so in circumstances entirely dissimilar from those described in the other four accounts. For according to Amiens, this third embassy was actually sent to Hainault to negotiate peace between England and France through the mediation of the count of Hainault. Only when Philip VI had reneged on his promise to negotiate and had unilaterally withdrawn from the negotiations did this embassy enter into discussions with potential allies. Nothing similar to these circumstances is so much as hinted at in the other four accounts.

Further examples could easily be multiplied but I shall content myself with a brief allusion to two other major episodes. The first is one of the most celebrated passages in the whole of the *Chronicles*: Edward III's attempted seduction of the countess of Salisbury over a game of chess. This episode occurs only in the Amiens MS and is not so much as hinted at in any other version, despite the fact that Le Bel and the A and B MSS both have extended accounts of Edward's infatuation. The attempted seduction is a gem, artistically and psychologically superior to any other episode in Book I (II, 340-2). It is hard to believe that any author once having penned such a scene could bear to drop it from subsequent editions of his work.

One final example: the story of the rise of van Artevelde. This is perhaps the most powerful piece of political analysis in the whole of Book I, and one which reveals an astonishing degree of sophistication. The account of the rise of van Artevelde given by Le Bel is a very crude and predictable story of the treachery and disloyalty of an upstart plebian towards his true lord, the count of Flanders. This is copied verbatim in Froissart's A and B MSS; and although the Rome version is considerably more refined, it is recognisably the same story. The Amiens version, however, is quite different. In place of the moralistic tale of the other four sources, we are given a complex analysis of the social, economic, political and diplomatic factors which made van Artevelde's career possible, if not inevitable. It is an analysis which has scarcely been bettered by modern historians, and it seems odd — to put it no more strongly — that an historian could produce such an analysis and then abandon it in favour of what is a patently inferior version of events.[46]

There are therefore good grounds for regarding the Amiens MS with very considerable suspicion. And yet this suspicion may ultimately prove to be unfounded. Incredible though it may seem, it is possible that Froissart produced such opposing versions of the same set of events as a matter of course, without making the slightest effort to reconcile them. In one particular instance, in fact, it appears that we may observe him doing this in Book I, in his description of the invasion of Normandy by Edward III in 1346.

Here, as in the cases analysed above, the basic narrative of all versions of Froissart's story is taken from the *Chronicle* of Jean le Bel. The A, B and Rome MSS repeat that story, with some elaboration it is true, but without serious modification. According to them, Edward III decided to land in the Cotentin peninsula, caught Philip VI entirely unprepared, and was thus able to disembark his army without opposition and launch it on its victorious path into Normandy.

The Amiens version could not very well be more different, and indeed has the appearance — as do so many other passages in the Amiens MS — of having been written to contradict the other editions of the *Chronicles*. For according to Amiens, Philip VI did, in fact, make quite strenuous efforts to resist the landing of Edward III, sending troops in advance of that landing to all the threatened areas. Moreover, he correctly anticipated the particular threat to the Cotentin peninsula and sent his marshal, Robert Bertran, to guard that region. Far from landing unopposed, therefore, Edward III had to fight a stiff battle on dis-embarkation, a battle which produced a casualty list worth recording in the Amiens MS.[47]

Once again, therefore, the Amiens MS is completely at variance with all other versions of the *Chronicles* and their source. In this case, however, we can see why. For whereas the A, B and Rome versions are based squarely on the *Chronicle* of Jean le Bel, the Amiens MS, although making some use of Le Bel, has also drawn on the *Life of the Black Prince* by Chandos Herald; and it is the contri-butions made by the *Life* which make the Amiens account so different from all the others. We know that Froissart used the *Life* elsewhere in Book I, so there is no need on this occasion to posit the existence of another author in order to explain the discrepancies between Amiens and the other editions. Why Froissart chose to follow Le Bel in three of his editions and Chandos Herald in the other, and why he apparently made no effort at all to reconcile the two stories, or to seek further evidence to support one or other of the alternatives, we have no means of knowing.[48] But if the Amiens MS is, in fact, the work of Froissart, then such insouciance was habitual; for there are countless other instances scattered throughout Book I where the content, the structure or the text of this manuscript is completely at variance with all other versions of the *Chronicles*.

But perhaps we should not be so surprised at this conclusion, nor doubt Froissart's authorship of the Amiens MS on these grounds alone. It has, after all, long been recognised that Froissart often presented his readers with alternative and conflicting versions of the same event, without making the slightest effort to reconcile them, as in the famous case of his two accounts of Aljubarrota in Book II, analysed below by Professor Russell. It has also long been known that many of the MSS which include more than a single book of the *Chronicles* have been put together from different editions of the separate books, and for this the author presumably bears some responsibility. In these circumstances it is perhaps not as incredible as it might at first appear that the A, B and Amiens versions of Book I are themselves each compilations of 'first' and 'second' edition elements.

The problems posed by the peculiarities of the Amiens MS and by the conflation of different editions within each of the first three versions of Book I create almost insuperable difficulties for anyone trying to trace Froissart's development as an historian. Indeed, in these circumstances, it may well be questioned whether the concept of 'development' is meaningful, for Froissart himself apparently did not think so. Despite the fact that his first three versions of Book I involved not merely rewriting and restructuring his narrative but the alteration, addition and suppression of a vast amount of *factual* detail, he apparently did not consider it important to keep his editions distinct. We are forced to conclude that he did not see his revisions as superseding his earlier efforts but simply as alternative — and equally valid — versions of events. Such an attitude must appear to us as methodologically deplorable and fundamentally unhistorical. It suggests that we have a very long way to go indeed before we can penetrate and comprehend the mind of even the most fully documented of medieval historians.

II JEAN FROISSART AND EDWARD THE BLACK PRINCE *

Richard Barber

THE Black Prince has been described by Shears as 'Froissart's greatest hero' (1930: 104). The purpose of this essay is to examine what Froissart actually knew about him, and what he actually thought about him, two seemingly simple questions with far more complex implications which may reveal something of the chronicler's methods and help us to estimate his real value as a historian.

On the face of it, Froissart's sources of information about the prince should be impeccable. Both he and Jean le Bel, his chief source for the early period, were Hainaulters, fellow-countrymen of Queen Philippa, and therefore *persona grata* at the English court; nor had the Hainaulters aroused any of the hatred directed against the Poitevins under John and Henry III, or the Gascons under Edward II. Le Bel had been on Edward's Scottish expedition of 1327 in the company of John of Hainault, uncle of Philippa; thirty-four years later, if we accept the date usually quoted for his arrival in England, Froissart joined the household of the queen. He was in her entourage until 1366, and rejoined her in England for a time early in 1367. He was with the Black Prince in Aquitaine in the winter of 1366. In all, he appears to have spent six or seven years closely connected with the English court, when the prince's reputation, and that of his companions, were at their height. On the face of it, he should be a prime witness.

But his presence at the court has been largely misinterpreted. Our only evidence for it, and for the dates at which it began and ended, are in the *Chronicles* themselves. The material derived from his poetry is not historical evidence, though his biographers have clutched at the straws to be found in the poems, such as Saturday 16 April,[1] or the *avolés* present at the port from which he sailed to England (Shears 1930: 13), to arrive at 1356 and 1361 as the dates for his crossing. Likewise, the autobiographical substance of his poems is thoroughly interwoven with poetic invention, and the historian can only admit that we know nothing definite of Froissart's youth and early manhood. Even the date of his birth is doubtful, though 1333 is the generally accepted date.

We must therefore turn to his own statements in the *Chronicles*. He tells us that he was in the English royal 'ostel' for five years: '. . . car de ma jonnesse je fui v. ans en l'ostel du roy d'Angleterre et de la royne, et si fu bien de l'ostel du roy Jehan de France et du roy Charle son filz.'[2] What does he mean by 'en l'ostel'? Some clue is given by his use of the same word in his account of his second visit to England in 1395, when he speaks of belonging to Richard II's household. Here he was clearly a guest, with no official standing, and I would suggest that

* All references to the *Chronicles* are to volume and page of the SHF edition unless otherwise stated.

25

his status in the 1360s was not dissimilar. He is reasonably precise in his use of titles, and would have told us if he had been a minor official in the queen's household.[3] Instead, he describes Queen Philippa as his patron, and if we look closely at his description of his activities in England, a consistent pattern emerges. Froissart went to England not as a historian or as a clerk, but as a budding author, with a number of poems to his credit, in search of a patron. This is confirmed, firstly, by the admittedly tenuous evidence of the poems themselves, many of which, broadly speaking, are presented as the work of a youthful writer. Then there is his statement in the prologue to the *Chronicles* that he had composed a rhyming chronicle when he was just out of school, which he presented to Queen Philippa on his arrival to England (I, 210). Again in another reference to Philippa, he claims to have been her 'clerk' and to have served her 'de beaux dittiers et trettiés amoureux' (KL XIV, 2).

Furthermore, the kind of material he claims to have gathered directly from the English court is all such as would interest a poet rather than a chronicler. The first episode is that of Queen Philippa's love for Edward when he came to the court of Hainault in 1326, a romantic episode which is much closer in spirit to the *Espinette amoureuse* than the bulk of the *Chronicles*. The second piece of evidence would seem to contradict this, but in fact ties in equally well with Froissart's literary activities. In 1365, Froissart went to Scotland, and the queen wrote to King David, the earl of Douglas, and the lord of Stirling and the earl of Mar:

> liquel, pour l'onnour et amour de la bonne roine desus ditte qui tesmoingnoit par ses lettres seelées que je estoie uns de ses clers et familiiers, me requellièrent tout doucement et liement. Et fui en la compagnie dou roi un quartier d'un an, et euch celle aventure que, ce que je fui en Escoce, il viseta tout son pais, par laquelle visitation je apris et considerai moult de la matère et ordenance des Escoçois, et sont de toute tèle condition que chi desus vous est devisé (I, 269).[4]

The immediate result of this journey was almost certainly not the Scottish history contained in the *Chronicles*, but the romance *Méliador*, of which the first version is dated variously to before 1370 or 1373 (Loomis 1959: 390). This vast work must have taken even so prolific a writer as Froissart some time to complete, running as it does to over 30,000 lines, and it is not unreasonable to think that he may have had it in mind as early as 1365. It is set for the most part in Scotland; and while it would be idle to pretend that the queen sent him there to work up the background for his projected romance, the important point is that on his return he used his experience to produce a romance, not a historical work.

This leaves only one journey, that with Sir Edward Despenser to the west country in 1366, which looks like a voyage of historical discovery, on the lines of his expedition to Béarn in 1388-9. But even here, the immediate use he made of his experiences was to create from it scenes in *Méliador*, as Professor Diverres has pointed out.[5] As with his Scottish journey, however, this journey is only fully described in the Rome version of the *Chronicles* (Diller 90). It suggests that Froissart, writing at a considerable distance in time from the events he described, was anxious to establish his credentials, and, quite rightly, mentioned his personal knowledge of important figures of the period as a means of guaranteeing the authenticity of what he wrote. This does not mean, however, that the original purpose of the journey was historical research, and apart from the enquiries at Berkeley into the death of Edward II, it does not appear as such a journey from the conversations that took place.

One other episode might be construed as portraying Froissart as actively engaged in historical work in this period. This is the scene at the birth of Richard II, when Froissart was actually at Bordeaux when the prince was born. However, its placing in the *Chronicle*, at Richard's death, shows that it could not have been written before 1400. In any case, the conclusion of the speech in which Sir Richard Punchardon instructed Froissart: 'Froissart, escripvés et mettés en memoire . . .' (KL XVI, 234) imputing to him a reputation as a chronicler, shows that it must have been invented: for there was no reason to expect Richard II to succeed to the throne until the death of his elder brother Edward in 1370.

I would suggest that on balance, Froissart's only historical effort up to his departure from England, was his juvenile verse-chronicle, and that he had no plan for a chronicle in mind before he left. Hence, his apparent value as an eye-witness is much diminished. So what we have for this period, and probably up to the late 1370s, when I believe he began to write the *Chronicles*,[6] are the *Chronicle* of Jean le Bel, supplemented and adapted by Froissart in the light of his researches; memoirs culled from conversations with various knights in the late 1370s, after the Black Prince's death; and Froissart's own memories, without any basis of records, of that period, when his prime concern had been a career as a poet. This last contention is borne out by entries in the accounts of Wenceslas of Bohemia and of Joan of Brabant; in April 1366 a gift to 'a certain Froissart, *dictor*, who is with the queen of England', if we are to translate *dictor* as *ditteur*, a poet, is recorded, and this is followed by other entries using the same designation, on 19 September 1367 and then from June 1370 onwards. He is also referred to as 'Fresset den spreker' in the accounts of John II de Chatillon, lord of Beaumont, in 1368-9, when he visited John at Beaumont for two days.[7] Indeed, it is worth bearing in mind the evidence that even after he had embarked on the *Chronicles*, 'in his own day he seems to have considered himself principally a poet, and only secondarily a chronicler' (Kibler 1976: 77). Although we know of at least one presentation copy of the *Chronicles*, destined for Richard II in 1381, when he went to visit Richard in 1395 it was his poetry that he presented to the king. Likewise, at the court of Gaston Fébus in 1388, he read *Méliador* to the count. This is not to deny his early and keen interest in history, nor the importance he attached to his *Chronicles*, but to set his historical work in the context of a busy life with many other preoccupations.

When we come to evaluate Froissart's record of events, we have also to look at the context. Clearly he was not writing an 'official' chronicle such as that of St Denis, or even a chronicle based largely on documents and official material, like the English writers Robert of Avesbury and Geoffrey le Baker. Froissart rarely quotes a document, though he had undoubtedly seen a number of important state papers, and on occasions offers an accurate paraphrase of such items.[8] Equally, he used other chronicles extensively, describing his collection of such manuscripts with pride. Yet this makes him very much a secondary authority: and the first question is whether he ever knows more than other chroniclers.

The answer, as always, is that he knows both more and less. But there are specific problems in using Froissart's account of events which do not apply to other chronicles of the period. Any modern historian with a specific knowledge of a particular medieval period can usually point to errors or muddled passages in a given medieval chronicle. But in most cases, such passages stand out, because the chronicler hesitates and contradicts himself or becomes vague. Froissart, with great literary skills at his disposal, glides smoothly over such problems, giving a spurious air of confidence. Two specific passages can illustrate this: the landing of the Black Prince and John of France in England in 1357, and the arrival of the Black Prince in Aquitaine in 1363. John and the prince sailed from Bordeaux on 11 April 1357 and landed in Plymouth early in May; the royal entourage then made its way at reasonable leisure across England via Salisbury, Sherborne and Winchester. The journey is well documented, in the prince's accounts and in the English chronicles, and we have what is probably an eye-witness account of the 'entry' into London on 24 May, an elaborate ceremonial pageant in which only King John struck a sombre note, dressed in a black robe trimmed with miniver, 'like an old chaplain' (Barber 1978: 152, 260). If we turn to Froissart, we find a rather different story: the prince left Bordeaux with the king in a heavily armed flotilla:

'Car il estoient enfourmé, ains leur departement à Bourdiaus, qui li troi estat, par lesquelz li royaumes estoit gouvrenés, avoient mis sus en Normendie et au Crotoy deux grans armées de saudoiiers, pour aler au devant des Englès et yaus tollir le roy de France; mès onques il n'en veirent nul apparant. Si furent il onze jours et onze nuis sus mer, et arrivèrent au douzime ou havene de Zanduich. Puis issirent li signeur tout bellement hors des naves et des vaissiaus, et se herbergièrent en le ditte ville de Zanduich et ens ès villages environ. Si se tinrent illeuch deux jours, pour yaus rafreschir et leurs chevaus. Au tierch jour, il s'en partirent et s'en vinrent à Saint Thumas de Cantorbie.

Ces nouvelles vinrent jusques au roy d'Engleterre et à le royne, que leurs filz li princes estoit arrivés et avoit amenet le roy de France: si en furent grandement resjoy, ce fu bien raisons; et mandèrent tantost as bourgois de Londres, que il se ordonnassent si honnourablement comme il apertenoit à tel signeur recevoir que le roy de France. Chil de le cité de Londres obeirent au commandement dou roy, et se vestirent par connestablies très richement et ordonnèrent de tous poins pour le roy recueillier; et se vestirent tout li mestier de draps different li uns l'autre.

Or vinrent li rois de France et li princes et leurs routes à Saint Thumas de Cantorbie, où il fisent leurs offrandes, et y reposèrent un jour. A l'endemain, il chevaucièrent jusques à [Rocestre], et puis reposèrent là. Au tierch jour, il vinrent à Dardeforde, et au quart jour à Londres, où il furent très honnourablement receu; et ossi avoient il esté partout de ville en ville où il estoient passet. Si estoit li rois de France, ensi qu il chevauçoit parmi Londres, montés sus un blanc coursier, très bien arret et appareilliet de tous poins, et li princes de Galles sus une petite noire haghenée dalés lui. Ensi fu il aconvoiiés tout au lonch de le cité de Londres jusques à l'ostel de Savoie, liquelz hostelz est hyretages au duc de Lancastre. Là tint li rois de France un temps sa mantion. Et là le vinrent veoir li rois d'Engleterre et la royne, qui le reçurent et festiièrent grandement, car bien le savoient faire; et depuis moult souvent le visetoient et le consoloient ce qu'il pooient (V, 82-3).

The Amiens manuscript tells the same story, though with less detail:

Or avint que, sus le quaremme et environ Pasques, li prinches de Galles, par l'acord et consentment des Gascons, se parti de Bourdiaux à grant navie et belle et bien pourveue de gens d'armes, et enmena le roy Jehan en Engleterre, monseigneur Phelippe son fil, et tous les seigneurs prisonniers qui adonc estoient à Bourdiaux. Si ariva celle belle navie en Engleterre au port de Douvres; si missent hors des vaissiaux chevaux, harnas et touttes autres coses, à grant loisir, et reposèrent trois jours à Douvres. Au quart, s'en partirent, et vinrent à Saint Thummas de Cantorberie, et y fissent li seigneur leur offrande. Depuis, chevauchièrent il tant qu'il vinrent à Londres, où li roys englès et la roynne rechurent à grant joie le roy Jehan, et fu mennés à trompes et à nakaires et à touttes solemnités au palais de Wesmoustier, où il fu bien festiiés. Et fu li roys Jehans logiés assés priès de là, en ung moult très bel hostel et grant que on appelloit Savoie, qui est dou duc de Lancastre. Depuis fu il tranmués de là au castiel de Windesore, et tous ses hostels. Et alloit li roys de Franche cachier, voller, lui deduire en bos et en rivierre tout enssi qu'il li plaisoit; et estoit souvent visetés et conjois dou roy d'Engleterre, de madamme la roynne, sa cousine germainne, et de leurs enffans, et lui faisoient toutte l'amour et le courtoisie qu'il pooient (V, 300).

Leaving aside the question of which is the prior version, and whether Froissart has expanded or condensed his first draft, the basic outline of how his account arose seems reasonably clear. Froissart believed that the prince and the king had landed at Sandwich, a port which he himself had passed through in 1365 (VI, 92). This belief may have been a deduction from the story of the attempted rescue of the king given in the A/B version, since a fleet assembled in Normandy and at the mouth of the Seine (Le Crotoy) would be little use against a flotilla in the western approaches of the Channel. But around this fundamental error, Froissart builds a convincing edifice of detail, derived from his own knowledge of the road from Sandwich to London. The details of the king's reception are equally realistic, but clearly derive either from his imagination, or, more probably, from experience of other similar occasions. The eye-witness account in the *Anonimalle Chronicle* contradicts his two main points: that Londoners were dressed in one colour, not many different colours by trades, and that it was the king who was meanly attired by contrast with the prince (Galbraith 1927: 40-1).

The second example of a 'reconstruction' based on an initial wrong premise is the prince's voyage to Aquitaine in 1363. The prince left England after long delays on 9 June, from Plymouth, and arrived at Lormont, outside Bordeaux on 29 June (Barber 1978: 178-9). Froissart has this to say in the Amiens version, which is here fuller than the A/B version:

Assés tost apriès, se departi d'Engleterre li prinches de Galles et de son hostel de Berkamestede à vingt lieuwes de Londres, où il s'estoit tenus tout le temps en grant reviel avoecquez madamme la princhesse sa femme .... Si vint madamme la roynne d'Engleterre, environ le Noël, à Berkamestede prendre congiet à son fil le prinche et à sa fille le princesse, et fu layens avoecq yaux environ cinq jours, puis s'en retourna à Windesore et tint là son Noël. Et tantost après le festes, li princes et li princesse et tous leurs arois vinrent à Hantonne et entrèrent là ens ès vaissiaux appareillés pour yaux. Si nagièrent tant et singlèrent avoecq le conffort dou vent qu'il arivèrent à le bonne ville de le Rocelle, où il furent recheu à grant joie, moult festiiet et bien honneré; et leur dounna on et presenta grans dons et biaux jewiaux.

Si tost que messires Jehans Cambdos, qui grant tamps avoit gouvrenné le duché d'Acquittainne et touttes les terres appertenans et respondans à celle, sceut la venue dou prinche et de la princesse, qu'il estoient avenut et arivet à le Rocelle, il en fu durement joieans et se parti de Niorth, où il se tenoit, et s'en vint à belle compaignie de chevaliers et d'escuiers deviers monseigneur le prinche. Si se conjoirent et festiièrent grandement, quant il se trouvèrent et encontrèrent. Assés tost apriès, vinrent veoir et conjoir le prinche li signeur de Poito et de Saintonge qui estoient ou pays, et par especial chilx bons chevaliers messires Guichars d'Angle, qui avoit juret et voet, ou kas que li roys de Franche l'avoit rendu au roy d'Engleterre et quitté de foy et d'oummaige, qu'il seroit ossi loyaux au roy d'Engleterre qu'il avoit estet au roy de France; et bien le moustra depuis voirement, si comme vous orés avant en l'istoire (VI, 275-6).

We know from Froissart's own evidence that he was at Berkhamstead in 1361:

Et pur ce que le prince et la princesse se devoient partir d'Angleterre et alerent en Aquitaine tenir leur estat, le roy Edouard d'Angleterre, madame la royne Phelippe ma maistresse . . . [et] leurs enffans, estoient la venus oudit manoir veoir le prince et la princesse (KL XVI, 142).

In this passage, he is correct as to the year, for we know from the prince's accounts that there was a family gathering at Berkhamstead at Christmas 1361; but the earlier passage is wrong, because the prince spent Christmas 1362 at Restormel in Cornwall, and there was no question of the prince's imminent departure at Christmas 1361, although preparations were beginning to be made for the voyage. For someone who was at the English court at this time, Froissart's account is almost incredibly misinformed, implying a departure from Southampton about February 1363, when the actual departure was from Plymouth four months later, and the prince actually came to Windsor in late January and again in April, evidently to see the king. As to the arrival in France, the confusion of events is considerable. Froissart clearly had received some account of the prince's journey to receive the homage of the lords and towns of Aquitaine from July 1363 to April 1364, which took him from Bordeaux along the Dordogne and then back to Angoulême, Saintes, La Rochelle and Poitiers, before he went south to Agen for Christmas 1363. It is from this visit to La Rochelle that Froissart seems to have derived the idea that the prince landed there. Yet it is his version that is still to be found in every modern account, so convincing is his tone.[9]

From 1363 to 1366, Froissart is not well-informed about Aquitaine, nor does he pretend to be. Interestingly, this is also a period when other chronicles provide little information, and his relative silence indicates that he himself relied on other texts for his basic knowledge. Yet some news of the prince's doing must have reached Queen Philippa; again, the only possible conclusion is that he was not recording such information in the 1360s with a chronicle in mind, and that his text was probably composed when his memory of events was already dim, perhaps as much as twenty years later.

This idea is supported by Froissart's account of the Spanish campaign. Although he was himself in Aquitaine in the winter of 1366-7, and was at Bordeaux for the birth of Richard II, he did not accompany the prince to Spain, being sent back from Dax on a mission to the queen (KL XV, 142). He has some valuable material on the preparations for the campaign, including the quarrel of the Black Prince with the lord of Albret, which would account for that lord's behaviour in 1369-70. But for the campaign itself he relies on the account contained in Chandos Herald's verse life of the prince; the latter is generally dated to 1385 on the strength of line 1816, which says that the Spanish campaign took place almost twenty years before the date at which the poet was writing. Although Chandos Herald's life must be later than 1376, the vagueness of his expression — 'ne passa mie des ans vint', and the fact that 'vint' is a rhyme-word, means that the dating is not secure. If Froissart did use the poem as we now have it, it means that the Amiens and A/B versions in the form in which they have come down to us date from the decade 1380-90, and probably from the latter years of that decade. The second possibility, that Chandos Herald, known to be an eye-witness and participant in the Spanish campaign, and — as a herald — trained to record such events, derived his account from Froissart, seems to me quite implausible. The third possibility, that Chandos Herald had written an earlier account of the Spanish campaign which he re-used in the life of the Black Prince and which Froissart also used, is attractive, but cannot be supported by any hard evidence.

To illustrate the difficulty in assessing these possibilities, let us look at some specific instances. Firstly, there is the account of the prince's crossing of the Pyrenees. In tabular form, we get the following results:

1. Chandos Herald (2243-2311)

The vanguard under the duke of Lancaster crosses first, with Thomas Ufford, Hugh Hastings, William Beauchamp son of the earl of Warwick, the lord of Neufville, Chandos (constable of the host) and the men from the companies: the lord of Rays, the lord of Aubeterre, Garsis du Castel, Gaillard de la Motte, Aimery de Rochechouart, Robert Camyn, Creswell, Briquet, Richard Taunton, William Felton, Willecok le Boteller, Peverell, John Sandes, Shakell, Hauley. They were followed by the marshals and Devereux: one marshal was Stephen Cosinton, the other Guichard d'Angle, and they carried the banner of St George. In all, more than 10,000 horse.

Amiens (VII, 261-2)

Omits the names of Creswell, Briquet, Sandes, Shakell and Hauley, but otherwise identical. The names are deformed — Camyn becomes Cheni, Felton becomes Clicleton.

A/B (VII, 7-8)

Alters order — marshals come before Chandos. *Omits* only Sandes, Shakell and Hauley.

31

2. Chandos Herald (2312-2360)

The prince's battalion follows, led by the prince, Pedro and the king of Navarre. With them were Louis de Harcourt, Eustace d'Auberchicourt, Thomas Felton, the lord of Parthenay, the Pommiers brothers, the lords of Clisson, Curton, the lord de la Warre, Robert Knolles, the viscount of Rochechouart, Lord Bourchier, the seneschals of Aquitaine, Poitou, Angoumois, Saintonge, Périgord, Quercy, Bigorre, and 4,000 others, 20,000 horse in all.

Amiens (VII, 262-3)

Adds title of Harcourt, names of Pommiers brothers, Thomas Despenser and *substitutes* Agenois for Angoumois, Rouergue for Périgord; *omits* Saintonge, Knolles. Different order. Gives 8,000 horse.

A/B (VII, 8-9)

Adds title of Harcourt, lords of Pons, Puiane, Tonnay-Boutonne, Argentan, William Felton, Richard Punchardon, Neil Loring, messires d'Aghorises (Degori Says), the lord of Pierrebuffière. *Omits* Pommiers brothers, Clisson, Curton, de la Warre, Knolles, Bourchier, *substitutes* Agenais for Angoumois, Rochelle for Périgord, Limousin for Poitou. Total 12,000 horse. Of the added names, Degori Says is mentioned elsewhere in Chandos Herald (2721) as being in Spain. The lord of Pian (Puiane) was seneschal of the Landes, and Thomas Wettevale (Wetenhale) was seneschal of Rouergue, so these are variations on the list of seneschals. Sir Neil Loring was the prince's chamberlain, and was almost certainly on the expedition. Curiously, Chandos Herald never mentions him anywhere in his poem. Thomas Balastre (Bannastre) was given letters of protection for Aquitaine (Rymer 1830: 731). Richard Punchardon was at Bordeaux in 1366 (KL XVI, 234). I cannot trace references to the other Gascon lords in this period: none are in Chandos.

3. Chandos Herald (2361-2386)

The rearguard crossed the next day led by James, king of Majorca and the count of Armagnac, with Bérard d'Albret, the lord of Mussidan, Bertucat d'Albret, the bour de Bretueil and the bour Camus, Naudon de Bageran, Bernard de la Salle and Lami. No figure given for numbers.

Amiens (VII, 263)

Adds lord of Lesparre, Aimery de Tarse, lord of Chaumont, lord of la Barde, Soudich of Lestrade. None of these names occur elsewhere in Chandos Herald.

A/B (VII, 9)

Adds names omitted from the main body (2, above) except for Bourchier and de la Warre. Also *adds* new names in rearguard in Amiens list. The following added names are unique to this version: the count of Périgord, the viscount of 'Quarmain', the lords of Rosem and Condom, 'Hortingo'. Figure of 10,000 given for number of horse.

In this passage, Amiens has a very small amount of extra information: A/B contains rather more but seems to derive from Amiens. Both are fundamentally the same lists as in Chandos Herald. The additions could easily have come from oral sources, conversations with knights who were on the expedition. The same general remarks hold good for the rest of the account of the campaign, in that the course of events is described in the same sequence and general style, but minor details, particularly lists of names, are altered. For present purposes, the important point is that Froissart is almost certainly using an existing poem or chronicle for the one passage on the Black Prince where his account is really reliable.

For the last years of the Black Prince, Froissart seems to rely on material deriving from French rather than English sources. Two points in his narrative offer good evidence for this. Firstly, there is the account of the proceedings leading up to the renewal of war in 1368-1369, which describes in detail the proceedings in Paris, while giving only in outline the reaction in Bordeaux and London, contrasting Charles V's strictly legal approach with the Black Prince's impotent boasts from his sickbed and Edward III's outraged fury and threats to the French ambassadors.[10] This can be explained by Froissart's absence from the English court after 1367; from 1370 onwards he was moving in circles which were likely to receive news of Aquitaine from France rather than England. It is possible that he drew on a French chronicle for the events of 1368-9, so detailed is his account, while continuing to use Chandos Herald's poem for information about the English view of affairs. All that we know of his movements at this period is that he was at Beaumont in Flanders some time in 1368-9. There is no positive evidence that he returned to England after his visit to Brussels in September 1367.[11]

The second point is the account of the siege of Limoges, which Froissart appears to have obtained from a source distinctly hostile to the English and anxious to make propaganda out of it. This could either be the French court, or that of Pope Gregory XI, because one of his nephews was held captive after the siege until at least 1375. Yet there is little trace of such propaganda in either French chronicles or papal letters. Froissart describes the events following the breach of the city walls as follows:

Cil de piet y pooient bien entrer par là tout à leur aise, et y entrèrent, et coururent à le porte, et copèrent les flaiaus et l'abatirent par terre et toutes les bailles ossi. Et fu tout ce fait si soudainnement que le gens de le ville ne s'en donnoient garde. Evous le prince, le duch de Lancastre, le conte de Cantbruge, le conte de Pennebruch, messire Guiçart d'Angle et tous le aultres, et leurs gens, qui entrent ens, et pillart à piet qui estoient tout apparilliet de mal faire et de courir le ville et de occire hommes et femmes et enfans, car ensi leur estoit il commandé. Là eut grant pité; car hommes, femmes et enfans se jettoient en genoulz devant le prince et crioient: "Merci, gentilz sires, merci!" Mais il estoit si enflammés d'aïr que point n'i entendoit, ne nuls ne nulle n'estoit ois, mès tout mis à l'espée, quanques on trouvoit et encontroit, cil et celles qui point coupable n'i estoient; ne je ne sçai comment il n'avoient pité des povres gens qui n'estoient mies tailliet de faire nulle trahison; mais cil le comparoient et comparèrent plus que li grant mestre qui l'avoient fait.

Il n'est si durs coers, se il fust adonc à Limoges et il li souvenist de Dieu, qui ne plorast tenrement dou grant meschief qui y estoit, car plus de trois mil personnes, hommes, femmes et enfans, y furent deviiet et decolet celle journée. Diex en ait le ames, car il furent bien martir![12]

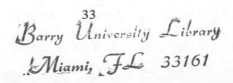

There is some support for Froissart's allegations – provided that he is not the source of their information – in Thomas Walsingham and in the *Chronique des quatre premiers Valois* (Luce 1862), who both speak of widespread slaughter: 'he killed almost everyone he found there . . .' 'he put many of the citizens to death . . .' Yet local chroniclers say nothing of this massacre. The chronicle of the abbey of St Martial in Limoges puts the deaths at 300, which would be less than the estimated number of the citizen militia (Barber 1978: 226). All sources agree that the city was razed, but a captured rebel city was technically at the mercy of its conquerors, and although such devastation was rare, it was by no means unusual. There is another possibility, that the scene is of Froissart's own invention. Froissart is writing a literary as well as a historical work, and the Black Prince is one of the main protagonists. Here was a heroic figure who came to an untimely and melancholy end after a long illness. The literary figure for such a career would have been that of the wheel of fortune, well known from the Arthurian romances – and Froissart on several occasions compares Edward III's court to that of Arthur. So the siege of Limoges becomes part of the dark descending aspect of the Black Prince's career, the reverse of the shining scenes of chivalry at Poitiers.

For the strength and the weakness of Froissart's portrait of the Black Prince, and of much of the early part of the *Chronicles*, is that it is conceived in literary rather than historical terms. Its strength lies in the vital portrait he presents, the high ideals he offers, its weakness in the historical imprecisions and errors. I do not want to suggest that literary considerations overrode Froissart's continual search for what really happened, his determined effort to gather historical evidence from oral and other sources, but only that when his material fell into a recognised literary pattern, he could not resist moulding it to fit a formula; and equally when his material was defective, he used his literary skill and imagination to gloss over the lacunae.

The most valuable element in his record of the prince's deeds is his portrait of the man and of his companions. Even if literary values colour his great set-pieces, such as the prince's chivalrous behaviour after the battle of Poitiers, it tells us a great deal about the attitudes of his heroes. I have studied these set-pieces elsewhere, in examining the legend of the Black Prince as an ideal hero of chivalry and Froissart's contributions to it (1978: 244-50). But there is another side to Froissart's attitude to the prince. As victor of Crécy and Poitiers, Froissart presents the prince as the flower of knighthood, for in his scheme of things only such a paragon could win such victories. He sees also that the prince was an incompetent ruler, out of sympathy with his Gascon subjects and able to take up the cause of an unjust and unpopular king like Peter of Castile. The moderation of Sir John Chandos is contrasted with the prince's obstinacy over the hearth-tax, and, according to the Amiens version, Chandos also opposed the prince's decision to support Peter (VI, 361-2; VII, 69). Indeed, if we really want Froissart's 'greatest hero', it would probably be either Chandos or Sir Walter Mauny, both of whom appear as paragons, one of military skill and statesmanship, the other of chivalry and knightly deeds.

Froissart does not set out to provide us with a specific portrait of any of his protagonists, despite his literary approach to history. He is still primarily concerned with deeds and actions, not with history as biography. Yet he is no longer a chronicler in the old medieval tradition. A comparison between the different versions of Matthew Paris' work or of the fourteenth century St Albans chronicle and the different versions of Froissart shows that Froissart's reworking is primarily literary: it is not condensation nor wholesale incorporation of old material into a 'new' chronicle. He seeks to strike a new balance, to achieve the right effect. For in Book I of his work, Froissart is a historian, rather than a chronicler, if the distinction may be allowed. He is writing at a distance in time from the events he describes, recreating the past from such material as he can obtain, whether oral or written. He is consciously creating a literary work with a purpose, a purpose which differs from the record set down by medieval chroniclers in that it is selective and secular: he wishes 'to encourage all valorous hearts and show them honourable examples' (Johnes I, 3). Froissart is not concerned with mere events, the portents of God's wrath or favour, but is closer to the attitude of the first modern historians. His first book should be set beside Clarendon's *History of the Rebellion*, a similarly brilliant but often factually erratic assessment of a recent past, rather than beside his medieval predecessors.

In sum then, Froissart's account of the Black Prince is not a primary authority, but foremost among the secondary authorities, written from a distance in time, with the advantages of hindsight and leisured assessment as well as the disadvantages of inaccurate or lost information. Furthermore, because of his great literary talents, the most memorable moments in his account of the prince have a legendary rather than strictly historical quality, drawing on the kind of anecdote told about great men after their death. We cannot ignore Froissart in writing the history of the Black Prince's age; we have to admire his literary achievement; but, as historians, we must also treat his work with the greatest of caution.

III THE AGE OF CHARLES V *

John Bell Henneman

JEAN FROISSART loved heroes and heroic deeds. The French, who began to discover their national identity in a period of grave trials, had need of heroes and found some very improbable ones: a frail, studious prince with an aversion to pitched battles; a rough Breton warrior who combined brigandage with bluster and managed to get himself captured by the enemy five different times; and finally, fifty years later, a teenage peasant girl who believed the saints had given her a military mission. To consider how Froissart, the chronicler of heroism, dealt with the age of Charles V and Du Guesclin is no easy matter in these days when an 'anti-hero syndrome' prevails in intellectual circles. Films and literary works now glorify characters who feel alienated or rejected; 'investigative' journalism seeks to expose the foibles of those in power; revisionist historians produce uncomplimentary reappraisals of the respected leaders of the past and cast doubt on the credibility of formerly trusted sources.

Charles V ruled France in a time of victory; his predecessor and successor are associated with great disasters in French history. Does Charles owe his reputation to good luck? It has been suggested recently that the early death of John II enabled Charles to profit from achievements that should be credited to his father (Cazelles 1974: 26), and that Charles himself made serious errors late in his reign but was rescued from the consequences of these mistakes by his own early death (Palmer 1972: 3). As for Froissart, can modern historians regard him as a respectable practitioner of their craft, or must he suffer the fate of his famous fifteenth-century successor, Philippe de Commynes, who was recently denounced for his 'unparalleled mendacity' (Vaughan 1973: 234)?

It is perhaps a symptom of the French need for heroes in 'the calamitous fourteenth century'[1] that the successful Charles V has pre-empted a much larger part of the century than the years covered by his actual reign. Modern French historians, who have honoured most of their medieval monarchs with biographies or regnal histories, have not produced such studies of the unfortunate John II and Charles VI. It has become traditional to begin the period of Charles V with the aftermath of the battle of Poitiers in September 1356, when the capture of John II thrust the young dauphin into the limelight. After his death in 1380, the king continued to cast a shadow, particularly between 1388 and 1392, when his former counsellors (the Marmousets) were able to dominate the royal government. Only in 1392, when Charles VI's first attack of insanity facilitated the dismissal of these officials, did France begin to plunge into the disasters associated with

---

* All references to the *Chronicles* are to page and volume of the SHF edition unless otherwise stated.

this reign. These thirty-six years, from the capture of Charles V's father to the insanity of his son, covered most of Jean Froissart's adult life, the years in which he did the bulk of his travel, research, and writing.

It has been said that Froissart first left his native Hainault in 1356 to seek a patron in England (KL I, i, 35-8). This dating of his first trip is questionable, but it is with the events of 1356 that his account begins to include significant new materials not reproduced from the earlier chronicle of Jean le Bel. Perhaps the very battle that made an important political figure of the future Charles V also fired the imagination of the young Froissart and helped decide him to chronicle the events of his time. By 1392, most of his travels were behind him and he had progressed into the fourth book of the chronicle he had begun to write in earnest more than twenty years before.[2] With the end of Jean le Bel's work in 1362, Froissart becomes fully original. Changing patrons and political circumstances led him to revise his first book and modify his strong initial sympathy for the English, but he retained his commitment to accuracy and the changes in emphasis do not entitle us to dismiss him as a mercenary publicist.[3]

There is no doubt that Froissart tried strenuously to get the facts and report them. He travelled widely, interviewed witnesses, and sought access to official documents which he quoted or paraphrased. Like most historians, however, he searched only for information that he deemed significant; and like most chroniclers (and their modern successors, the tabloid newspapers), he reported what he thought would interest his intended audience. Consequently, he included material that we might dismiss as trivial, while failing to do justice to matters now considered to be of prime importance. Because he was a better and more interesting writer than most medieval chroniclers and most modern historians, posterity has conferred on him the fame that he desired, but if we are now to evaluate him as an historical source he must pass sterner tests.

Froissart's ability to tell a good story has made him attractive to writers of narrative, event-orientated political history, a style that nowadays is unfairly dismissed as old-fashioned. When it was most in vogue, this method was practised by historians whose perceptions of the political process were coloured by nineteenth-century attitudes towards the nobility of the *ancien régime*. Social, economic, and institutional historians have distrusted narrative sources, Froissart included, and have demanded the greater precision of official documents. Many contemporary historians have allowed themselves to become intrigued by 'popular culture', and nearly all of us have been influenced by the 'new social history' associated with Marc Bloch. Perhaps the most striking feature of current historiography is a pervasive 'anti-élitism' that induces scholars to neglect, if not reject, a writer like Froissart, whose main concern was to relate the great deeds of the great personalities of his age. It is possible, however, that the increasingly sophisticated methods of modern historical scholarship can be applied to a 'new political history' that will examine the phenomenon of leadership and policy-making — the behaviour of élites in a military and political context. The period of Charles V offers a fertile field for such a study, and our ultimate assessment of Froissart as an historian of this period may hinge upon his contribution to this kind of research.

Our inquiry must begin, however, in a more conventional manner. If Froissart was interested in great events and great personalities, how well did he deal with the great events after 1356, as judged by current historical scholarship? At the outset, we are in for some disappointment. The political crisis at Paris between the autumn of 1356 and the summer of 1358 clearly ranks as one of the most important aspects of this whole period, with major implications for the future constitutional development of France. Yet Froissart's account, which virtually reproduced the faulty report of Jean le Bel, was not changed or augmented significantly in later versions and provides little of value to modern historians.

The crisis involved, among other things, unusually frequent meetings of the Estates General, which had already convened three times in ten months, had granted taxes in return for promises of reform, but had utterly failed to deliver the funds that might have made the Estates indispensable and the reforms effective. Meeting again in an atmosphere of disaster, the Estates of October 1356 had no king to deal with. The Dauphin Charles lacked both experience and prestige, and the most visible manifestation of the government was a group of royal officials. Not only were these associated with mismanagement of finances and unpopular manipulation of the coinage, but many of them had risen from the ranks of the Parisian bourgeoisie. They were universally disliked – by nobles, by advocates of governmental reform, and especially by the prominent bourgeois of Paris and the other northern towns who envied the power and wealth they had gained in royal service. With the French army beaten and no money to pay troops, and with much of the north-western nobility opposing the crown in support of the captive Charles of Navarre, Normandy and the Île de France were embroiled in brigandage and civil war.[4]

The assembly of Estates, apparently very large, delegated to a smaller, but still sizeable, group the task of drawing up proposals. More than thirty members of this commission were regarded by the royal officials as their particular enemies.[5] These officers prevailed upon the dauphin to reject the proposals and dissolve the Estates, but some members remained in session illegally to hear inflammatory speeches. In the next few months the dauphin failed to obtain money by other expedients, was intimidated by the Parisians, and finally had to recall the Estates. In March 1357, he issued a lengthy ordinance of reform at the behest of this assembly.[6]

Contemporary sources, written from differing points of view, present various accounts and interpretations of these and subsequent political developments at the French court.[7] The Froissart-Le Bel version is riddled with errors. The Estates of October 1356 are said to have delegated all authority to a commission consisting of twelve members of each order. The actual commission seems to have been much larger and its task was merely to draw up proposals. One of these called upon the dauphin to replace his advisers with a council made up of appointees of the Estates. Froissart does not mention the assembly of early 1357, nor the great ordinance issued in March. He does refer to the unauthorised liberation of Charles of Navarre late in 1357, but places this event after the famous murder of two marshals in the dauphin's presence in February 1358.[8] This last event (to which Froissart wrongly adds a third victim, Simon de Bucy) drove a decisive wedge between the nobility and the bourgeois critics of the government. It also had much to do with the circumstances in which the dauphin assumed the regency in March 1358 (Froissart calls him regent eighteen months earlier) and left Paris to negotiate with the nobles.[9] Froissart mentions the dauphin's departure but not until after he discusses the Jacquerie that in fact occurred three months later.[10] It is curious that Kervyn de Lettenhove, whose edition contains extensive notes, did not attempt to clarify this muddled chronology and point out the more obvious errors. Simon Luce, with his far greater knowledge of the French government archives, did make this effort, and for those interested in Froissart's accuracy in reporting political events, Luce's edition is the only acceptable one in any language. We are now aware of some mistakes by Luce, but these are the sort one would expect to turn up during a century of further scholarly effort.[11]

It has been pointed out, in fairness to Froissart, that his is one of the first major chronicles that can be, and has been, checked for accuracy by comparison with the increasingly abundant archival material at our disposal.[12] The real question is why Froissart, who took such pains to obtain accurate information about some things and rewrote large parts of his chronicle, did not make the effort to find out more about the French political and constitutional crisis of 1356-8. One can only conclude that it did not interest him. The royal chroniclers at St Denis, the embattled financial officers, and critics of the government or the aristocracy all had strong reasons for wishing to record their versions of these events, as well as some access to the royal archives. Froissart's concern was with heroic deeds and feats of arms; one finds little of either in the political struggle that followed John II's capture. In thinking of Froissart as a chronicler of the great events of his day, we must remember that the events in question were those that he perceived as important. For milestones in the development of taxation, representative assemblies, or institutions of government, we must look elsewhere.

These considerations may explain why Froissart has not been valued as a source by institutional historians, but there is a good deal more to this period than institutional history. We shall continue our inquiry by considering four 'subject areas' in which Froissart's comments (and his omissions) may be revealing. Three of these relate to Charles V as ruler of France: (1) the events of 1358-64 and the problem of who controlled French policy; (2) Charles V's relations with the nobility and his choice of those who served him; and (3) the events of 1378-83 and what they imply about French leadership. The fourth area, which relates to broader questions of social history, is his treatment of military activity – both the sordid side of war (brigandage and acquisitiveness) and its glamorous side (chivalry, military etiquette, and the pitched battle). Each of these 'subject areas', and Froissart's treatment of them, deserve closer study from modern scholars. No broad conclusions can be attempted in these pages, but it may be possible to suggest avenues of inquiry that should utilise Froissart.

The murder of Étienne Marcel and the dauphin's recovery of Paris at the beginning of August, 1358, mark the point at which the French could give serious consideration to ransoming their king. The task was made extremely difficult by the rising level of brigandage and the intermittent hostility of that enemy of the Valois, Charles 'the Bad' of Navarre, who still commanded an important following in the region of his Norman lands. His intrigues in 1358 helped to wreck one treaty for the release of John II, but the French at this date were hardly ready to raise a ransom anyway. A second, harsher treaty, negotiated at London in 1359, was rejected by the dauphin's government in May. Edward III again invaded

France, but not until the autumn. Although generally victorious, he could not take Reims or Paris, nor force a major engagement with the French, and in the spring of 1360 he concluded a treaty with the dauphin at Brétigny. More moderate than the document of 1359, it was ratified at Calais in October when John II was released. The dauphin had supervised a remarkable fiscal effort to secure the first ransom payment, and in December 1360 an important royal ordinance stabilised the silver currency, established the gold franc, and set up the *aides* and *gabelle* — indirect taxes that were to finance the rest of the ransom and also happened to be the first regular peacetime taxes in French history.[13]

Back in his kingdom for what would be slightly more than three years, John II had to contend with the continuing disorders of unemployed troops, whose two most famous actions were the seizure of Pont-Saint-Esprit late in 1360 and the defeat of a royal army at Brignais in April 1362. In 1361, John appropriated the duchy of Burgundy as his inheritance, provoking a new rupture with Charles of Navarre. The companies of brigands, after being paid a large sum to go to Spain, poured back into France after participating in a battle between the warring counts of Foix and Armagnac in Gascony. John II spent many months in Languedoc in 1362-63, mostly discussing a crusade with the pope at Avignon. Meanwhile, several French princes who were hostages in England negotiated a new treaty that promised Edward more lands in return for their release. The French government did not ratify it, but one of the royal hostages, Louis of Anjou, broke parole and refused to return to Calais. The Estates of northern France, convened at Amiens late in 1363, authorised a new direct tax (*fouage*) to combat brigandage, and heard the king announce plans to return to England. After just four months there, John died, just as Franco-Navarrese hostilities in Normandy were reaching a critical stage. While Charles V was proceeding with his coronation, the royal commander, Bertrand du Guesclin, broke the power of Charles of Navarre by defeating his forces at Cocherel.[14]

Such, in brief, were the events that now seem to have been most important for French political history between 1358 and 1364. Froissart, not surprisingly, ignores the crucial question of how the French set about raising the money for the ransom. He says nothing about taxation, not even mentioning the *fouage* granted in 1363, which ultimately paid the salaries of so many of the troops whose exploits he described. Nor does he mention the stabilisation of the coinage, a valuable concession to the nobles and long a major political issue in France. To be sure, when Froissart acquired most of his first-hand knowledge of French political issues the monetary question had receded into the past.

Even if he did not write about these years until long afterwards, we might expect Froissart to have had some contact with the French fund-raising effort and the establishment of the new currency if he actually travelled to Narbonne in 1360 and thence to Paris as Kervyn de Lettenhove has suggested. What makes it especially doubtful that he ever took such a trip is his handling (or mishandling) of a subject in which he was much interested: the activities of the companies of brigands. His trip would have been complicated, to say the least, by those companies known as the Tard-Venus, who eventually took Pont-Saint-Esprit at the end of 1360. Froissart places the battle of Brignais a year too early (the spring of 1361 rather than 1362), and has it *followed* by the capture of Pont-Saint-Esprit and very shortly by Seguin de Badefol's occupation of Anse (which actually occurred in 1364).[15] Luce, whose notes point out the actual dates, did not pursue the matter, nor did he try to explain the chronicler's errors.[16] They are certainly not the mistakes of a first-hand observer, particularly one with Froissart's passion for the details of military activities. It is virtually inconceivable that he was in southern France in this period.

In actually describing battles like Brignais and Cocherel, Froissart is convincing in his presentation of details,[17] and much the same can be said of the English campaign of 1359, about which, we may infer, his principal informant was a participant, Eustache d'Auberchicourt.[18] Even if his informants were self-serving, they offer valuable evidence on the values of the military class and contemporary notions of proper tactics. He offers us an interesting picture of the unbeaten but frustrated Edward III in the Beauce during the spring of 1360, being talked into the negotiations that quickly produced the treaty of Brétigny (VI, 4). He had first-hand access to documents that accompanied the ratification of this settlement at Calais.[19]

One of Froissart's most intriguing inaccuracies concerns the abortive second treaty of London in 1359. This document was rejected by the dauphin, who assembled the Estates for that purpose at the end of May. According to Froissart, Charles of Navarre and the dauphin, having become reconciled, were together when the treaty was delivered to France and concurred in opposing it.[20] Now the Franco-Navarrese peace was not concluded until some months later, so this account is clearly erroneous, although Charles the Bad had reasons for not welcoming this treaty.[21] Froissart's story, however, concludes with a supposed quotation from John II in London, to the effect that his son had been gulled by Charles of Navarre into rejecting the settlement.[22] Even if the king never uttered these words, they cannot be dismissed as mere fabrication. The chronicler surely talked to somebody who had been close enough to John to be aware of his feelings. Recalling this when writing about the treaty, he probably assumed that the Franco-Navarrese reconciliation had come early enough to fit the testimony he had heard. John knew well that his son had come under the influence of Charles the Bad in 1355-56, to the point of very nearly becoming a tool in intrigues against the French monarch (Cazelles 1958: 259-60). Not having seen the dauphin since the day of Poitiers, John was in no position to judge the extent to which political adversity had matured him.

The place of Charles V in history depends in part on our assessment of John II. Froissart takes note of two of the most controversial incidents in John's last years: his prolonged absence in Languedoc discussing a crusade with the pope and his decision to return to England at the end of 1363. These actions have persuaded some historians that the dauphin, rather than John, controlled the French government in the early 1360s, and have also caused John to be stigmatised as an empty-headed exemplar of chivalric decadence. The English-speaking world has long been influenced by the superb translation of Edward Perroy's highly literate history of the Hundred Years War. One of the eminent French historians of this century, Perroy stands out as perhaps the most severe of John II's critics, but a recent article by Raymond Cazelles has challenged his assessment of the king.[23] Was, for instance, the crusading scheme a lot of anachronistic foolishness, reflecting John's desire to fulfil his father's earlier vow without regard for the exhaustion of his realm or his own questionable record as a battle-field commander? In thinking so, Perroy was prepared to accept one of Froissart's explanations while rejecting the other. Froissart acknowledged the king's concern for his father's vow, but added that John had a second motive — to rid the country of brigands (VI, 83). The weight of evidence suggests that this second motive was paramount in the king's mind. It was certainly a major concern of Urban V, who devoted most of his pontificate to devising more or less plausible crusading schemes to rid Europe of its undesirable excess of men-at-arms.[24] Similar motives had influenced Urban II in 1095. Realists may have questioned the practicality of an expedition to the Levant or the Balkans, but the first attempt to send the *routiers* to Spain had just failed, and the king of Cyprus was in the West, seeking reinforcements. Perroy would have done better to take seriously Froissart's second explanation for John's crusading scheme. The king was fully mindful of the plight of his realm.

In discussing John's return to England, Froissart mentions his desire to 'make excuses' for Louis of Anjou's escape to France, but does not imply that the royal sense of honour was the main reason for the trip. He makes the visit seem more like a reunion with family than a return to captivity.[25] Perhaps Froissart was being tactful: others (Newhall 1953: 116) thought John merely wished to escape to the pleasures of the English court. John doubtless intended to conduct negotiations, to replace the defunct 'treaty of the hostages' or to deal with the reasons for lagging payments of the ransom. Contrary to some opinions, the *aides* and *gabelle* were quite adequate to provide the necessary funds, but much of the money had to be diverted to deal with brigandage.[26] Just before leaving France, John had obtained the new *fouage* from the Estates for this purpose. Having explored the prospects of a crusade to employ the Companies elsewhere and having obtained additional funds from his own subjects, John must have felt entitled to demand more cooperation from the English monarch who had been unwilling or unable to suppress the troops that his campaigning had brought to France. Froissart took particular note of how Brittany, excluded from the Anglo-French treaty, had become a major base for these soldiers (VI, 50-2). If Edward hoped to receive in full the ransom payments to which he was entitled, he might be persuaded to help stamp out the brigandage that delayed those payments. Froissart does not enlighten us on the matter, but he offers little support for Perroy's harsh judgment of the king.

Although he left the dauphin in charge of the government during his absences in Languedoc and England, John does not seem to have relinquished control over policy. His rule was not, however, very effective. Despite peace with England, regular tax revenues, and the best intentions, his government seemed paralysed in the face of the brigand companies. Even if John, rather than his son, had benefitted from the army financed by the *fouage* of 1363, that tax was not so much a triumph of royal policy as a last resort, by which the Estates applied to a large area the sort of fiscal remedy already tried by assemblies in smaller regions when they found that the crown could not help them expel the *routiers* (Henneman 1976: 206-28). Once levied, the tax helped Charles V pay his troops regularly (Contamine 1972: 146), thus improving his standing with the nobles and contributing to the military successes that have given his reign a favourable reputation. In this as in other respects, Charles V was blessed with good fortune, not because he had a clever and foresighted father but because France, in her misfortune, was deprived of many options and forced to adopt as policies 'the commonplace tasks which alone remained within her power' (Perroy 1951: 149).

When we consider Charles V's relations with the nobility, we find that Charles may be contrasted strikingly, and on the whole favourably, with his father in the kind and calibre of men he chose to serve him. John II had been roundly criticised for surrounding himself with dishonest *parvenus*, among whom even some of those with titles were the ennobled descendents of wealthy Parisians.[27] His use of such people may have been a partial cause and partial result of the disaffection of large numbers of north-western nobles from the first two Valois monarchs.[28] Charles V inherited some of his father's men, and Perroy reflected a general view when he said that Charles relied on 'small fry' (1951: 148). Cazelles, however, has questioned this generalisation (1974: 26), and as we shall see, the new king actually drew heavily for support on that very segment of the nobility which had opposed his predecessors (Henneman 1978: 954-5).

Among the servants inherited from John were two military commanders from petty noble families — Arnoul d'Audrehem and Bertrand du Guesclin. Both were 'small fry' and both proved singularly inept in pitched battles, but both had been loyal to the Valois at a time when many nobles with similar backgrounds were becoming soldiers of fortune without consistent allegiance. Audrehem had risen to the rank of marshal and was royal lieutenant in Languedoc. Du Guesclin's renown was essentially local until his victory at Cocherel. Charles V treated the two men very differently. Du Guesclin was loaded with honours, entrusted with important missions, and eventually made constable. Audrehem was removed from his post in Languedoc and gradually eased out of the military leadership. In treating them so differently, Charles V must have been judging the two men on their ability to deal with the Companies. In Languedoc, where Audrehem had been unable to cope with their depredations, Charles installed his brother, Louis of Anjou, as royal lieutenant. Louis had youth, energy, and royal blood, but such qualities never made John of Berry effective in Languedoc. Anjou's great skill was in dealing with the *routiers*. He could punish ruthlessly those who crossed him, but Froissart repeatedly notes the presence of *routier* captains in Anjou's service. Only in his command did they serve the Valois on a regular basis.[29] Froissart makes equally clear the respect with which the *routiers* regarded Du Guesclin, and Perroy suggests (1951: 148-9) that the Breton warrior, something of a brigand himself, was adept at mastering these freebooters and knew how to utilise their skills most effectively. Du Guesclin's recruitment to the Valois cause may have been the work of John II, but it was Charles V who knew how to flatter him and select him for the most appropriate assignments.

Even before his father's release, Charles had found other men he could trust. Jean de Conflans, one of the marshals murdered in 1358, was an early defector from the opposition.[30] Pierre de Villaines, 'the Stammerer', appears throughout the pages of Froissart. Although one of the 'small fry', he remained a prominent figure for half a century after the dauphin enlisted him in the 1350s.[31] Many nobles from important families are found among the prominent military commanders of Charles V. The great majority came from the north and west, including many who had been hostile to the earlier Valois kings and had supported Charles of Navarre (Henneman 1978: 953-5). Charles V was adept at winning the loyalty and support of nobles with real ability, important connections, or both. The 'small fry' who served Charles were valued for their abilities. No doubt the time was ripe for a *rapprochement* with the aristocracy, but Charles managed to exploit the situation without in turn being exploited. Froissart's occasional allusions to those who 'turned French' are but a partial indication of the crown's progress in rebuilding support. Charles V became reconciled with the Harcourt family and enticed Enguerrand de Coucy back into French service.[32]

His most important catch, however, was Olivier de Clisson, a Breton lord whose family was of more recent prominence than Du Guesclin's but was extremely well-connected and thus more influential among the Breton aristocracy. Clisson's father had been executed by Philip VI, who confiscated some of the family lands.[33] As early as 1360, the dauphin returned some of these possessions (VI, lxxvii, n.2). Clisson, however, continued to support the anti-French faction in Brittany and fought against Du Guesclin at Auray in 1364.[34] After the treaty that recognised John IV as duke of Brittany, Clisson became fully reconciled with the French crown. By 1370, in fact, he had broken completely with his duke and had begun to play a crucial role in the French army and government (Jones 1970: 48-55, 94-101). In giving the impression that Clisson became a trusted royal councillor as early as 1365, Froissart seems to have been anticipating events by a few years, but in saying of Clisson that 'without him nothing was done', our chronicler reveals how contemporaries in the 1370s perceived the Breton's influence at court.[35]

Many prominent nobles resided in the large principality of Aquitaine that the treaty of Brétigny assigned to England, and their dealings with the king of France are an especially interesting feature of Charles' relations with the nobility. Throughout the pages of Froissart, we find lists of military leaders who were present at different engagements. Among those who appear most frequently were the great lords of Poitou, who fought on the French side at Poitiers (when many lords of Normandy, Brittany, and the north were absent) and fought repeatedly on the English side once the treaty required the transfer of their homage to the prince of Wales. There were many defections from the English cause after the resumption of hostilities in 1369, but the Poitevin lords, as a group, were the most steadfast in standing by the Black Prince. The French did not succeed in regaining their support until the reconquest of Poitou was virtually assured by the naval battle off La Rochelle. Such, at least, is the impression Froissart gives us.[36]

In the southern, or Gascon, regions of Aquitaine, however, it was a different story. There the leading lords were reluctant to accept their transfer to Plantagenet suzerainty, and while they did serve the Black Prince through the Spanish campaign of 1367, there were early signs of friction.[37] When the Prince levied a *fouage* in Aquitaine to restore his depleted finances, the protests of the Gascon lords created such an uproar that Froissart, for the first time, became interested in the issue of taxation. There followed the famous appeals to the French court, which Charles V accepted only after a year of careful political groundwork in the south-west. The war resumed and the king gave handsome pensions to the rebel lords for, in effect, defending their own lands against the reprisals of the English.[38] Having recently been in Bordeaux, Froissart was particularly well-informed about these events and the personalities of the participants. Historians would be well advised to re-examine his account as part of a comprehensive new study of the political behaviour of the nobility throughout Aquitaine. Why do the Poitevins, in striking contrast to the Gascons, appear to have been more loyal to their legal overlord than other regional aristocracies in France?

As for Charles V, his cultivation of, and cooperation with, the nobility, both great and small, must be seen as a cornerstone of his policy and a key to the success of his reign. When one considers broadly the reigns of the first five Valois kings (1328-1461), one finds that all of them except Charles V were troubled by factional struggles, as cliques of nobles vied with each other for royal favour or influence at court. It is hard to believe that only Charles V recognised that the nobles were (as Perroy put it) 'the only class that counted' (1951: 126). Yet he understood them and their foibles, knew how to conciliate them and use their talents, and created a milieu in which they could pursue not only their own interests but also those of the monarchy. His mastery of the nobility paralleled Du Guesclin's mastery of the *routiers*, and perhaps their common skill in handling people is the real link between these two unlikely 'heroes' of late fourteenth-century France. As for the nobles, they were not merely being manipulated. They were well aware of their interests and how to pursue and protect them. Perroy was the victim of nineteenth-century assumptions when he dismissed the nobles as being 'devoid of any political sense' (1951: 130).

We must not allow our own assumptions to be formed by Christine de Pisan. Charles V was capable of errors and he certainly made some at the end of his reign. In his eagerness to have a pope at Avignon, he gave too-hasty recognition to Clement VII in 1378. The action may have seemed politically appropriate at the time, but the government of his successor would have reason to deplore it. Had Charles supported Urban VI, the Schism could not have endured; his action, once taken, could not be reversed by any French government without the implicit, and unthinkable, admission of having been schismatic. In addition, the king's personal animosity towards Louis II of Flanders and John IV of Brittany led him to overplay his hand in these two fiefs, thus inviting dangerous new English interventions (Palmer 1972: 3, 18-20).

The king's most famous 'blunder' was his deathbed cancellation of the *fouage*, the tax that really paid for the royal army. Although Froissart characteristically ignored this action, it has provoked an endless debate among modern historians, who have failed to reach any consensus about his motives.[39] We know that the royal policy of avoiding pitched battles was a calculated risk that exposed the French countryside to repeated ravages (Palmer 1972: 5-8). Such misery became intolerable when the momentum of the French reconquests slowed down. Revolt against taxes at Montpellier had led to Anjou's recall from Languedoc earlier in 1380 (Henneman 1976: 299). Even a healthy king would have had difficulty stemming the reaction against taxes. The tax Charles cancelled was the one that most irritated the nobles and bore most heavily on the afflicted countryside. His death, however, left as regent Louis of Anjou, who was associated with harsh fiscal exactions. The towns, which paid the bulk of the remaining taxes, rose in anger, and a crisis was at hand.[40]

Philip, duke of Burgundy, who had vital interests at stake, responded by over-throwing Charles V's plan for a regency. The young Charles VI was declared an adult, the *aides* and *gabelle* cancelled, and the Estates convened. Although

Anjou's ally, Clisson, did become constable (and later the leader of the anti-Burgundian faction), Louis himself steadily lost influence in the government and departed for Italy in 1382. Under Burgundy's leadership, the government extricated itself from an awkward situation in Brittany by making a new treaty with John IV, and it obtained new taxes after difficult negotiations. The French army crushed the Flemish rebels at Roosebeke in 1382 and then felt strong enough to reimpose the *aides* and *gabelle* and suppress the resultant revolts.[41]

In describing these events, Froissart combined insight with ignorance. His position on the Schism was essentially Clementist, but he shows a striking lack of conviction on the subject, notices bad behaviour on both sides, and seems to treat the entire issue as a political one. Perhaps he himself was merely being politic.[42] He is most revealing about the animosity between Charles V and his great vassals of Brittany and Flanders, and portrays vividly the desire of the Breton lords to preserve the autonomy of the duchy (which Charles V threatened), provided that John IV renounce the aid of the English.[43] On internal French politics, Froissart is sharply pro-Burgundian and clearly ignorant of the ordinance that had named Louis of Anjou regent. He portrays a dying Charles V who was deeply suspicious of Anjou's cupidity, and has Anjou seizing power when the king died.[44] Although this description is contrary to what actually took place, it leaves no doubt about Anjou's reputation. Throughout his career, Philip of Burgundy was fortunate in enjoying a 'good press' from the French chroniclers.[45] Obviously upset at the English rebellion of 1381, Froissart conveys a vivid impression of class conflict in this period. A French defeat at Roosebeke, he thought, would have led to serious uprisings in France with disastrous results for the French nobility; the French victory in Flanders, while a political blow to the English, was quietly applauded by the English aristocracy.[46]

In writing his chronicle, Froissart devoted by far the most space to what we must assume was his greatest interest — the conduct of war. His treatment of this subject will be considered in another chapter, but something must be said about it here because it bears so heavily on our understanding of the age of Charles V. In this last of those subject areas we set out to examine, our concern will be limited to a few aspects of the problem that relate particularly to French politics and society in the quarter of a century that followed the battle of Poitiers.

Froissart has been criticised for emphasising the 'glamorous', rather than the 'sordid', side of warfare, but we should note that he did not ignore the latter. We find many references to pain and brutality, the slaughter of innocent people, and the evident desire of the nobles for booty and lucrative ransoms.[47] What he does is to treat these things as a matter of routine, not requiring elaboration because his audience would know that they were an inevitable part of warfare. In this respect, he differed little from military historians of other times. Not until quite recently have writers really considered warfare from the point of view of suffering, human costs, or the feelings of ordinary participants. What really irritates the modern reader is not Froissart's lack of emphasis on the misery of war, but rather the way in which he stresses the glamorous side of things — the great feats of arms, the valour, the etiquette. In doing so, however, he was reflecting the attitudes of the military class of his own day, telling his audience the things they wanted to hear and, like most military historians, viewing military engagements mainly from the point of view of those in command.

More to the point, Froissart's saga of military exploits has to deal with two sets of contradictory impulses, both of very ancient origin. The first of these contradictions arises from the fact that throughout human history the warrior has generally been accorded an honoured and prestigious place in society as opposed, for instance, to the tradesman or agricultural worker, yet the practice of war has always implied the possibility of physical agony. To reconcile the pain with the prestige has required the development of a mythology or etiquette. The most effective military mythology has been the sacred cause, the notion of fighting for or against something definite. We can only surmise that the French crusaders who set out in 1096 were better motivated than those who went to Aragon in 1285. It is less difficult to compare the motivation of the French armies of the 1790s with those of a century earlier, or that of American combat troops in 1943 with their successors in 1968. Now the fourteenth century was a time that suffered from, among other things, a sort of historical hiatus between causes. The religious ideal of the crusade and the tradition of feudal loyalty had both lost their vitality, while the spirit of nationalism and the new religious zeal of the Reformation had not yet appeared. Consequently, the mythology that alone makes combat psychologically endurable was in a state of disrepair. Personal honour and pecuniary gain were all that were left. They were not always compatible, but even when they were it was more comfortable to talk about the former while thinking about the latter.

Each of these motivations was, in essence, highly individualistic in character, and this brings us to the second of the contradictions implicit in fourteenth-century warfare: the tension between individual action and group discipline. In most military encounters, a disciplined fighting force has the advantage over troops fighting as a group of individuals, although technological factors can modify this rule. If anything, the advance of military technology (if we may call it that) places a greater premium on cohesion and discipline. In the pages of Froissart, we find a continuing tension between individual action and disciplined tactics. As an admirer and chronicler of heroism, Froissart stresses individual action, yet his accounts make it clear that in the large engagements the advantage lay with the side that managed some degree of coordinated tactics. He is a particularly useful source for guerrilla warfare, small operations, and actions constituting outright brigandage. It was in this area that individualism still counted for something. Du Guesclin, that strutting egotist, could be, and was, a hero in this milieu. In pitched battles he was a failure, except at Cocherel, where he cunningly exploited the egotism of a kindred spirit on the opposing side and induced the enemy to abandon superior positions against the better judgment of their experienced commander.[48]

One of his few vivid portrayals of the discomforts faced by the fighting man is also found in his discussion of Cocherel, where he calls attention to the oppressive heat that made the hours of waiting so difficult for men in armour to endure (VI, 119). This factor may have been important in influencing the behaviour of armoured, dismounted knights in battlefield conditions. They had to operate under physical conditions that increased the difficulty of playing a waiting game and reinforced the tendency to rush headlong into combat with all the risks that such action entailed.

The behaviour of French knights in battle during the fourteenth century is in fact an important problem that historians need to re-examine. The spectacular defeats and their immediate consequences, which are well-known, evidently led Charles V to make a particular point of avoiding pitched battles. His explicit instructions to this effect have been chronicled by Froissart.[49] It was a policy that invited destructive English raids and precluded total victory (Palmer 1972: 5-7). Yet the subsequent disasters at Nicopolis and Agincourt have made it hard for historians to criticise Charles for his defensive posture. Why, however, did the French perform so badly in battle? Were they unable to adjust to new technology or tactics? Did each defeat breed a psychological need to try again and prove that the traditional tactics worked? Was Charles V a tactical genius or a coward? Did he aspire to be a 'universal spider' luring his enemies to their doom, or was he merely a cautious man of conservative temperament? Was there a basic defect in French generalship, and if so, did Charles perceive it?

Such questions did not torment historians schooled in the assumptions of the nineteenth century. Knowing that traditional feudalism was in decay, and influenced by the achievements of the revolution of 1789, they found it easy to perceive the nobles of the fourteenth century as anachronistic relics of a bygone age. They were the victims of their own 'vainglory' and were beaten by lowborn archers and pikemen. Froissart would not have been happy with this assessment, but Kervyn de Lettenhove (I, i, 429-30) detected in his writings a criticism of the decline of chivalry: courtesy was giving way to covetousness. Perhaps the real problem was that courtesy itself had changed. Once it had embodied the concept, encouraged by the clergy, that the true knight's mission was to protect the weak against the strong. Now it was essentially a code of etiquette observed by members of the upper class in dealing with each other. Johan Huizinga's picture of later chivalry suggests a society in decay (1954: 67-107). For Maurice Keen, however, the fourteenth century marked the elaboration of an international law of arms, which regulated the behaviour and treatment of combatants.[50] In this sense, the remnants of the old chivalry can be seen as a remote ancestor of the modern Geneva Convention.

Whatever we may think of fourteenth-century chivalry, however, the fact remains that the French nobility still constituted an important and vital social class, whose 'political sense' Perroy vastly underrated. Historians who treat these people as anachronisms in the fourteenth century are themselves guilty of anachronism. We cannot, therefore, evade the critical question of why the nobles, who were, above everything, supposed to be military experts, proved so unsuccessful in pitched battles. Froissart was not merely trying to excuse unsuccessful commanders by blaming their failures on bad counsel (KL I, i, 438). In many instances, sound advice was given, but rejected; sound tactical plans were abandoned in the heat of battle; the tactical importance of a rearguard was recognised, but the best commanders did not wish to command it.[51] We are left with the contradictions already mentioned: the only things deemed worth fighting for (i.e. risking life and limb for) were personal honour and financial gain, but these were essentially individual goals, incompatible with the collective tactical discipline that alone could assure victory. Charles V, who understood his nobles so well, may indeed have grasped this fact, in which case his policies were justified. Such a conclusion cannot be documented, however, without a careful re-examination of French military behaviour using the methods of modern scholarship. In such an endeavour, Froissart cannot fail to be an extremely important source.

In reviewing Froissart's treatment of the age of Charles V, we need not be unduly troubled about his inaccuracies in reporting or dating political events or his utter lack of interest in institutional history, as long as we are properly aware of them. We should, however, be wary of his editors and translators and prefer Luce to the others when considering Book I. Nor need we be troubled by his love of heroes and heroic deeds. If we ourselves are not unduly influenced by the tradition of Christine de Pisan (or that of Edward Perroy), we can read Froissart without finding Charles V or Du Guesclin exalted beyond their talents. They were two of the great figures of their age, and are often shown at their best, but they are also portrayed in more controversial or less flattering terms. The erroneous notion that Charles presided over an age of unbroken French success would never be derived from a careful reading of Froissart, but the reader must be alert to his own assumptions as well as those of the chronicler.

It is possible to predict a resurgence of interest in Froissart as an historical source for this period if historians recognise the importance of undertaking a 'new political history'. We need to restudy the French nobles — their attitudes, their economic interests, and their behaviour in war and politics. Even in moments of humiliation in battle, factional strife, and destructive brigandage, they were of crucial importance to French society. In calling them the only class that counted, Perroy was not exaggerating very much, but the notion offends our twentieth-century egalitarianism, and they have counted far too little in the work of our best contemporary scholars.

IV CHARLES VI AND RICHARD II *

J. W. Sherborne

ON his journey to the court of the count of Foix in the autumn of 1388,[1] Froissart made the invaluable acquaintance of Sir Espan du Lion, who was to delight him by the knowledgeable answers he gave to his many questions about the history and politics of the regions through which they were travelling. 'If God grants me health', he told the knight, 'not a word of yours will be lost. They will all be chronicled, provided God grants me health to return to Valenciennes' (XII, 115). But Sir Espan disappointed Froissart in one important respect, and the chronicler records the evasive replies he received to his several inquiries about the fate of the count's heir, Gaston. Eventually, Froissart was obliged to seek the information elsewhere, from one of the veterans of the court. Young Gaston, he then learnt, had been accidentally killed by his own father, in a moment of rage. The young prince had believed a promise by the king of Navarre that his father would be reconciled with his wife, if a pinch of magic powder was sprinkled over his father's meat when the boy served him at dinner. As it turned out, the powder was a poison which killed a pet dog when the suspicious count sprinkled some on the animal's food.

This story is rehearsed in all seriousness by Froissart and both the manner and the matter of his account are too typical of much of his approach to historical writing. The entire episode has clearly been conceived as 'a good story' rather than as a piece of historical reconstruction. The evasiveness of Sir Espan is a dramatic device to arouse the reader's curiosity, and when that curiosity is eventually satisfied by the telling of the tale, Froissart has achieved his purpose and has no more to say. There is no attempt to question the witness, to test his veracity, to query the probability of the story, or to seek to penetrate behind its obviously fabulous details in search of some residual element of factual truth or of a feasible political interpretation. For all his intelligence, Froissart was not a 'modern' man who would discount a tale of this kind. Rather he revelled in fairy stories and was learned in centuries of mythology. In his writings he passes back and forth between the worlds of reality and fantasy; perhaps they were never in fact for him entirely separated from each other.

It is crucial to our assessment of Froissart the historian to appreciate the diversity of his literary skills. The author of the *Chronicles* was also a poet and a writer of chivalric romances. In the long winter evenings at the court at Orthez, he alternated between writing up the notes for his *Chronicles* (XII, 65) and

---

* All references to the *Chronicles* are to volume and page of the SHF edition unless otherwise stated.

reading to the count sections of his enormously long and unreal chivalric romance *Meliador*. Meliador was the son of Patrick, duke of Cornwall, who, among his numerous ventures, rescued a damsel threatened by a bear, and, after shipwreck on the Isle of Man (peopled, as he thought, by the ancient Hebrews), and a crossing to Aberdeen, entered the castle of his beloved disguised as a pedlar of jewelry. The tale enthralled the count, who demanded total silence while Froissart read and questioned him earnestly about the meaning of certain passages. To Gaston of Foix the fantasies of *Meliador* did not belong to a world apart from the competitive society in which he lived; and for Froissart the composition of his poetry was not consciously dissociated from that of the *Chronicles*. His descriptions of the courts of Edward III and Charles VI are not sharply differentiated from those of court life and its festivities in such poems as *La Prison Amoreuse*. Richard Barber has recently drawn attention to a most revealing example of Froissart's conflation of his literary and historical materials. In rewriting Jean le Bel's account of the battle of Crécy in the *Chronicles*, Froissart has added a section in the manner of his poem *Meliador* into Le Bel's text in describing the movements of King Philip of France on the dreadful evening which followed the slaughter of his army. This insertion was deleted from subsequent editions,[2] but the fact that it was ever penned at all points to a mental world and a scale of values very different from those of a modern historian. For all his many protestations of his unceasing pursuit of the truth, through endless questioning of witnesses or of those who had a claim to be well-informed (II, 265-6), Froissart was quite capable on occasion of inventing facts in order to enhance the verisimilitude of his narrative, or of manipulating both facts and text to achieve a dramatic purpose. If anything was sacred to Froissart, it was not 'the facts' but the demands of a strong story line. He was undoubtedly one of the great literary talents of the later Middle Ages; but if at times the application of a strict factual critique to his majestically dynamic prose may seem pedantic and unappreciative, we may exonerate ourselves from a charge of pettiness by recalling the standards which Froissart himself asserted were intrinsic to his enterprise.[3]

Froissart was not at his best when writing of the accessions of Richard II and Charles VI. His treatment of the unhappy, nearly parallel experiences of England and France, whereby within little more than three years the crowns of each country passed to a minor, is permeated with ignorance or error, or a combination of both. We may pardon him for giving mistaken dates for the deaths of Edward III and Charles V, who died on 21 June 1377 and 16 September 1380 respectively, and not, as Froissart states on 23 June 1377 (VIII, 230) and near Michaelmas 1380 (IX, 287-8). Of greater importance is that his treatment of the backgrounds to the coronations at Westminster and Reims, and the aftermaths of these great ceremonies, is unreliable. Neither in England nor in France is the scene adequately set.[4]

Froissart's virtual silence about England in the 1370s cannot have been determined by choice. He may have been happiest when describing the sight of a great army drawn up in battle array, or writing of knights fighting for their honour, but he was also interested in the battles of words and of interests which occurred in councils or in the English parliament, a body which he never really understood; he had no analogy in France on which to draw. Had Froissart known of the critical events of the last decaying years of Edward III, or of Alice Perrers, or of the Good Parliament, we may be sure that he would have found the space and the time to tell the tale. Sir Peter de la Mare, who had expressed concern about the conduct of business in the king's household and who, speaking for the Commons, had accused some who were close to the king of corruption, was unknown to Froissart. As for Alice Perrers, the king's mistress, who was reputed to have filched the rings from the corpse of her royal lover, Froissart would have been distressed that he had had no chance to write of her.[5] He had always found words to describe the gossip of the great. He knew his readers would enjoy it, as much as he enjoyed it himself. Had he known, therefore, of the hugely unpopular policies of John of Gaunt after the Good Parliament was dissolved, and of the almost hysterical rumours of his intentions, he would not have reported, as he did, that after the death of Edward III John of Gaunt 'had the government of the kingdom' (KL VIII, 392). It would be difficult to imagine a comment which indicated greater ignorance of English political life at this time.

Quite apart from his ignorance, moreover, Froissart has the atmosphere all wrong. To be appreciated properly, the minority years of Richard II's reign must be seen against the background of suspicion which accompanied his accession. During the last years of Edward III's reign, the risk, if not the practice, of the abuse of royal revenues and patronage to private advantage, prompted an almost obsessional anxiety among the politically articulate. Between October 1377 and January 1380, the king's councillors were under oath to protect the royal heritage, and with respect to all taxation granted for the defence or common interest of the realm. After a generous grant of two subsidies in November 1377, the Commons grew in recalcitrance; and while they were unable to fault the accounts of the war treasurers which were laid before them during the Gloucester Parliament of October 1378, they refused to concede the necessity of a grant in anticipation of the campaigning needs of the following year. In January 1380 the Commons asserted that a standing council was no longer necessary in view of the king's age and his assumed ability to manage for himself.[6] This was both tendentious and wishful thinking and, apart from the subsequent saving of the daily allowances paid to members of the council, there was no improvement in the quality or the cost of government.

Mounting tension over financial problems was not the only symptom of disquiet. The successes of Charles V's strategy were increasingly impinging on the domestic scene. We may cite one example of the way in which English sentiment was heavily swayed by French initiative. In 1380, as in 1377, the enemy used their naval strength skilfully, harassing the English coast-line and prompting fierce outcry from the shires attacked, who complained bitterly about neglect of the defence of the realm. The Franco-Castilian fleet even sailed up the Thames and burned Gravesend that summer. As in 1377, no English fleet was at sea in 1380; and although the council would no doubt have defended their decision to devote funds available to Buckingham's expedition, it was inevitably exposed to criticism.[7] None of these issues, however, reached the ears of Jean Froissart, who has nothing at all to say about the naval raids of 1380. His silence is indicative of the patchiness of the information which came his way and also of his incomplete understanding of the English domestic scene in these crucial years.

By contrast, Froissart's account of the Peasants' Revolt of 1381 is one of the more informed sections of the *Chronicles*. Not that it is by any means faultless. Sometimes incidents which are uncorroborated elsewhere may or may not be true; sometimes Froissart is demonstrably wrong. The importance attributed to the Londoners at the start of the revolt (X, 97-8) is nowhere confirmed and can be rejected on grounds of improbability. The harrassment of Joan of Kent, the king's mother, on her return from Canterbury to Westminster (X, 99) is not reported elsewhere. Froissart's presentation of the meeting at Smithfield on Saturday 15 June as happening by chance (X, 117-8) is unacceptable, and the influence of John Ball upon Wat Tyler, as shown in the radical demands made by Tyler at Smithfield, is not described. After Tyler's death, no other chronicler mentions the seizure of banners earlier granted by the king (X, 122-3) or the destruction of letters patent of pardon and manumission issued under the king's seal (X, 130). It is unlikely that the earl of Salisbury (a man regularly misplaced by Froissart) vetoed a night sally from the Tower in the darkness of the night of 13-14 June (X, 110), and it is hard to credit that the king's council knew 'before any man stirred' that there would be rebellion and that 'nevertheless nothing was provided by way of remedy' (X, 99). Froissart's famous remark — often misunderstood — that the revolt was due to 'the ease and riches that the common people were of' (X, 94) tells us more about his social prejudices than about the common people and the causes of the revolt of 1381. Finally, Froissart could not resist a good story, however improbable. When the night skies of London were glowing with flames from buildings fired by the rebels, an army under Edmund, earl of Cambridge, numbering nearly 3,000 men, was waiting at Plymouth to leave for Portugal. Cambridge was in touch with the capital but was not recalled. Froissart has a story that the army ventured out of port in bad weather because it feared attack by rebels from Southampton, Winchester and Arundel. Once out of harbour it waited for a fair wind to carry it overseas. It is a good story but — as Froissart well knew (X, 135) — Cambridge did not in fact sail until the end of June, and by then quiet had been restored to London.

Nevertheless, there are good things in this narrative, although it is unfortunate that Froissart does not name his source or sources. Heavy taxation had tried the patience of the socially inarticulate in both town and countryside beyond breaking point. There was widespread savaging of royal agents of varied callings in the summer of 1381, and much talk of traitors in the government. The king himself was young and blamefree, but what, for example, of Simon Sudbury, the chancellor and archbishop of Canterbury? He was unfairly accused of prospering through defalcations of royal taxes. Froissart catches these themes well (X, 94-124).

He also portrays effectively the emergence from virtual anonymity of the young Richard II. His actions in June of that year when confronted by the rebels at Mile End and at Smithfield (X, 112-24), suggest that here was a spirited young man capable of swift response when confronted by a frightening situation. But Froissart's subsequent analysis of Richard's character does not fulfil the promise of this early sketch. Richard had not advanced far into his teens before he had made it clear that he intended to enjoy his regality, to be king in deed as well as in name. He would be his own judge of propriety in the way he exercised the prerogative of an office hallowed by the sacrament of the coronation. Richard's preoccupation with the rights of kingship was perhaps a reaction to the fact that he regularly found himself on the defensive against the criticism that government should be more of a joint enterprise, shared by the king and his *proceres*, than he allowed. In the 1380s Richard countered this with caustic, opprobrious rejoinders. Better at talking than at doing, he was basically a weak man.

Little of this emerges from Froissart's narrative and it is doubtful whether an historian could analyse the character of the English king to this effect, or indeed coherently to any other effect, on the basis of what Froissart wrote. This is a characteristic defect of the *Chronicles*. With the partial exception of Thomas of Woodstock, earl of Buckingham and later duke of Gloucester, no figure of importance in English politics in Richard II's reign appears in more than one-dimensional form; and even Buckingham was far more complex than the tub-thumping stereotype found in the *Chronicles*.

Nor does Froissart successfully portray the situation of Richard II and the quality of his rule. Near the end of his work, in looking back over the reign, Froissart wrote that for twenty-two years Richard had reigned 'in great prosperity and with much splendour' (KL XVI, 233), a conclusion which was far from accurate. Froissart continues that there had never been a previous English king who had lavished such huge sums in keeping up his royal estate (KL XVI, 233). When he wrote to this effect, we can be sure that Froissart was echoing an opinion widely current in England. Many of Richard's subjects thought that he spent too much money on the wrong things. They also thought that he wantonly wasted money which had been levied by taxation for a defined purpose such as the defence of the realm. Had Froissart been better informed than he was, he might have demonstrated that the charge of excessive expenditure at court is a thread which runs almost throughout the reign. It is first heard in the November parliament of 1381, when Richard was no more than fourteen. And it was heard again in the words of a Commons' petition of February 1397, the petition initiated by Thomas Haxey, which had voiced the thought that there were too many bishops and ladies about the king's person, who were costing him money which he could ill afford. Words of this nature touched Richard on a raw spot; and as his father and grandfather had also kept expensive courts we may feel some sympathy for him. Edward III, no doubt, assumed that the keeping of a colourful, extrovert court was as much a duty to his subjects as a privilege of kingship. His subjects should be proud of their splendid king, and most of the time they were. But Edward III had commanded confidence of a kind never encompassed by his grandson. Why this was so emerges only in the most generalised manner from Froissart's narrative. The weaknesses of Richard II's character are never really explored.

Much the same could be said of Froissart's account of the early years of the reign of Charles VI which gets off to an even worse start than the uninformed background to Richard II's minority. For Froissart's account of the death of Charles V is a mélange of falsities in which virtually every factual statement is wrong. We are at once tested in our judgement. There are two possibilities. The first requires the generously sympathetic premise that Froissart had the bad luck to collect his information from one or more unreliable sources. Alternatively, — and in view of the scale and character of his errors this view seems preferable — we must admit the likelihood that Froissart invented his account of the death of Charles V.

He gets the date, the place, the cause, and the company about the dying king wrong (IX, 279-89). On his deathbed, Charles did not abolish all taxation, as Froissart wrote, but only the *fouage*. His passing at Beauté-sur-Marne (not St Pol) was caused by a heart attack and not by the belated action of a poison administered to him twenty-two years previously by the king of Navarre, a poison which (so Froissart solemnly informs us) was destined to kill him in a matter of days once an incision, made in his arm by the finest doctor in western Europe some years previously, ceased to suppurate. The heart attack which killed him made him far too ill to deliver the instructions which Froissart attributes to him as to how France was to be governed during the minority of the heir to the throne, instructions which can but be apocryphal in view of the precise ordinance regulating the minority issued by Charles V in 1374.[8] Finally, Froissart's story that the dukes of Berry, Bourbon and Burgundy were summoned to hear the final wishes of the dying king, Anjou being ignored because of his notorious greed, is wrong on all counts. Charles V would not thus have treated the man who had been designated regent in 1374; and, in any case, there were in reality no royal dukes at all present when Charles V died.

After these sins of commission, Froissart then further shows his ignorance. In pursuit of Charles V's provisions for the minority, the dukes of Berry and Burgundy claimed the guardianship of Charles VI, producing a tense antagonism between themselves and Anjou which was a source of public alarm. In the end, it was agreed that Charles VI should be crowned immediately, and that after the coronation Anjou's regency should cease. Thereafter, in name though not in fact, Charles VI should fully exercise the royal powers with the guidance of his uncles and the duke of Bourbon. On 30 November more detailed provision for the government of the realm was made when it was agreed that there should be a standing council of twelve permanently resident in Paris, of which Anjou should be president.[9] It is interesting that both in England and France a scheme of government involving a standing council was adopted. Of all this, however, Froissart was as unaware as he had been of events surrounding the death of Edward III and the accession of Richard II in England, but with much less excuse. His combination of fantasy and ignorance is dismaying. The fact that he was so comprehensively uninformed about a crucial sequence of events in French domestic history occasions a deep-seated anxiety in the critic.

Froissart's portrait of the new French king, though superficial and impressionistic, conveys some sense of his personality and of the manner in which he was manipulated by his uncles to serve their political interests. Both characteristics are evident, for example, in his narrative of the French invasion of Flanders in 1382 in support of Count Louis de Male against his rebellious subjects. The moving spirit was the duke of Burgundy, heir to the county; but he aroused

Charles' interest by the timely reminder that the count of Flanders was his vassal. The technique worked. Charles VI's response, as reported by Froissart, has the ring of truth. 'If I am to reign with honour and glory, it is necessary that I learn the art of war. I have never worn armour. It will give me great pleasure to try my strength and to humble the pride of the Flemings' (X, 252-4). It is wholly improbable that Charles used these words, but they encapsulate Froissart's image of the king. The qualities projected are those of a spontaneously ebullient youth, thirsting for combat in the cause of his kingdom against the impudent burghers of Ghent led by Philip van Artevelde. The ensuing description of the battle of Roosebeke, which is not without historical merit, is a literary *tour de force* (XI, 44-59). Great care was taken for the protection of the fourteen-year-old boy (such was also the age of Richard II at Smithfield in June 1381) who smelled blood and saw death in battle in a way Richard II never did. Charles, as portrayed by Froissart, discovered in victory a divine blessing, for he ordered a chapel to be built on the battle-site. He, too, remembered the French humiliation at Courtrai eighty years earlier; and when the body of the dead Flemish leader was brought to his presence, he kicked it.

Similar qualities of youthful exuberance, martial ardour and political naivety appear in other episodes in the *Chronicles* concerning Charles VI. In November 1386, for instance, when there were justifiable doubts about trying to cross the Channel to invade England in poor weather, Charles announced that he was not afraid. He had boarded ship and was sure he would make a good sailor. 'If no one will follow me, I shall have to go by myself', he added (KL XI, 375-7). Again, in 1385, after the ladies at court had decided that Isabella of Bavaria, the bride chosen for the king by the duke of Burgundy (to serve his own interests), was a suitable young lady, it was suggested that Arras would be a city becoming the great occasion. To this, Charles rejoindered, 'Why do we have to go to Arras? What is wrong with Amiens (where he was at the time)? I won't have any further delays' (XI, 231). Here was the epitome of a wilful young man. It is probable that Froissart, who with poetic licence did not hesitate to remark upon the king's enjoyment of his marital night, overplayed the Peter Pan-like quality in Charles. In November 1388, for example, when Charles was nineteen, Froissart first invents drinking and dancing at Avignon under the direction of Pope Clement VII, and then explains that it is important that his audience should understand that the king was 'still young' (KL XIV, 38).

Although he gave some attention to the characters and domestic problems of the two young kings, Froissart's prime interest was always in the 'great feats of arms' in the war between England and France, an interest much stimulated by the spectacular events which followed the renewal of the war in May 1385, after a sixteen month truce. In three successive years, England was threatened with invasion. To these events, Froissart devoted some of his lengthiest and most memorable passages, beginning with the French invasion through Scotland.

On 1 June 1385, Jean de Vienne landed at Leith at the head of the first French army to campaign in Britain since the reign of King John. De Vienne and his men, the 'flower of the knights and squires of' France, were not impressed by

King Robert of Scotland, who had 'red, bleary eyes' and was unbelligerent. Edinburgh, 'the Paris of Scotland', was small, and the men of Scotland 'rude and worthless'.

Froissart first describes a Franco-Scottish raid over the border into north-east England, which withdrew northwards when news arrived that an English army was approaching from the south (XI, 212-18, 253-8). He knew a fair measure about the English king's first venture into the field, describing later the retreat of the army to England and how its break-up was precipitated by a serious row between Richard and his uncle, John of Gaunt. There was, indeed, a sharp disagreement between Richard and Gaunt, but the account of its cause is at variance with English sources and wholly unacceptable. Froissart says that outside the walls of Aberdeen, it was agreed by Richard, his uncles, a number of other magnates and 'the greater part of the army', that the army should return to England through the western march in an attempt to intercept De Vienne when he came back to Scotland from Carlisle, which he was trying to capture. Robert de Vere, the earl of Oxford, however, went to the king's tent by night and warned him that John of Gaunt was plotting his destruction. He wanted to expose the king to the hazards of the narrow passes over the Cumberland mountains in winter time — the date was in fact early September — where Richard would be at the mercy of a Scottish ambush. What Lancaster most wanted, said de Vere, was the king's death and the throne for himself. Next morning, when Richard rounded on Lancaster, the duke defied any man to impugn his loyalty. He would follow the king wherever he wished (XI, 273-4). And so the army returned to England by the route by which they had invaded, 'but not before they had destroyed the greater part of that country'. Here Froissart was correct. The Scottish Lowlands were savagely scorched. Thus ended Richard's one real military venture. He never drew his sword. So much for the son, who was quite unlike his father. Not even Froissart could project the makings of a chivalric hero on Richard. De Vere's motive eluded Froissart, but not the king's dependence on him. Not only was he the heart and soul of the king's council, but if he had told the king that black was white and white black, Richard would have believed him. More than one English writer was perplexed by de Vere's hold over the king.

The accounts of the argument between Richard II and Gaunt which appear in English sources are greatly to be preferred. During August 1385 the army arrived outside Edinburgh without striking a blow and it was at this point that the debate about strategy took place. Gaunt advised a crossing of the Firth of Forth and the pursuit of the Scots into the Highlands. Richard angrily countered that if the army crossed the Forth, it would disintegrate through lack of supplies. Gaunt was then showered with accusations of bad faith. The extensive abuse directed at him by the king went beyond and behind the immediate situation and was caused by Richard's pent-up distrust of his uncle. Relations between the two had been bad for some time. In 1384, Gaunt was believed in all seriousness to be plotting the king's death, and less than a year later Gaunt believed that his own life was at risk.[10]

Another weakness of Froissart's account is his failure to see the Scottish campaign in its proper strategic context. The French invasion of Scotland was to have been part of a two pronged attack upon England, with the bulk of the

French forces falling on the south of England from Sluys. Since Froissart believed that this second force was to have gone to Scotland to reinforce de Vienne, he was in no position to appreciate either the seriousness of the threat to England, or the gamble the English were taking in their invasion of Scotland, leaving their rear dangerously exposed. Even the English Channel fleet disbanded on 31 July, leaving the south coast open to attack.[11] Only the attack on Damme by the men of Ghent on 14-15 July saved the situation for the English by diverting the French invasion forces to the relief of Damme. The invasion was postponed until 1386, by which time Ghent had at last made her peace with the duke of Burgundy on 18 December 1385 (Vaughan 1956: 35-8).

Sensing the momentous events to come, Froissart went to Sluys to see what was happening for himself in 1386; and there, as he stood looking out to sea, he saw a 'whole forest of masts'. Here were sights to cure those sick of a fever or gnawed by a toothache. 'Never, since God created the world', he wrote, 'had so many ships and great vessels been seen together as there were that year in the port of Sluys and off the coast between Sluys and Blankenberg, for by September their number amounted to thirteen hundred and eighty-seven.' (By chance, it seems, his total was just one more than the number of years which had passed since the birth of Christ!) Surely, no historian should be pedantic about facts when confronted by rhetoric of such dimensions. One more sentence from the same paragraph must suffice: 'From the port of Seville in Spain right round to Prussia, there was not one big ship at sea on which the French could lay their hands that they had not seized.' As for supplies, there was 'everything that could be thought of and (commodities) which in days to come will seem incredible to those who did not see it.' Jack Straw had seemed menace enough in 1381, but by comparison in 1386 Leviathan was now at hand. Sensing that Judgement Day was near, many English spent their cares away, borrowing from all who were foolish enough to lend. As they prepared, the French chattered as though their ancestral enemy had already succumbed, with all her menfolk slaughtered and her women and children brought to France and held in slavery (XIII, 75-101).

Here we have magnificent prose of almost cosmic dimension; and it is this quality, combined with the archetypal themes which are regularly spiced by Froissart's perceptive worldliness, which have provided an enduring place for Froissart's *Chronicles* in literature. In our age of fastidious professionalism, Froissart has properly been demoted by historians as a source. The price to be paid for the pleasure of reading the *Chronicles* is the jarring exercise of perpetual vigilance in relation to factual and conceptual accuracy, and such vigilance is no less necessary in 1386 than on other occasions, despite the fact that Froissart was an eye-witness. One illustration must suffice. Historians have been much exercised in explaining the cancellation of the invasion project in November 1386 and part of the debate has been dictated by what Froissart wrote. He asserts that John of Berry caused a delay in the departure of the fleet through deliberately obstructive delays in coming to Sluys. It is true that Berry was late, but so indeed was Charles VI himself. It is not until 29 October that we can be sure that Charles was at Sluys: Berry, we know, was two days behind the king.[12] Thus we may reject statements of the repeatedly neglected summons of Berry to Sluys by the king and by Burgundy. Dr Palmer has written of this episode, 'How Froissart came to make such a mistake when he was actually at Sluys at the time

58

is something of a mystery'. Dr Palmer is further puzzled because, as he correctly says, Froissart 'gives the most circumstantial account of what happened' at Sluys (1972: 77-8). Yet are the difficulties as serious as is suggested? Froissart had no textbook on the laws of evidence on his desk when he wrote. One never has the feeling that his presentation was inhibited by the possibility of error or of correction by another who was better informed. Modesty and restraint were not virtues honoured by Froissart. Sadly there are numerous sections in the *Chronicles* where Froissart opted for writing a good story although the scanty material he had at his disposal called for restraint. Finally, the fact of physical presence does not necessarily lead to good testimony, nor could Froissart's presence at Sluys by itself enable him to be a reliable reporter of debates within the king's council.

Events at Sluys had their counterpart in England and, as is so often the case, Froissart was ill-informed about them. He was unaware, for instance, of the crucial parliaments of October 1386 and February 1388 and for this reason the structure of his narrative is gossamer thin. Had he been questioned about the character of parliamentary impeachments or appeals, he would have been obliged to admit that he had never heard of them. He was also unaware of the political importance of Michael de la Pole and of the attack upon him in October 1386. On the other hand he knew, as we have already seen, of the huge unpopularity of Robert de Vere, earl of Oxford, and he also knew the names of several of the chamber knights who were prominent among the king's 'evil councillors'. He was aware that a reform commission was established, but apart from the reference to Thomas of Woodstock's prominence, almost everything he wrote about it is mistaken. He states, for instance, that the commission was appointed after a meeting at Windsor on 23 April 1386 at which spokesmen from London and other towns confronted the king with their complaints. The townsmen, we are told, took this initiative at the suggestion of Duke Thomas, to whom the Londoners had appealed for help. Gloucester had replied that no profit would result from any initiative that he might take: Richard II would not listen to him. We are told that after Gloucester, the most active member of the commission was the archbishop of Canterbury, whose surname was Montague. One victim of the commission's purge is said to have been the treasurer, named as Alexander Neville, archbishop of York. Eventually, the confrontation between the king and his fierce opponents was brought to a close after the battle of Radcot Bridge by a request from Westminster that the king should return from Bristol and that the reconciliation should be symbolised by a fresh coronation and the renewal of homage and fealty to the king (XIV, 19-72).

This incoherent presentation of the events of 1386 to 1388 is chronologically muddled and there is no indication that the events described extend over a period of two years. The use of the technique of interlacements adds to the problems of understanding. But, as is often the way with Froissart, among the blanket-fire of facts and fictions showered upon the reader, there is at least one moment of important insight. It is to be found in an invented exchange between Richard and his critics at Windsor. The king makes two remarks which admirably express the royal point of view. As he is bullied into discussing the appointment of a reforming commission, he firmly states that none should believe that he would allow his policies to be dictated to him by his subjects. Secondly, he counters criticism of his government by saying that he does not know what basis there was for criticism of his friends; he could find no fault himself. In reply, he was told that he was ignorant of what was happening in England. It was not in the interest of those whom he trusted to keep him informed of what was happening in the realm. If they did so, they would lose their capacity to enrich themselves at his expense (XIV, 28-30). Finally, Froissart accurately reports the distress of Richard II and his queen at the execution of Sir Simon Burley. Froissart also expresses his own dismay; for Burley, he says, had been an honourable man in the years he had known him (XIV, 41-2).

In the final decade of the fourteenth century, Froissart was at the height of his powers and a man of wide and lengthy experience. It also happens that he was either personally present at some of the greater events he describes, or was able to collect his information from those involved in decision-making. Here, at least, we might therefore expect to find accurate and informed reportage. But while elements of this are from time to time visible, Froissart's narrative continues to be spattered with errors, misunderstandings and sheer invention.

His account of the insanity of Charles VI, for instance, is typical both in its insights and its flaws. Once again, the story with which we are presented (KL XV, 35-42) is graphically realistic; but our confidence in the array of detail in Froissart's text is shaken by the fact that there is one very serious error. This is the statement that John of Berry accompanied the king on his ride from Le Mans to Brittany. This was not the case, for Berry was in fact in Avignon at this time, conducting important business which had been assigned to him (Lehoux 1966: 291-2).

This is not the place to examine the aetiology or the symptoms of the king when he went out of his mind; but it is interesting that when Froissart first mentions that the king was indisposed, he says that he did not look after himself properly. In the spring of 1392, as the peace negotiations at Amiens were drawing to a close, the king was taken by a fever. After a period of rest and a change of air at Beauvais, he soon recovered and went to Gisors to hunt. Later in the year, in July, there was again concern about his health, while he was leading his army to attack Duke John of Brittany. Berry and Burgundy did their best to persuade Charles that he was in no fit state to proceed. His doctors also recommended caution. But Charles angrily contradicted them, saying that he was in better health than they were. He warned his critics that they would suffer if they tried to impede him. In 1392, the king was only twenty-three years of age; and from this year the tragic disintegration of France, which had such depressing consequences after 1400, had its beginning. The attack of 1392 was comparatively mild; but with the passage of time, the king's bouts of insanity became more frequent and more prolonged. His next attack came in June 1393, when the peace negotiations at Leulingham were nearing their end.

Charles had chosen to stay at Abbeville, a pleasant town on the river Somme, where the climate was thought to suit his health. He was zealous for peace and anxious to expedite a conclusion to the negotiations, if easy access to him might be helpful. Negotiations began shortly after Easter (6 April) — not, as Froissart writes, 'soon after St George's day' (KL XV, 110) – and lasted in the first instance until 29 April. On the previous day the truce was extended until Michaelmas 1394 and not, as Froissart reports, for a period of four years (KL XV, 121). These mistakes are all the more interesting in that Froissart had himself taken up residence in Abbeville in order to enhance his capacity to glean accurate information. They are by no means the last or most serious of his errors. The dukes of Berry and Burgundy led the French delegation and the English representatives were led by Lancaster and Gloucester. Neither the archbishop of York nor the bishop of London was present as Froissart reported. The conjunction of Lancaster and Gloucester is interesting and important, because Froissart describes the latter as very popular with the English commons and with those who preferred war to peace. He also reports that Gloucester was an angular and difficult negotiator who doubted the honesty of the French, believing them to be unscrupulous equivocators, specious and dissembling. When Robert the Hermit was sent to mollify him, Gloucester said that he had come in good faith as a negotiator, but in his opinion and that of most English subjects, a pre-condition of peace negotiations should have been the restoration to England by France of all lands subtly taken away from her since 1369. Froissart claims that Gloucester had at a later date – presumably in 1395, when he was in England – rehearsed this to him as the gist of what he had said to Robert (KL XV, 120-1).

Part way through the negotiations the two delegations reported to their kings in writing what progress had thus far been made. The English dukes, Froissart believed, sent a messenger to the king from Calais, who returned with an enthusiastic endorsement on their achievement to date, together with encouragement to proceed to a conclusion. Thus Froissart; but in fact, as the monk of St Denis correctly reported, Lancaster and Gloucester returned to England (Bellaguet 1840: 78). They did so with urgency, as there were disturbances in Yorkshire and a revolt of threatening proportions in Cheshire, where men had risen believing that the English delegates were willing to surrender Richard's claim to the French throne, as well as to withdraw the privileges of Cheshire. Of this Froissart knew nothing. Clearly the rebels in Cheshire did not regard Gloucester as a warmonger. About 20 May negotiations were renewed and were continued for the greater part of a month (Palmer 1972: 184). Berry and Burgundy had received the same measure of encouragement to proceed further from Charles VI as Richard II had given to his delegates. Both Froissart and the monk of St Denis gained the impression that there was progress between the English and French at Leulingham. Froissart heard talk in Abbeville to the effect that a peace had been agreed on the basis of certain articles accepted by both sides. Unfortunately, he was unable to establish the basis of the agreement, learning only that the truce had been extended (KL XV, 108-23). In the same way, the St Denis author could not establish either the form or the content of what had been agreed – *formam et modum tractatus* (Bellaguet 1840: 82). Some years ago, Dr Palmer discovered the text defining what – as a result of hard bargaining – had been accomplished by June 1393 and those issues which remained for further discussion and settlement in order that a final peace might be concluded. Dr Palmer's opinion that the articles indicate that 'a final peace was well within sight by the summer of 1393' is arguable, but one cavils at the use of the words 'treaty' or 'provisional treaty'. *Les articles qui ont este parlez et traictiez pour parvenir a bonne paix final entre les roys de France et Dangleterre* might more appropriately be described as a *working agreement*.

Dr Palmer also believes that we may extract from Froissart's text an indication of a 'secret peace' between the two delegations, but this conclusion is not readily apparent. He has suggested that Richard II granted the duchy of Guyenne to John of Gaunt and his male heirs in perpetuity, to be held as an *apanage* of the French crown (1966: 81-95). Dr Vale has already expressed his doubt about this conclusion, for as late as 1394 Richard repeated what he had already said more than once before, namely that the grant to Gaunt was for life only and that sovereignty was reserved to the English crown. It is familiar to historians that the Gascons took considerable exception to Richard's grant in 1390 and that its legitimacy was questioned by them. In the end the propriety of the grant was considered by the king's council at Eltham on 22 July 1395. The conclusion of the legal experts appointed by the king was that the gift was invalid by reason of earlier grants made to the duchy by Edward III and Richard II himself. These were to the effect that the lordship of Gascony might only be alienated to the heir to the throne. The fact that no reference to a promise of the succession of the duchy to Gaunt's heirs was made in the minute of the decision reached at Eltham on 22 July seems to represent a very difficult impediment both to the acceptance of Dr Palmer's hypothesis (1972: 154-63) and to Froissart's report of the refusal of the Gascons to accept the alienation of the duchy to Gaunt and his heirs upon which Dr Palmer's hypothesis is in some measure founded (KL XV, 157-9).

Froissart's narrative of the Gascon revolt was, he states, retailed to him first-hand by Sir Richard Stury, a member of the king's council, on his visit to England in 1395, the very year in which the issue was being thrashed out. If he could be so mistaken in these circumstances, when can he be trusted? Other statements in his account of this visit are disconcerting. He tells us that after the council of Eltham he remained in the king's company for three months, staying at several places in the Home counties such as Kingston, Chertsey and Windsor (KL XV, 141-82). The reader's suspicions about Froissart's integrity here is aroused by an analysis of the places at which letters under the Great Seal were authorised after 22 July. From this analysis we find Richard II at Northampton on or about 1 August and at Nottingham on 1 September; on 16 September he was at Worksop. We do not know what the explanation is of this itinerary; but if Froissart had, as he said he had, stayed with the king after the council at Eltham, we should expect him to refer to the king's journey into the Midlands. One has to attribute falsehood to Froissart here. A pity, for his description of his visit to England is one of the most delightful sections of the *Chronicles*. He tells us that he believed that a return to the country where he had once been treated with gracious courtesy would make him live longer, perhaps the most lavish compliment our author could pay to England. In his renewal of the acquaintance of Sir Richard Stury was a most happy event, and Froissart could scarcely have found another who was so admirably qualified to answer the questions which were put to him. Finally, it is interesting to observe that Froissart had such easy access to Richard II; he never enjoyed such a privilege with Charles VI.

Froissart's description of the closing years of Richard II's reign is composed at the level of epic travesty. Most of his facts are wrong, and the *Chronicles* fail to enhance our understanding of the springs and character of the king's policy. Froissart was not helped by his ignorance of the existence of the parliament of September 1397 and of its adjourned session at Shrewsbury in January 1398. Of the year 1397, Walsingham wrote, 'In this year the king began to play the tyrant', but one would not know what the St Albans writer had in mind by reading Froissart. By way of apology for Froissart, it should be said that there are defects in all the narratives written in England describing the events of 1397 to 1399. Also, it makes a change to read a text which is not a resumé of the *Record and Process*. Such information as reached Froissart, and it cannot have been much, was evidently thin and garbled. Having heard that Gloucester had been murdered at Calais, he chose, it seems, to invent the story of death by strangulation. He reverses the roles played by Mowbray and Bolingbroke in their disastrous argument. Froissart has the king reducing the duration of Bolingbroke's exile from ten to six years. This gesture was invented as a dramatic way of assuaging Gaunt's disquiet. We would think better of Froissart had he used a rhetorical escape line by admitting that 'events in England were confused at this time and I have been unable to learn as much as I would have wished. In due course I may, through further inquiries, learn more'. But an admission of this nature was incompatible with Froissart's pride. When the king of England and the son-in-law of Charles VI had been deposed, we may imagine that Froissart envisaged an expectant audience looking to him, the historian, to tell them what had happened and why. He felt it incumbent upon himself to fulfil their expectations and as a result he paid yet a further price in credibility.

V THE BRETON CIVIL WAR *

Michael Jones

ON 7 September 1341 Philip VI made it known that he would accept the homage proffered for the duchy of Brittany by Charles of Blois, on behalf of his wife, Joan of Penthièvre, and that he thereby rejected a similar request first made to him by John of Montfort, respectively niece and half-brother of the late Duke John III. Twenty-five years later on 13 December 1366 Charles V, Philip's grandson, thankfully admitted John of Montfort's son into his homage for the duchy in a tense ceremony at the Hotel St Pol in Paris.[1] In the interim there had been waged a bitter, often bloody, civil war for succession to John III, in which the original claimants had received military support from England and France.

The course of this war is graphically and most comprehensively described in some of the finest passages in Froissart's *Chronicles*. Episodes like the elder John of Montfort's blitzkrieg of 1341 and the heroic defence of Hennebont by his wife in 1342, or accounts of the sieges of Brest, La Roche Derrien and Rennes, and the battles of La Roche Derrien (20 June 1347), of the Thirty (26 March 1351) and of Auray (29 September 1364) are highlights which successive generations have avidly perused. Dramatic confrontations, powerful character-isation, stirring, patriotic speeches and lively dialogue, cliff-hanging suspense with rescue in the nick of time, all and more than the usual ingredients of chivalric history are displayed, often with consummate artistry. Yet leaving literary qualities aside, the question — how valuable to the historian are the successive redactions of these events related in the *Chronicles*? — has often been and still needs to be posed.

There are no good contemporary Breton accounts of the civil war, and surviving sources from the later fourteenth and fifteenth centuries not unnaturally recognised the rightfulness of the outcome which had resulted in the Montfort family gaining power and consolidating its position. Although writers like Guillaume de St André and the author of the *Chronicon Briocense*, both in ducal employment (c.1380-1416), or in a later generation, Pierre le Baud (fl.1460-1505), drew on oral traditions and on written sources, some of which are now lost, for the period of the war, these writers often have a propagandist purpose on behalf of the Montfort dynasty (Jones 1976: 144-6, 163-5). The independent or novel factual content of their work is slight in comparison with that provided by Jean le Bel, Froissart, writers in the St Denis tradition, or by those English chroniclers (Murimuth, Avesbury and Geoffrey le Baker) who were contemporary with events, or like Henry Knighton were later able to draw on authoritative

---

* All references to the *Chronicles* are to volume and page of the SHF edition unless otherwise stated.

64

sources.[2] From Jean de St Paul in the mid-fifteenth century (La Borderie 1881: i-xxii), most native Breton authors relied heavily and usually uncritically on Froissart, seldom writing more than a paraphrase of those picturesque episodes already noted.[3] If the Benedictine historians of the eighteenth century, Dom Lobineau (1707a: 311-80) and Dom Morice (1750a: 245-320), started to produce more scholarly syntheses, based on their prodigious efforts in collecting the literary and documentary evidence relating to the duchy, the general structure of their accounts was still determined by the outline provided by Froissart.

The rediscovery of the unique manuscript of Jean le Bel's work in the mid-nineteenth century, followed by the critical editions of Froissart's chronicle by Lettenhove and Luce shortly afterwards, called for a reassessment of the latter's account of the Breton civil war. In 1871 Dom François Plaine launched a wholesale attack on Froissart's credibility as an historian of that war. Doubts were now seriously cast not merely on some manifestly incorrect details or on some of the more fantastic individual deeds of prowess, but on the occurrence of whole campaigns which Froissart had recounted with a wealth of substantiating detail, much but not all of which he had derived from Le Bel. The ferocity of Plaine's attack, to which he returned several times, provoked the greatest of modern historians of the duchy, Arthur de la Borderie, to a series of critical studies in which Plaine himself came under severe scrutiny. For although he had an enviable ability to uncover novel pieces of evidence and to pose new questions about that which was already known, his cavalier handling of historical sources and a naive approach to some problems requiring a rigorous knowledge of diplomatic, left him open to devastating counter attack. Eventually La Borderie's researches culminated in the very comprehensive treatment of the war which was published in the third volume of his *Histoire de Bretagne* (1899).

La Borderie was able to utilise not only his own immense knowledge of all the sources of Breton history, but also the labours of an outstanding generation of editors, inspired by Siméon Luce, and which included the Moliniers, Moranvillé and Lemoine. If he lacked the standard editions of Le Bel and the *Grandes Chroniques* which Jules Viard (aided by Eugène Déprez) was to produce after his death, La Borderie had nevertheless mastered all the significant contemporary literary sources for the war, and Lemoine, in particular, had made available to him information drawn from the Public Record Office in London. As a result his account of the period remains the standard one; it may be supplemented, especially by reference to Déprez's work, and modified in detail. New scholarly editions and the predominating concern with documentary sources have enabled a clearer picture of the tangled sequence of events to emerge.[4] But as Froissart's work so influenced earlier generations, so La Borderie's has largely shaped serious debate in the twentieth century. Moreover, since he was largely prepared to vindicate the broad outlines of Froissart's account, after his examination of the *Chronicles*, through this modern exegete, whose account is ignored with peril, Froissart's version of the Breton civil war continues to dominate historical writing.

Occurring as it did between 1341 and 1364, all or part of the civil war was treated in the three redactions of Book I of the *Chronicles*. The major points of difference between these successive versions must be emphasised in so far as they concern Brittany. In the first redaction (composed from 1369 onwards, and in

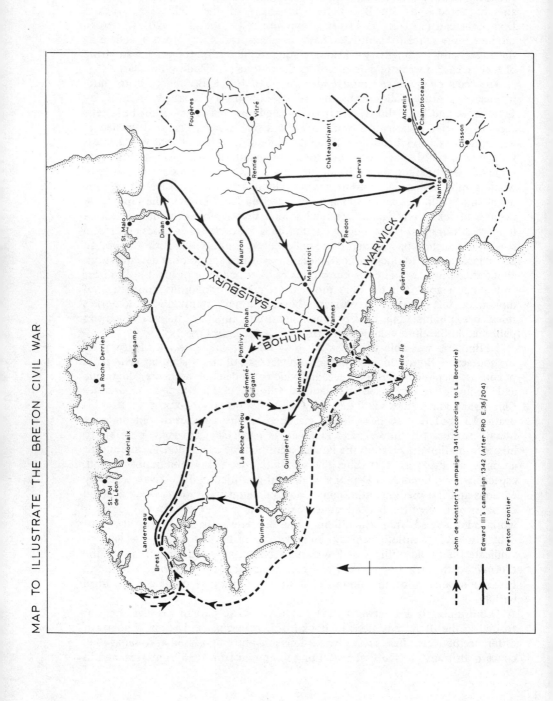

MAP TO ILLUSTRATE THE BRETON CIVIL WAR

Fougères
Vitré
Ancenis
Champtoceaux
Clisson
Châteaubriant
Derval
Rennes
Nantes
St. Malo
Dinan
Mauron
Redon
Malestroit
WARWICK
Guérande
SALISBURY
Rohan
Pontivy
Vannes
BOHUN
Guingamp
La Roche Derrien
Guémené-
Guigant
Hennebont
Auray
Belle Ile
Morlaix
La Roche Periou
Quimperlé
St. Pol
de Léon
Landerneau
Quimper
Brest

John de Montfort's campaign 1341 (According to La Borderie)

Edward III's campaign 1342 (After PRO E.36/204)

Breton Frontier

what Luce has termed its revised form, from 1378 although, as argued above (11-12), there is room for debate on this issue), Froissart largely follows Le Bel on the origins and early course of the war. His dependence is evident from the start when he borrows the description of the methods of composition used by the earlier writer in passages relating to Brittany, and Froissart does little thereafter but paraphrase his model.[5] Many of the picturesque phrases which have been taken as particularly characteristic of his style find their origin in Le Bel's work. John of Montfort, half-brother of the late duke, for example, was not, according to Le Bel 'extrait de l'estoc de Bretaigne' (I, 247). He is similarly described by Froissart in MSS of the first redaction as the man 'qui n'estoit point extrais de l'estok de Bretaigne' (II, 88). In the Amiens MS the context changes a little but the key phrase remains: 'Lequelx ne venoit mies dou droit estock de Bretaingne' (II, 267). In the case of his wife, the countess of Montfort, she is always for Le Bel as subsequently for Froissart 'the one who had the heart of both man and lion'.[6] Conversely, knights are conventionally and repetitively described as 'terribly brave' and 'very valiant' as were Garnier de Clisson, Miles and Waleran, castellans of Champtoceaux, Henry and Olivier de Spinefort and many others.[7]

All Le Bel's errors, whether those relating to particular events and personalities or those simply induced by ignorance of geography, are reproduced. Confusion seems to reign at every level — actual inland locations like La Roche Periou situated 35 km from the sea are, according to Le Bel and Froissart, lapped about with tidal waters, distances are telescoped, and conventional descriptions of the sites of 'a fine town' or a 'very strong castle' are taken over without more ado, whether they are appropriate or not. Even if La Borderie's suggestion that Le Bel and Froissart both habitually confused Dinan and Guémené-Guigant (now Guémené-sur-Scorff) is accepted, the conventional nature of the description repeated several times, that the town was 'only enclosed with a palisade and ditch' is completely at variance with what is known of the defences of Dinan, whilst recent excavations at the castle of Joyeuse-Garde near Landerneau — the Goy-la-Forest of Froissart — revealed very modest defences contrary to the chroniclers' description.[8]

The catalogue of trivial and, indeed, of more serious errors is almost endless. Armies march in a bewildering series of eccentric movements and castles are in the hands of commanders who, according to other records, were known to be far away, safely incarcerated by their opponents, dead or frankly mythical. Generations of historians, for instance, have argued whether the name of the commander at Brest in 1341 was Garnier or Gautier de Clisson but neither he nor Olivier de Clisson, captain of La Roche Periou, both allegedly cousins of the (historical) Olivier III, sire de Clisson, have ever been identified from authentic record sources (La Borderie 1899: 427). The time scale, like that of distance, within which most events take place is purely conventional and few actual dates are proffered. When they are, they are often highly inaccurate. In the first redaction only two dates are seriously advanced for Breton affairs during the whole of the period 1341-3 — 'about All Saints Day' (1341) for the capture of Nantes by the French, and 'the beginning of May 1342' for the delivery of Rennes to Blois, whilst a truce concluded shortly afterwards was to run to Pentecost. In the second redaction Nantes is said to have been captured on

20 October *1340* and in the third redaction this is revised to c.19 November (1341) which is probably closest to the actual date. In the second redaction there is a hopeless muddle over events of 1342 which are attributed to 1343.[9]

Where Le Bel does occasionally admit his ignorance and abbreviate the narrative accordingly, Froissart in the first redaction wisely follows suit. In a few instances only does he add details, presumably, though the point can hardly be demonstrated, from his own personal knowledge. For instance he added the names of Bourchier and Despenser to those lords accompanying Robert of Artois from England to Brittany in 1342, whose names he found originally in Le Bel's account, and we know from other evidence that he had contacts with both these families when he was in England.[10] But for the rest in the first redaction it is only in his narrative of the decisive battle of Auray that Froissart clearly displays his own undeniably independent abilities as a chronicler in the chivalric mode. For virtually all the other material relating to the war in the duchy down to 1356 (the year in which by his own admission he began to take an interest in history) in the first redaction, even in the revised form contained in the MSS of Luce's group B, Froissart followed Le Bel. He thus naturally shared with his predecessor the generally pro-English interpretation of events.[11]

In the second redaction, that contained in the Amiens and Valenciennes manuscripts and generally dated to the years 1376-83 (but see above: 11-12), when Froissart reached the commencement of the Breton succession war, he now commented at much greater length before introducing his narrative. His explicit claims must be quoted; they provide a yardstick by which he invited others to measure him and so indirectly a warrant for the critical modern scholarship lavished on his *Chronicles*:

> Many minstrels and singers in their turn have made up songs about the Breton wars, corrupting by their contrived rhymes the real course of events. This greatly annoyed both Master Jean le Bel, who began to write a chronicle about them in prose, and myself, Jean Froissart, who within the limits of my power, loyally and correctly continued that work, for their contorted verses and songs in no way recounted the true state of affairs. Now you may see how we have done so in completing it through our own considerable efforts, for one achieves nothing of note without great anxiety and travail. I, Jean Froissart, immediate successor to Jean le Bel in this work, went and visited the greater part of Brittany and asked lords and questioned heralds about the wars, captures, attacks, invasions, battles, rescues and all the other fine feats of arms which have happened there since 1340 up to the latest time mentioned in this book, both at the request and expense of my own patrons and for my own satisfaction, to establish my account on as truthful a basis as I could, for which I have been greatly rewarded (II, 265-6).

Whilst the debt to Le Bel is thus clearly acknowledged, Froissart's treatment of the common material is now altogether much freer both in the sense that he manipulates it with greater assurance, compressing and changing the emphases by omission or by introducing entirely new passages, and in the language he uses. Additional sieges are added, for example, to the summer campaign of 1341, and in describing the feats of the countess of Montfort under the year 1343, there is a magnificent description of a naval battle in which she valiantly fights, fully armed, at the head of her forces in an engagement, the details of which are necessarily incorrect in almost every particular.[12] Similar embellishments are added to other episodes, whether real or fictitious, which form the core of his account, many of which are of the kind which Froissart imagined would inspire future generations of knights to behave in accordance with the strict etiquette of chivalric practice. The heroic role of those individuals who appear as *leit-motiv* in the *Chronicles*, like Walter Mauny and Robert of Artois for the Anglo-Bretons and Olivier de Clisson and Hervé de Léon for the Franco-Bretons, are consistently emphasised. Outstanding archetypal deeds of prowess like the battle of the Thirty or the jousts at the siege of Rennes are included at appropriate points when Froissart's main theme is no longer Breton affairs but the war in some other theatre. For after the battle of La Roche Derrien, in which Blois was captured and led off to captivity in England and the greater Breton nobility were severely depleted by death and capture, both the first two redactions treat the later stages of the war as a minor theme, isolated episodes of which occasionally gain prominence, but in which quite significant battles like that at Mauron (14 August 1352) are surprisingly neglected. On the other hand the character of the war is brilliantly encapsulated in a few short passages in which the career of the adventurer Crokart and the activities of English garrisons are evoked.[13] But there is no attempt to describe in detail the guerilla warfare and obscure sequence of sieges (La Roche Derrien in 1347 and Rennes in 1356-7 excepted) which formed the core of the account of the years 1341-3 and continued to provide material for other contemporary writers.[14] But despite these omissions, the second redaction is much fuller in its history of the duchy during these troubled years. Le Bel apart, the only other chronicles to approach Froissart's comprehensive coverage are the *Grandes Chroniques* and the early fifteenth-century compilation largely based on the same material from St Denis, the *Chronographia regum Francorum* (Viard 1905).

Froissart was himself the first to comment on the possibility that his treatment of the civil war was influenced by a desire to please his patrons. In the Besançon MS, one of the earliest copies of the A group of manuscripts, which according to Luce contain the first version of the text, he writes:

> One might say that I deliberately falsified this great history out of favour for what I received from Count Guy of Blois, who made me write it and who paid me more than I expected, because he was much more like a son than a nephew of Count Louis of Blois, full brother of St Charles of Blois, who as long as he lived was duke of Brittany. But truthfully it is not so. For I do not wish to recount anything but the truth and to act impartially, blaming neither one side nor the other. Indeed nor would the gentle lord and count, who forced me to begin to write this account, have wished me to do otherwise than relate the truth (I, liii-iv).

For the most part this disclaimer can be accepted at its face value. In the general prologue to the second redaction Froissart tried to establish his impartiality by balancing the names of the great heroes on the English side during this phase of the Hundred Years War by equally worthy names from the French side. As he explains, even in the darkest hours of defeat there were many valiant knights who had comported themselves with distinction from Philip of Valois downwards. Among those included at this point only in the Valenciennes MS of this redaction is the name of *Messire Charles de Blois* — the copyist of the Amiens MS was unable to decipher his original and left a blank (I, liii). Elsewhere, once again speaking of Count Guy of Blois, Froissart comments favourably on his high lineage and social connections. But this is essentially the limit of his eulogy of the Blois family. It is in the presentation of the parcel rather than in any significant change in its contents that this version is notably different in so far as it concerns Brittany. For apart from a topical reference to the popular cult of Charles of Blois and recognition of the legitimacy of Blois's claim to Brittany, there are few other alterations to the main body of the text to change the interpretation of events in order to make Blois appear in a more favourable light.[15] In passing it may be noted that since the official commission sitting at Angers between 9 September and 18 December 1371 did not finally pronounce in favour of the canonisation of Blois, ultimately achieved with Dom Plaine's assistance this century, and that since French royal policy in support of Blois's claim to the duchy of Brittany manifest from 1341 was reversed by Charles V in 1378, Froissart's version in this redaction poses interesting questions about the dating of the Amiens MS. On the traditional interpretation such favour towards the Blois family could be explained by the manuscript being antecedent to the reversal of royal policy; if it were written after the case of John of Montfort came before the court of peers in December 1378, such favour might be indicative of undue and increasing partiality on the part of the author for his patron.[16] This ambiguity apart, most of the modifications in the Amiens MS are of a factual nature, perhaps reflecting Froissart's own increasing knowledge of events and personalities. For example, the movements of Blois during the years 1342-3 are chronicled a little more closely. Family details are more correctly given, and the subsequent fate of the hostages for his ransom in 1356 are traced.[17] But his dilemma, when presented by Louis of Spain with the demand to deliver two English hostages whom he knew Louis was planning to execute, is just as poignant in the first as in later redactions; whilst the undoubted heroism of Blois, in particular at La Roche Derrien and Auray, is as fully portrayed in the first and third redactions or even more so.[18] Nor does Froissart give favourable prominence to the activities of Joan of Penthièvre, unlike the sympathetic treatment accorded to the countess of Montfort who, long after she had left with Edward III in February 1343 for an exile from which she never returned, is described continuing the struggle in the duchy with the aid of English lieutenants.[19] Indeed, the intransigence of Joan of Penthièvre in defence of her rights in 1364 and her speech stiffening the resolve of Blois to hazard all on a final battle is the first occasion on which she took a directing part in affairs as described by Froissart (VI, 325-6). This contrasts sharply with her position when studied from administrative and diplomatic documents.[20] The claim, then, that he did not deliberately or unduly falsify his narrative, even in the interests of powerful and rich patrons, when describing events in Brittany seems to be a fair one.

The main characteristics of the third redaction, that contained in the Rome MS and compiled between 1400-5, for the Breton civil war which require comment are structural, factual and literary. In the first place, unlike the earlier versions which in some form cover the whole war, the third redaction contains only an account to the time of the battle of La Roche Derrien (1347). Moreover, since the story of that battle is recounted in a separate chapter, essentially the redaction contains, within one long coherent section, an artistically satisfying account of the years 1341-3, only momentarily broken up by a single chapter on Scotland (Diller 462-600). In the earlier versions Scottish affairs, Edward III's amorous advances to the countess of Salisbury (toning down the more lurid story of her rape found in Le Bel), the foundation of the Order of the Garter and other miscellaneous matters often break up the flow of the narrative. Froissart had originally taken the sequence from Le Bel but it is clear that he already felt some unease, for example, in the transposition from Breton to Scottish affairs in the first redaction which occurs during a period of swiftly moving events in the duchy recounted under the year 1342. Now in the third redaction Froissart deals with the period from the opening of the succession dispute to the truce of Malestroit (19 January 1343) as a whole. Thereafter, preserving the fiction that the truce was carefully observed by all parties, which confuses his chronology of events like the execution of Olivier III de Clisson (2 August 1343) and the other Breton and Norman traitors (29 November 1343 and April 1344), he only notices subsequent Breton matters when it is absolutely necessary.[21] In comparison with the brief but closely factual accounts of the best English chroniclers, who all provide evidence on the small expeditionary forces sent to the duchy by Edward III after his return to England, Froissart ignores the skirmishing which went on as the Anglo-Breton administration strengthened its hold.[22] To the end he persists in an error for which Le Bel was originally responsible but for which equally he had craved indulgence should it turn out to be incorrect. That is, he continued to state that John of Montfort died in prison at the Louvre to which he had been consigned after being seized at the capitulation of Nantes in the autumn of 1341.[23] In reality, after being released on parole (in all probability in 1343) he escaped to England around Easter 1345 and did homage for the duchy to Edward III.[24] Like an earlier departure from Paris by Montfort, this one was apparently dramatic and worthy of retelling in Froissart's finest style. But this time the scoop fell to the St Denis writers to describe. They were then able to gloat at Montfort's swift demise when he returned to the duchy with William Bohun, earl of Northampton, in the summer of 1345. Montfort's final delirium and the augury of a parliament of crows gathering about the lodgings where he lay on his deathbed are touches of which Froissart might have been justly proud! (Viard 1937: 255, 258).

In terms of factual accuracy, the third redaction superficially offers a much greater precision of reference. Dates have been revised sensibly as demonstrated above. The names of those involved in specific actions and the names of towns and castles besieged are more comprehensive, as a comparison of the account of events in the summer of 1341 in this redaction and earlier ones shows clearly.[25] Although there are still fundamental misconceptions about the course of events, the strategic objectives of campaigns, and the motivations of individuals, as a later section of this paper will demonstrate, the overall pattern is a more balanced one, with fewer entirely absurd flights into fantasy.

From a literary point of view, dialogue is imaginatively used to evoke a fuller emotional response in the Rome MS. John of Montfort's interviews with Garnier de Clisson and Philip VI, the appeal to and encouragement of her supporters by his wife, Blois's exchanges with Louis of Spain, are here used economically but effectively to advance the story (Diller 120-5). Professor Diverres long ago noted how Froissart developed traditional direct speech in French historical works into realistic dialogue by the time he came to write his third book about 1390. His remarks *à propos* Froissart's treatment of dialogue in the sections relating to his journey to Béarn in 1388 are as appropriate for the third redaction of events in Brittany where dialogue is equally 'an essential part of narrative, a means of varying the tempo of a passage, of carrying the action forward and of giving substance to the characters . . . often introduced to mark a particularly dramatic incident' (Diverres: xxvi). In the same way, as Professor Diller pointed out, the interior monologue has a similar function when the character, finding himself in a critical position, thinks aloud in steeling himself to use every conceivable ruse to escape from his predicament. A clear example is when Montfort, having appeared in the court of peers, recognises that if he stays in Paris to await Philip's sentence, it is unlikely that he will remain at liberty, so he makes a clandestine escape, reaching Nantes before the king is aware he is not in his lodgings (Diller 122). In its refashioning of a story already twice told at length, this third recension displays few signs of tiredness. The literary imagination is still fertile and the form of presentation represents that preoccupation with 'fine language' for which Froissart is sometimes prepared to sacrifice objective historical exposition in his later years (Diller 24-31). For where around the year 1400 could he have turned to gain reliable information on conversations, which if they had taken place, had occurred some sixty years earlier?

This raises the whole question of Froissart's sources for his various accounts of Breton matters. In common with other parts of the first redaction the obvious source is the work of Le Bel, on which the close reliance of Froissart both for form and content has already been amply demonstrated. But this simply pushes us a stage further back. From where did Le Bel obtain his information? Modern opinion seems to suggest that the Breton sections of this earlier chronicle were written about 1358 and that Le Bel principally used oral testimony.[26] The only written sources to which he refers are by *jongleurs*. These he dismisses as 'so full of humbug and lies that I dare not repeat them' (I, 3; II, 10, 21), and in his turn Froissart, as noted above, scathingly dismissed them too (II, 265). The only work to have survived which could possibly fit into this category during the 1350s is the poem on the battle of the Thirty, written by someone familiar with eastern Brittany c.1355. It has been suggested that both Le Bel and Froissart (at least by the time of the third redaction) had seen copies of this work; neither acknowledges a specific debt but a number of verbal similarities make this a distinct probability (Bush 1911-12: 516).

At about the time Froissart was completing his second redaction, two mediocre writers, Guillaume de St André and Jean Cuvelier, were working on their respective verse lives of John IV of Brittany and Bertrand du Guesclin, both of which necessarily touched upon the civil war (Charrière 1839). No doubt Froissart's condemnation of 'contrived rhymes' could be made to include these rambling pieces, but again there is no direct evidence that he consulted either. In fact, like Le Bel before him, it seems Froissart neither used nor required literary sources for his account of the Breton civil war, nor apart from documents incidentally relating to the duchy in the treaty of Calais (24 October 1360), which he exceptionally quoted at length in the second redaction, did he normally have recourse to official material (VI, 34-46). His nonchalant citation of alleged truces and treaties, which may have some basis in reality, but which often seem to be introduced for literary effect, to enable him to change location and so on, is particularly evident in his handling of diplomatic incidents concerning Brittany.[27] Unlike many contemporary chroniclers, Froissart did not very evidently use newsletters, of which several sent to England by commanders of expeditionary forces to Brittany survive and were clearly accessible.[28] Apart from Le Bel, whom he significantly calls the first historian of the Breton wars, Froissart spurned or was ignorant of other contemporary historical works dealing with the duchy. The major sources of this kind are the *Grandes Chroniques*, which for the period 1340-50 is apparently contemporary, the *Chronique normande*, originally compiled c.1369-73, or the many adaptations of the material gathered at St Denis, all of which must be used by modern historians to fill gaps in Froissart's narrative after the truce of Malestroit.[29]

For Brittany, then, Froissart's classic method of gathering material was by personal interview of participants, eye-witnesses or those who could recollect family tradition about events; in short almost anyone whom he could persuade to talk to him. For the most part they remain anonymous. Minor alterations and additions, even in the first redaction, to the list of Englishmen who accompanied Artois and Bohun in the summer of 1342 (which he derived originally from Le Bel) suggests that Froissart had talked to Englishmen about their experiences in the duchy (n.10). Sometime between late April and December 1366, Froissart passed through Brittany *en route* for Bordeaux, but the only Breton who helped him and was specifically named was a certain Guillaume d'Ancenis whom he met at Angers shortly before his journey to Béarn in 1388 (KL I, i, 153-5). Ancenis was a cadet of one of the oldest noble families in the duchy, whose cousin, the lord of Ancenis, Froissart claims to have met at Sluys in 1386; certainly the Ancenis family receives much fuller recognition in the third redaction.[30] But for the most part the events on which Ancenis provided the chronicler with new material were much more recent ones like the capture of the constable of France, Olivier IV de Clisson, by John IV at Vannes on 26 June 1387, and on the family history of Du Guesclin, rather than on the civil war period, of which there is but an echo in some later exploits of Du Guesclin and his companions (XIV, 4-19).

It is probable that Froissart interviewed Even Charruel, one of the heroes of the battle of the Thirty. In a corrupt manuscript of the second redaction Luce discovered this interesting addition:

> . . . car bien vingt deus ans puissedy j'en vich ung seoir à la table du roy Charle de Franche, que on appelloit monseigneur Ievain Caruiel. Et pour chu que il avoir esté l'eun des Trente, on l'onnouroit deseure tous aultres. Et ousy il moustroit bien à son viaire qu'il sçavoit que cops d'espées, de daghes et de haches valloient, car il estoit moult plaiiés (IV, 340-1).

Taking Froissart at his word, the encounter must have occurred c.1373-4, and in all likelihood whilst Charles V was in Paris. Luce had misgivings about this date; a reference, which appears unambiguously to provide evidence that Froissart was in Paris in 1364 had been discovered, and he suggested that the copyist of the manuscript might well have added a supplementary *X* in the phrase *XXII ans puissedy* (IV,xlv). But if the problem is seen from Charruel's point of view, the date 1373-4 appears the more likely one. In 1364 Charruel, who clearly loved to be in the thick of fighting wherever it might be, was alongside Du Guesclin in the capture of Mantes on 7 April, of which he became captain, and a few weeks later he fought heroically at Cocherel.[31] Thereafter, most of the Breton troops in royal pay returned to the duchy to join Charles of Blois in the campaign which led to his defeat at Auray. A visit to Paris in the midst of this feverish military activity is improbable; in 1373-4, however, with the duchy temporarily in the hands of Charles V and his lieutenants, Du Guesclin chief amongst them, such a journey to Paris would be entirely appropriate for there were many Breton knights who had gone there to enjoy largesse.[32]

The only other named informant on Breton affairs is Guillaume de St Mesmin, a surgeon and astrologer, whom Froissart met at a monastery near Montpellier, again in 1388.[33] With a degree of foresight which is hardly exceptional, he had warned Blois about the dire consequences of giving battle at Auray. He could well have provided other details on the household of Charles and Joan, but this is not explicitly stated. Froissart remains, perhaps not surprisingly in view of the patronage of the Blois family, from whom over the years he seems to have gathered more precise information on Brittany, remarkably reticent about his specific sources.[34] Clearly he had authoritative English informants on the duchy like Windsor herald who told him of the battle of Auray and members of those aristocratic families who fought there either in 1364 or earlier. Although he says he visited the duchy (in 1366 in all probability) how long the visit lasted, where he went and who he met, are all matters for speculation (KL I, i, 154). He does not appear to have visited the duchy again, nor to have established direct contact with the Montfort family. It is possible that during John IV's many journeys outside the duchy, Froissart met some of his entourage. He notes, for instance, the death of Montfort herald in Flanders in 1383. But very often the quality of the later information which he recounts on Breton affairs reflects common rumour rather than an authoritative source.[35]

There can be no question here of correcting in the light of modern knowledge all the factual inaccuracies revealed by patient editorial work. In completing this assessment of Froissart's work as an historian of the Breton civil war, the examination of a few key episodes must suffice. Those chosen are his explanation of the origins of the war, Montfort's summer campaign of 1341 and the treatment of naval affairs during the first phase of the war, all of which are first described in Le Bel's chronicle, the siege of Rennes which Le Bel briefly mentions, and finally, the battle of Auray for which Le Bel provided no model.

The succession war is introduced in the first redaction (II, 86 ff) with the briefest of preambles after the statement that the duke of Brittany died on his way home after the 1340 campaign had been concluded by the truce of Esplechin (25 September 1340). The rights of the respective claimants are hopelessly confused by Le Bel (I, 244 ff), who admits candidly that he does not even know the name of the late duke. He then retells a story about John of Montfort being the uterine rather than the consanguineous brother of John III, so that he did not 'issue from the true house of Brittany'. This seems to reflect Valois propaganda, which finds its fullest expression in the *Chronographia regum Francorum*. It comes strangely from a chronicler who is traditionally considered pro-English.

74

Froissart not only took over this account in his first redaction but persisted in repeating it in the two following redactions (II, 87-8, 266-8). Whilst nearly all the French chroniclers who deal with the genealogical intricacies of the succession are confused (in marked contrast, for example, to the text-book clarity of Avesbury's exposition), the following tables will demonstrate the peculiar blend of generalised knowledge, ignorance and misrepresentation contained in the accounts of Le Bel and Froissart and require little further comment, except to say that much of the genealogical information provided by these writers for the Breton civil war appears to be similarly flawed.[36] Attributed relationships 'the cousin of X' or 'the uncle of Y' are all suspect until otherwise established.[37]

Once the disputed succession question arose, the strategic importance of Brittany was bound to lead to the involvement of England and France. According to Le Bel and Froissart it was Montfort's appeal to Edward III which stimulated English intervention, and the reasons why Edward seized the opportunity to intervene in the duchy have been no better explained by modern historians than by the words which Le Bel put into Philip VI's mouth, when he attempted to forestall Edward by sending troops to the assistance of Blois: 'He could do us no greater harm and obtain no better entry into our kingdom than by coming that way, especially if he should obtain the province and fortresses of Brittany . . .' (I, 264). Froissart repeats this and although concrete evidence of Edward III's intentions remains slight, what there is suggests that he did take the initiative in 1341. But both kings had been planning their respective policies in the full knowledge of John III's eventual childlessness (Le Patourel 1958: 186-7). Under the year 1334, for example, the anonymous continuator of the chronicle of Guillaume de Nangis (who wrote contemporaneously with events and before the outbreak of the civil war), has a report of John III's proposal to leave Brittany to Philip VI 'in order to avoid the dangers which would befall the kingdom should the duchy fall into the hands of a woman, namely his niece who said she had claims to it . . . but certain Bretons opposing this, the negotiations remained incomplete . . . and finally it all came to nothing'.[38] A few years later Philip gained a much more personal interest in the Breton succession when his nephew married that ducal niece. In the interim her hand as the duke's heiress had also been sought in 1335 by Edward III for his younger brother, John of Eltham, whose premature death in 1336 put an end to this scheme.[39] But the exchange of embassies and formal grants suggest that diplomatic relations between the two courts remained close, in any case they are virtually all the evidence we have.[40] In 1339 the service of Breton sailors with the French fleet and in 1340 that of John III himself with the French army, provided Edward III with an adequate excuse to confiscate the earldom of Richmond from the duke. But he had not done so at the time of John's death; clearly he wished to remain on friendly terms with him. Similarly Philip VI had equally sought to avoid any very serious breach with the late duke although there were important matters relating to ducal coinage and judicial rights which had been much debated. Whilst within the duchy, if there had been baronial opposition in 1334, little is known of any other causes for discontent or of the formation of rival groups anticipating the divisions of the civil war.[41] In this respect modern historians are little better informed than fourteenth-century chroniclers about the prelude to the war.

Turning to the campaign of 1341, a crux is reached. The original account is

75

Genealogical table constructed from the information contained in the three redactions of the *Chronicles*

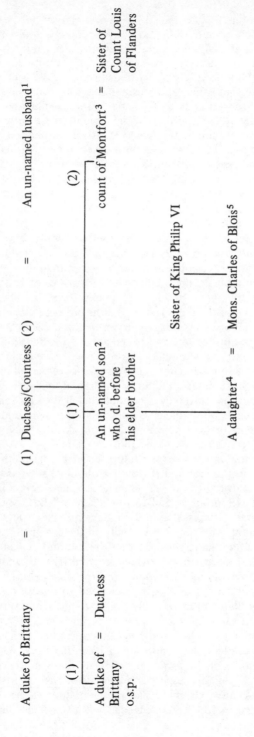

A duke of Brittany = (1) Duchess/Countess (2) = An un-named husband[1]

(1) = Duchess Brittany (2)

A duke of Brittany o.s.p.

An un-named son[2] who d. before his elder brother — count of Montfort[3] = Sister of Count Louis of Flanders

Sister of King Philip VI

A daughter[4] = Mons. Charles of Blois[5]

1. MS Rome states he was count of Montfort.
2. MS Rome calls him John of Brittany, count of Penthièvre.
3. MS Amiens adds, and had issue a son and a daughter.
4. MSS of Book III call her Joan. MS Rome adds, called Joan, countess of Penthièvre by right of her mother.
5. One MS of the first redaction adds, younger son of Count Guy of Blois. Amiens MS adds, younger son of Count Louis of Blois.
   MS Rome states he was son of Count Guy and brother of Count Louis of Blois.

Simplified table to illustrate the genealogy of the Breton ruling house

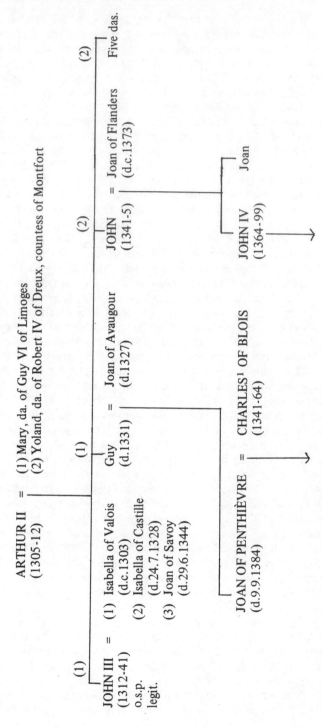

ARTHUR II = (1) Mary, da. of Guy VI of Limoges
(1305-12)   (2) Yoland, da. of Robert IV of Dreux, countess of Montfort

(1)   (1)   (2)

JOHN III = (1) Isabella of Valois   Guy   = Joan of Avaugour   JOHN = Joan of Flanders   Five das.
(1312-41)   (d.c.1303)   (d.1331)   (d.1327)   (1341-5)   (d.c.1373)
o.s.p.   (2) Isabella of Castille
legit.   (d.24.7.1328)
             (3) Joan of Savoy
                 (d.29.6.1344)

JOAN OF PENTHIÈVRE = CHARLES¹ OF BLOIS   JOHN IV   Joan
(d.9.9.1384)   (1341-64)   (1364-99)

1. Yr. s. of Guy, count of Blois, and Margaret of Valois, sister of Philip VI.

77

Le Bel's. It is embellished in the first two redactions of the *Chronicles*, whilst in the third, although abbreviated (and it now appears that many of the towns and castles which gave themselves up, did not require much persuasion), nevertheless the main outlines of the story remain. That is to say, John of Montfort, hearing of the death of his brother, hurried to Nantes, and decided with his wife to call the barons and other representatives of the duchy to a feast to do homage. In the interval before the appointed day, he rushed to seize the ducal treasure at Limoges (for the late duke was also viscount of Limoges), and returned to Nantes to find only Hervé de Léon had answered his summons. So leaving his wife, but accompanied by Léon and the troops he had hired with his treasure, he went to besiege Brest first and then several other strongholds. It was the confusion of this subsequent itinerary, followed by an account of a brief visit to Edward III, prior to an appearance before the court of peers at Paris, which first seems to have sparked off serious doubts about the veracity of the *Chronicles*.

It seemed impossible to compress all this action into a timescale already prescribed by what was known from other sources. Luce and La Borderie, in particular, introduced some order into Froissart's account, but much remained uncertain. If they accepted, for example, Montfort's flying visit to the English court, subsequent generations of scholars, whilst being far from unanimous, have in general adhered to the view expressed by Lemoine that the visit never took place.[42] But even if this complication in Montfort's itinerary is removed, the sequence of events in the summer of 1341 is still difficult to disentangle.

John III died at Caen on 30 April 1341. On 16 May the news was already known in England and in early June messengers left to meet John of Montfort.[43] Yet in the duchy things appear to have remained calm for on 15 June the late duke's executors were peaceably sorting through his effects at Nantes. The document recording their activities is now significantly in the Public Record Office, but nowhere does it suggest they were acting under duress.[44] Moreover as late as 11 July, Charles of Blois seems to have been conducting himself with due propriety. For a document issued then in his name simply styled him 'lord of Penthièvre', a courtesy title acquired by his marriage. Nor is there any other evidence to confirm military disturbances up to the time the two claimants appeared to present their claims for Brittany at Paris in the latter half of August.[45] If the chroniclers' accounts of Montfort's progress have any basis, it is surely that of the self-styled duke receiving pledges of loyalty from his new subjects during a tour of inspection of the towns and castles of the ducal demesne as a precaution lest his proffered homage should be rejected at Paris (La Borderie 1899: 425-9). It was only after Montfort's precipitate flight (probably to be dated between 1 and 4 September) that serious military operations began as the St Denis chroniclers more accurately suggest and, consequently, Froissart's account of the summer campaign is a wild travesty.[46]

It would be possible to examine in yet greater detail the whole chronology of this phase of the war, where almost every sentence which Le Bel and Froissart wrote requires minute critical attention. But one final example may be chosen to demonstrate the general pitfalls of trying to marry literary and documentary sources to produce an acceptable account, which are so much a part of Froissart scholarship. The war at sea engaged the chroniclers' interest almost as much as that on land; in the early stages of the civil war, the struggle between England

and France to gain control of the peninsula and with it a vital section of the lines of communication between the Channel and the Bay of Biscay hardly needs re-emphasis. From the outset, whatever his ultimate intentions were in supporting John of Montfort, Edward III had shown that a predominating concern was control of the Breton coastline through garrisoning certain ports and coastal castles (Jones 1972a: 72-4). Later in the war when the opportunity offered itself for the king to overrun the whole duchy, it was allowed to slip away because by that time the Anglo-Breton administration was firmly entrenched, particularly around Brest and on the south-western coastline.[47]

The standard account of the war at sea during this period remains Charles de la Roncière's *Histoire de la marine française*. Normally very reliable because of close acquaintance with administrative records, the chapter on the Breton war (1899: 462-70) is marred by giving credence to stories found in Froissart which even the chronicler on maturer reflection or in the light of new information thought prudent to edit or to omit. In the second redaction (III, 8-13, 208-12) the action between Artois and the countess of Montfort (returning from a visit to England which is as legendary as her husband's in 1341) and Louis of Spain off Guernsey is finally ended by a storm which blows Louis so far off course that he finds himself attacking the kingdom of Navarre! More prosaically, in the third redaction (Diller 566-7) the two naval forces engaged in the summer of 1342, are prevented from meeting by the providential storm. Such a change warns us that the description of similar naval actions may be equally fabulous; administrative documents show considerable activity off the south-western coastline of the duchy at this stage. English exchequer records have still not been fully exploited. What they show, and this may help to clear up some of the confusion displayed in contemporary chronicles (shared by those modern historians who have rigidly tried to interpret the dates given for the sailing of fleets) is that many expeditions, made up of numerous contingents, sailed at different times from a variety of ports so that it is often misleading or impossible to give a single exact date for their departure and arrival.[48]

The two final episodes − the siege of Rennes and the battle of Auray − may be discussed much more summarily, for they have been exhaustively covered by modern scholars. The siege of Rennes occurs at the point when Froissart is beginning his own independent career as a chronicler no longer primarily guided by Le Bel. In some manuscripts of the first redaction his account is relatively brief, emphasising chiefly the role of Henry of Lancaster as Le Bel did. But in others there is considerable development of a number of personal encounters, involving the young Bertrand du Guesclin and his cousin, Olivier de Mauny, of a type more usually associated with the style of the second redaction, where in this case little further is added except to make the roll-call of those defending Rennes more comprehensive.[49] The quality of Froissart's evidence in both versions is very much on a par with that of other chroniclers. The chivalric aspects of both redactions are carried to extremes in the work of Du Guesclin's eulogist, Cuvelier.[50]

For the battle of Auray which concluded the civil war, Froissart finally provides what is by far the fullest serious, contemporary account of an event in Brittany. His narrative is marred by a number of demonstrable errors of a venial kind − characteristically he misdates the battle by a week − but in other respects the accuracy of his factual information appears to be of a much higher standard than in the earlier parts of his *Chronicles* which deal with Breton matters. The reason for this seems obvious: in October 1364 Froissart was at Dover, following the court of Edward III who was conducting negotiations with the count of Flanders, when news was brought by a *poursuivant* of Montfort's victory. Froissart seized the opportunity and gained from the future Windsor herald as circumstantial an account as he could from which he later constructed his own narrative.[51] With such a source, it is to be expected that much of the information on those who participated in the battle would be accurate; what still needs careful handling is Froissart's treatment of the wider issues of strategy and diplomacy in the campaign. For instance, he states that Du Guesclin was deliberately sent to help Blois by Charles V; other records suggest he took French leave (VI, lxvii). But when Charles stopped his pay in September 1364 was this a prudent public relations exercise? The matter remains open to opposing interpretations and is typical of the ambiguities which arise through the use of the *Chronicles*.

Froissart intentionally in the second redaction set out to provide both contemporaries and future generations with the unvarnished truth about the history and course of the Breton civil war. Despite an increasing concern with literary style both in later books and in the third redaction of the first book, this insistence on the accuracy of his account is frequently reasserted whenever he touches upon Breton affairs (XIV, 3). But the methods he used to collect his material were little different from those of many contemporaries and he shared with them the strengths and weaknesses of these methods. Above all over-reliance on oral testimony in which distortion readily occurs through faulty memory, conscious or unconscious misrepresentation, misattribution and all manner of kindred defects, undoubtedly left Froissart at the mercy of some of his informants and undermined his efforts to achieve literal truthfulness (Thorne 1979). Furthermore the chivalric form emphasising individual achievement in which Froissart chose to present his history had a similar effect, glorifying as it did a particular way of life which had its own very stylised practices and literary devices and which was lived by ideals which, if shared by many, were practised by a minority.

For those, then, who simply want to know why the Breton succession war was fought, who took part and what happened, Froissart is a treacherous guide. Thanks to administrative documents, the nature of the legal arguments over the respective claims to the duchy and the subsequent character of the war, with its often harsh exploitation of the native population, can be studied in depth. So can diplomacy and the organisation of military expeditions, some of which, omnivorous collector of such information as he was, Froissart failed to chronicle. Yet for all these defects, many of which stemmed originally from his dependence on Le Bel, Froissart, perhaps better than any other contemporary, catches the flavour of the war and reflects contemporary attitudes and feelings; even in glorifying it and praising great names, he is aware of the suffering and cruelty war caused 'by which such great evil came into the world by land and sea' (KL II, 3). In his account of the Breton civil war, woven with increasing mastery into that much greater panorama of the conflict between England and France, there can be found *in piccolo* the same fundamental features of this extraordinary writer. For even were every word he wrote historically valueless — and the inconsistencies, confusions and contradictions of his various attempts to recount the Breton civil war have tempted some to assert that hypercritical view — there would be many, the present writer included, who would continue to read the *Chronicles* for sheer pleasure.[52]

VI THE WAR IN SPAIN AND PORTUGAL *

P. E. Russell

FROISSART'S ambitious attempt to deal with the historical consequences of the extension of the Hundred Years War to the Iberian Peninsula has usually earned him harsh criticism at the hands of modern scholars who have studied the same subject using both archival sources and the work of the various Peninsular chroniclers who were Froissart's contemporaries. Edouard Perroy, writing particularly about Froissart's treatment of the Lancastrian occupation of Galicia in 1386-7, dismissed him with the comment 'he accumulates improbabilities and errors to such an extent that his narrative is really unusable except as the source of a few colourful details'.[1] The observation echoes modern attitudes to Froissart's treatment of Peninsular history generally, though it may be noted that some scholars, when it comes to it, seem to find rather a lot of usable 'colourful details' in his work, specially when, as sometimes happens, he is the only chronicler to describe events at any length. It seems to me impossible to rehabilitate Froissart, generally speaking, as a trustworthy source of information about what happened, or why it happened, in the region with which we are concerned and I shall not attempt that in the present essay. His work, nevertheless, certainly merits a more sophisticated appraisal than the mere blanket disapproval it usually gets. It is, for instance, by no means all equally unsatisfactory, as I shall try to show, though we must, of course, avoid the trap of supposing that those portions of his narrative which cannot be collated with any alternative sources of information are any more likely to be reliable than the chronicler's verifiable norm is. The reasons for Froissart's unsatisfactoriness as a chronicler of Peninsular affairs must also be kept in mind; thus, unlike the authors of many chronicles of his time, he rarely arouses our suspicions that he is consciously inventing or fudging the happenings he describes, though he may well unwittingly transmit the inventions or fantasies of his informants as Tucoo-Chala has observed (1960: 20-2). It is not his good faith but his view of history and his methodology that can be called into question. Good faith will not, of course, excuse bad history but it leaves us with the duty to discover exactly why the vast amount of hard work that Froissart put into recording Peninsular affairs fails, on the whole, to produce the results he sought. One reason is obvious enough; his excessive faith in the reports of eye-witnesses. Though a belief that the testimony of eye-witnesses was the best evidence available to a historian was common ground between Froissart and, for example, his Castilian and Portuguese contemporaries, the latter were much less disposed than he to suspend their critical faculties when

---

* All references to the *Chronicles* are to page and volume of the SHF edition unless otherwise stated.

confronted by such evidence, or apparent evidence. He, it seems, could rarely bring himself to reject a good story, well-told, specially when the *mis-en-scène* was the 'besoignes des lointaines marches'. There is, of course, yet another reason for paying some attention to what Froissart has to say about events in the Peninsula, even on the occasions when we recognise his information to be seriously defective. The chronicler was a frequenter of the seats of power and of decision-making, as well as an intimate of the knights and squires on whom fell the task of implementing political decisions in the field by force of arms. If Maitland's well-known aphorism about the essential matter of history being what people thought or said about it has substance, then the *Chronicles* can be held to reflect, more than we might suppose, if not the real reasons why things happened as they did, at least the terms in which it was thought appropriate to explain them to those who had to do the fighting. In that particular respect Froissart, superficial and predictably ready-made as his treatment of historical causality usually seems to be, may well have the edge on more critically-minded and less easily satisfied chroniclers of his time.

Froissart's approach to the extension of the Hundred Years War to the Iberian Peninsula is, of course, basically war-oriented as he himself often stresses. Diplomatic history for the most part hardly enters his picture at all, though we now know, largely thanks to the secret seal registers of the crown of Aragon and to the great amount of incoming diplomatic correspondence preserved in Barcelona along with those registers, that, behind the actual military inter-ventions that the chronicler concerned himself with, England, France and all the Iberian kingdoms were enmeshed in a diplomatic labyrinth of projects and counter-projects for alliances, wars and conquests from which actual military action rarely emerged. For that reason Aragon, continuously wooed by England and France, hardly appears in the *Chronicles* at all until late in Book III, though it is only fair to say that, in this book, the diplomatic aspects of the Lancastrian expedition of 1386-7 do get some attention, too.

Before proceeding farther it may be appropriate to recall what, broadly-speaking, the scope of Froissart's treatment of Peninsular affairs is. Book I contains a long account of the Black Prince's campaign in Castile in 1367, together with an explanation of that campaign's immediate preliminaries and aftermath; it also deals, rather briefly, with Lancaster's assumption of the role of legitimist pretender to the Castilian crown consequent upon the assassination of Peter I, and with the course of the war at sea up to 1378 following the entry into it, on the French side, of the Castilian fleet. The invasion of Gascony and siege of Bayonne by the Castilian army of Henry II of Trastámara in 1374 — the only time a Castilian army left Spain to attack the English in Gascony — ought to appear in Book I but, because of a grievous error in Froissart's chronology, he has displaced this event to 1378 and hence to Book II. Book II contains his account of the Castilian invasion of Navarre in 1378-9 and a detailed history of Edmund of Cambridge's unsuccessful expedition to Portugal in 1381-2. Book III, finally, deals with the long Castilian attempt from 1383 to 1385 to conquer Portugal — an attempt that was brought to an end by the Castilian defeat at Aljubarrota. It also devotes a substantial amount of space to the Lancastrian expedition to Galicia in 1386 and to the Anglo-Portuguese invasion of Léon in 1387, ending with a very brief account of the settlement of Lancaster's dynastic

MAP TO ILLUSTRATE THE NAVARRESE CAMPAIGN, 1378-9

▲ Navarrese fortresses captured by Castilian Army

→ Routes of the Castilian advance on Pamplona.

–·– Route of Sir Thomes Trivet's attack on Soria

0 — 30 miles
0 — 50 km.

Peyrehorade

BAYONNE

Sauveterre

Fuenterrabia

Mauléon

San Sebastián

Guernica

Bilbao

Bidassoa

Nive

SAN JUAN DEL
PIE DEL PUERTO

Valcarlos

Tolosa

Roncesvalles

N A V A R R E

C A S T I L L E

Alsásua

Echarri-Aranaz

VITORIA

PAMPLONA

Aoiz

R. Arga

ESTELLA

Villatuerta

Beriain

Tiebas

Puente la Reina

Torralba

Mendigorria

Río Aragón

Lárraga

Haro

Viana

Lerín

Falces

LOGROÑO

Mendavia

NÁJERA

Funes

Calahorra

A R A G O N

Fitero

TUDELA

Cervera del
rio Alhama

Cascante

Tauste

Tarazona

C A S T I L L E

Río Duero

Agreda

Río Ebro

SORIA

ZARAGOZA

claims in Castile.[2] In Book III the chronicler offers us two different sets of perspective on the wars in Portugal which he presents in two different parts of the book and which he makes no attempt to collate. The first, he claims, was written up from information supplied to him at Orthez in 1388 by witnesses who had participated in these campaigns, mainly on the Castilian side. Later, when he had returned to Valenciennes and set to work writing this material up, he realised he lacked information from the Portuguese side so set off for Bruges to contact Portuguese informants in the Low Countries who could tell him what the Portuguese view of these events was (XII, 237-8). However, the two separate sources are both used side by side to make up the account of events in Castile and Portugal in 1386-7 and at least one of his sources here had served in the Lancastrian army itself, which is why his account shows a familiarity with events concerning it that cannot have been known to his Portuguese informants.[3]

Some features common to all Froissart's treatment of Iberian affairs may be noted first before we look at points of special interest in the way he handles individually some of the material listed above. It should be remarked that the chronicler himself never got nearer to the Iberian Peninsula than southern Gascony and Foix. We have his word for it that he had wanted to accompany the Black Prince's Spanish expedition in 1367 and, indeed, did join the prince at Dax, where the invasion army was assembled, at the end of 1366. He was, however, sent back to England on business (KL XV, 142). All his descriptions of the Peninsular scene are, therefore, second-hand ones. Despite this handicap he contrives quite well to build up a convincing impression of what making war there was like, particularly in Book III, and must have interrogated his informants with a view to securing this kind of local colour. However, he seems, particularly again in Book I, to be decidedly vague about political boundaries in the Peninsula. He thus speaks of the inhabitants of 'Lusebonne' renewing their homage to Peter I of Castile after the victory at Nájera and has them fighting, along with men-at-arms 'de Portingal', in the Trastámaran army (VII, 41, 51); though he knew the facts about the relation of Portugal to Castile when he came to write the later books, he evidently did not trouble to remove these earlier errors.[4]

Froissart's general treatment of Peninsular geography, and of Peninsular toponyms and proper names, is notoriously disastrous, though this is not universally the case. However, one may argue that critics have complained too much about his failure to present proper names in a decipherable form. It is admittedly disconcerting, for example, to find the famous constable of Portugal (who figures so prominently in the later parts of the *Chronicles*) — Nun'Alvares Pereira, count of Ourém and Barcelos — regularly presented as 'le conte de Navaire' or, sometimes, as 'messire Alne Perriere' (XIII, 161, 270); but, at least in the case of important personages, a correct identification can usually easily be made from other sources. Such distortions were, in fact, unavoidable; Froissart had to do the best he could from notes made of Peninsular proper names communicated to him orally by French-speaking informants who themselves must often have had scant idea of the original sound of the names to which they tried to give a French form. However, Froissart, no doubt correctly, does not seem to have thought his readers would be particularly interested in this problem for it must be admitted that he handles Iberian names only marginally better when he got them straight from someone like John I of Portugal's chancellor, Lourenço Anes Fogaça, who, as he says, 'bien et bel savoit parler françois' (XII, 241).[5] One of the chronicler's problems about these names was evidently that they sounded comical to French speakers. He tells us that when Fogaça told Lancaster the names of the Castilian dead and the Portuguese commanders at Aljubarrota, the latter laughed aloud and commented 'Je n'oy oncques mais nommer tant de fors noms, ne d'estranges, comme je vous ay ici oy nommer' (XII, 289). If true, it was hardly a tactful joke for the pretender to the Castilian throne to make.

The chronicler's persistent and inconsequential mishandling of Iberian geography and topography is a much more serious defect since it often makes it impossible to make sense of his narrative. I have already mentioned his treatment of the Lancastrian campaign in Galicia which, as Armitage-Smith pointed out long ago (1904: 321, n.1), allows him to make the Lancastrian marshal, Sir Thomas Morieux, capture a town in the heart of León and then return in the evening to Santiago de Compostela. What seems to have happened to cause such confusions is that Froissart has muddled up his notes for the 1386 campaign in Galicia with those of the Anglo-Portuguese invasion of León in the following year, perhaps because, as is probable, the Lancastrian garrisons left in Galicia continued military operations there in 1387 while the bulk of what was left of the Lancastrian army campaigned with the Portuguese in León. There are many other errors of this kind. In the case of the Aljubarrota campaign the chronicler reveals that he has only a vague awareness of distances and locations; he even manages to reverse the respective lines of march of the Castilian and Portuguese armies as they approached the battlefield! Book I has far crasser mistakes of this kind than any other. Thus the chronicler tells us that, among the territories ceded by Peter I of Castile to Charles II of Navarre as a reward for opening the passes to the Black Prince's army in 1367 was 'le ville de Saint Jehan dou piet des Pors et le marce de là environ' (VI, 210). The statement is repeated in all the variants. Now Saint-Jean-Pied-de-Port lies among the northern foothills of the Pyrenees only about thirty-five miles from Bayonne, in a region, therefore, the chronicler knew well. In his time it was the capital of the small Navarrese *merindad* (roughly province) of Ultrapuertos and could hardly have been further away from the dominions of the king of Castile. The Amiens MS scarcely improves matters on this occasion when it seeks to provide a rational explanation by saying that Saint-Jean 'marcist à Espaingne et à Galisse, et que li roys dans Pières li avoit tolue de jadis' (VI, 368). It seems clear that the place Froissart's informant had in fact told him about in this context was the Guipúzcoan port of San Sebastián (which was indeed ceded to Charles II at this time) and that the chronicler either could not read his own notes or had misheard what was said. The episode demonstrates his insouciant attitude to geographical exactness at this time, especially when we remember that, very shortly after perpetrating this howler, he describes, following the Chandos Herald poem, how the Anglo-Gascon army set out from this same Navarrese provincial capital on its way over the pass of Roncevalles to the royal seat of government in Pamplona. The passage from the Amiens MS just quoted also reveals another aspect of Froissart's total ignorance of Iberian political geography when he wrote Book I: he then plainly confused the far-off kingdom of Galicia ('Galice') with the Basque province of Vizcaya

('Biscaie').[6] There is no point in attempting to illustrate further the chronicler's often wholesale mismanagement of Iberian geography and topography. It is part and parcel of that mis-shuffling of incorrect with correct information which makes Froissart such a frustrating source for the historian of Peninsular affairs at this time. Nevertheless we should note that, had he wanted to, he could have avoided making such a mess of his topography. By his time information about the geography of the Iberian Peninsula was certainly available in France in various cartographical forms, some of which at least would have been accessible to the chronicler to settle his topographical doubts had he felt this problem to be significant enough to require special attention.[7] He obviously did not.

Allusions to the *Chronicles* by Spanish and Portuguese historians of the period, as well as by some of his critics elsewhere, tend to judge Froissart as if he was a strictly contemporary recorder of the events he discusses. This, of course, is not the case. Though the traditional chronology assigned to the various versions of Book I, for instance, has been recently called into question (Chapter I), it remains the case that this Book, which has much to say about Peninsular affairs up to 1378, cannot have been written, in any of the forms in which it has survived, until about 1390. Memories of the veterans who had taken part in the wars in Castile more than twenty years before must, by then, have become somewhat unreliable even by Froissart's not very exacting standards, which is, perhaps, why he was glad to be able to turn to the poem about the Black Prince's expedition as his main source material. On the other hand, Book III, composed not long after 1390, was written when the memories of those who had fought in the Portuguese struggle for independence in 1383-5, or had participated, on either side, in the struggle arising out of the Lancastrian expedition to the Peninsula in 1386-7, were still fresh and the chronicler's informants had only recently related them to him. This, as well as Froissart's better mastery of his trade in Book III, is, no doubt, one of the reasons why Book III's account of Peninsular affairs is written with a sense of authority and actuality, whether justified or not, that we often do not feel is present in his earlier accounts of events there.[8]

Finally it is appropriate at this point to note that some of the adverse criticism which the chronicler's treatment of these matters has earned him arises from factors extraneous to the *Chronicles* themselves. He was unlucky in the sense that, probably more so in the sections devoted to the Peninsula than in those written about other regions, so much of what he attempts to deal with — including the description of military campaigns — can be checked against contemporary documentary evidence of a kind that originates much nearer to the centre of the events concerned than he was able to get. Why, for instance, it may be asked, should scholars try to make sense of his confused versions of the Aljubarrota campaign when we possess, on the one hand, John I of Castile's own lengthy letter to the municipalities of his kingdom setting out exactly what had happened and why his army had been defeated (Russell 1955: 568-9) and, on the other, a narrative description of the whole action written up in surprisingly objective form by Pero López de Ayala (Rosell 1953b), himself a student of military history, a close counsellor of the defeated king and a field commander on the Castilian side during the battle? On the Portuguese side, too, we have the patient scrutiny and collation of contemporary Portuguese chronicles and documents bearing on the whole Aljubarrota campaign made half-a-century later by a remarkably advanced historiographer, Fernão Lopes (Machi 1975). The answer, I think, is not quite so resoundingly negative as has sometimes been suggested, but this kind of comparison does greatly diminish the essentialness of Froissart to students of these matters. Questions of the availability of archive material apart, it is unfortunate for Froissart's reputation as a chronicler of the wars in the Iberian Peninsula that there existed there in his time a tradition of vernacular chronicle writing a deal more advanced in its notions of the historian's task and in its methodology than anything Froissart at his best had any idea of (below). Compared with such sources it is indeed tempting to write off the French chronicler as merely a purveyor of minor anecdotes and colourful detail. In the pages that now follow I shall examine selected but representative portions of his account of the Peninsular wars in order to determine how far such root-and-branch dismissal is justifiable.

The account of the Black Prince's invasion of Castile in 1367 is the first major piece of writing devoted to Iberian affairs. It is also unique since most of it is taken not from oral testimony but from the poem on the life of the Black Prince written by the herald of Sir John Chandos about 1385.[9] The Chandos Herald accompanied his master, the constable of Aquitaine, on the expedition. Despite the fact that the poem we have was not written until nearly twenty years later, the exactness of its chronological and topographical information point to the employment of contemporary written records as well as the herald's own recollections. It is quite likely that these records were notes made at the time by the Chandos Herald since part of a herald's duties included making sure that his principal's deeds were recorded for his descendants. As far as the campaign goes, then, Froissart's reliability is that of his source and it is good. He begins to follow the herald's poem from about line 1776 and closely from line 2103. He continues to do so until the poem describes the departure of the prince from Castile in the autumn of 1367. The Amiens MS of Book I is the text most faithful to the poem, which is less closely followed in other manuscripts. As military history, the herald's account of the campaign is broadly supported by the chronicle of Pero López de Ayala (Rosell 1953a), by the Latin poem of Walter of Peterborough (Wright 1859) and by contemporary Castilian, Navarrese and Aragonese documents, though it alone goes into the fighting in detail and from the English side (Russell 1955: 83-107). Froissart's version of the events in Castile that led up to the usurpation of Henry II of Trastámara in 1366, of the process of decision-making that went on in Gascony after the ousted Peter I's appeal for help was received by the Black Prince, and his account of the final defeat and murder of the Castilian king in 1369 are his own. They show him uncritically repeating all the horror propaganda about Peter I sedulously circulated by the Trastámarans since the 1350s and put about in Europe by the usurper himself, by Charles V of France and by the papal curia to justify the attempt to replace the anglophile Castilian king by a francophile one. Froissart here clearly seeks to make his readers' flesh creep by depicting a king who in no way (as was indeed in reality the case) practised the chivalric virtues or had any time for them. Peter IV of Aragon, we are assured, told the pope that his Castilian namesake was 'bougre et mauvais crestyen' (KL VII, 84). The chronicler also repeats the story that Peter I was the son of a Jew whom queen Maria had

had substituted for her own baby when she found she had given birth to a daughter. On the other hand, the Castilian usurper is presented by the chronicler as 'li rois Henris, qui estoit larges, courtois et honnourables' (VI, 211). There is little about Henry of Trastámara's biography that suggests that the last two epithets were appropriate but he had plainly learnt, during his exiles in France, how to play the chivalric game for the benefit of French audiences. What is worth underlining is that, as we have seen, Froissart was in Gascony, and a visitor to the English camp at Dax, just before the invasion of Castile. His hostile description of Peter I may possibly be evidence that Trastámaran propaganda had had its impact even on the English and Gascon knights and squires who were now committed to replacing the king in exile on his throne. Froissart, indeed, has a great deal to say about the opposition to this scheme, both among the prince's counsellors and among the Gascon lords summoned to discuss the matter. There may well have been opposition which the Chandos Herald, realising that it hardly added to the glory of the prince's Spanish enterprise to suggest that its aim was to restore such an apparently unacceptable personage to his throne, chose to omit; when discussing the talk at the great council of the Gascon lords he limits himself to the observation 'Chescuns dist ce que li sambla / Bon affaire de cele emprise' (lines 1926-7). Froissart, in one of the recensions of Book I, makes the Black Prince admit that Peter I had performed evil deeds in great numbers but describes him as supporting the exiled king (i) because it cannot be tolerated by any king or king's son that a bastard should seize a throne legitimately held by a brother and (ii) because (more to the point) there were long-standing alliances between England and Castile which obliged the English to give military help to the Castilian ruler on request. While all this is quite plausible, we cannot be sure that it is not an attempt by Froissart to reconcile the stories about Peter I with which he has just regaled his readers with the undoubted fact that the prince, with his father's approval, decided to help the fallen monarch to recover his throne. It is, for instance, noteworthy that, though the Castilian king was with the army in Gascony when Froissart was also there too, his adverse criticisms of Peter I do not seem based on any personal or recent impressions of him nor do they mirror gossip about him picked up at that time, of which there must have been plenty going the rounds. To sum up: the effect of the incorporation of the Chandos Herald's text in this section of the *Chronicles* is decidedly damaging to Froissart's reputation as a historian of Spanish affairs since it serves to underline his credulity and his superficiality, not to mention his extraordinary disdain for topographical exactness, when he has to rely not on the poem but on oral sources. A further example of his uncritical attitudes is to be found in his account of the final defeat of Pedro I at Montiel in 1369 when he assures his readers that the loyalist army there contained great numbers of Jews (who naturally fled when battle was joined) as well as 20,000 Muslim troops supplied not only by the Moorish kingdom of Granada but also by the rulers of some of the North African states! Yet, for English historians, as always, there is some corn to be garnered among the chaff. The chronicler is the only source to mention that some English knights and squires served the Castilian king at Montiel (VII, 80, 82). He gives their names.

The chronicler's obsession with military affairs leaves a huge lacuna in his account of what really happened when the Black Prince returned to Gascony from Castile for, by silence, he leaves it to be supposed that his hero thereafter took no further interest in Spanish affairs. We now know that, until his eventual return to England, the prince, in fact, was continuously engaged in intense diplomatic negotiations with the various Iberian rulers, the aim of which was to mount another military invasion of Castile, in alliance with them. One of its chief purposes was to secure the Castilian crown for himself. It is, perhaps, unfair to blame Froissart, who only claimed to write military history, for not interesting himself in diplomatic history but the fact that he does not do so can often, as here, be seriously misleading. It is a mark of his progress as a historian of Peninsular affairs that, in Book III, he seems to be more aware that such diplomatic history also requires his attention.

The later parts of Book I are not impressive in their treatment of these affairs. Froissart's account of the marriage of John of Lancaster to Constance of Castile at Roquefort in September 1371 (VIII, 28-30, 283-5) attributes the union entirely to personal motives or to chivalric ones. According to one version, the Gascon lords pressed the marriage on the duke on the grounds that charity must be shown to the children of kings! The Amiens MS, as usual, is nearer reality when it suggests that Lancaster's motive was profit; by such a marriage he would be qualified to become the ruler of one of the greatest lands in Christendom. Of the real political and strategic grounds that enabled Lancaster to persuade the English government to agree to the marriage there is hardly a hint.[10] Froissart, moreover, attributes the Franco-Castilian alliance to Henry of Trastámara's concern over the Lancastrian marriage (VIII, 30-2), thus reversing the correct sequence of events in one of those superficially obvious, off-the-cuff, explanations of historical causality to which he is all too prone. The B manuscripts of the *Chronicles* even contrive to get the new duchess of Lancaster's parentage wrong, describing her as the daughter of a (non-existent) first marriage between Peter I of Castile and the daughter of the king of Portugal. This is one of the occasions when it is hard to believe that Froissart actually was the author of a statement attributed to him in the *Chronicles* so that we may have to do with a copyist's interpolation.

In Book II, the chronicler describes in considerable detail the war between Navarre and Castile (1378-9) in which England was involved as an ally of Charles II of Navarre (IX, 59-63, 99-119). This account merits particular attention because it warns us of the unwisdom of making blanket judgements about Froissart's handling of the wars in the Peninsula. Ayala, in his rather succinct treatment of the war in *D. Enrique*, thus deals with the question of the foreign help recruited by the Navarrese king very briefly, explaining that, as a result of a visit to Saint-Jean-Pied-de-Port for this purpose

> ... he was then joined there by an English knight called Mosen Thomas Trivet, with 300 lances, and the king of Navarre caused the defence of the castle of Tudela to be given to him. There also joined him a knight of Guyenne called Mosen Perducat de Lebret, with another 300 lances, and to him the king gave charge of the castle of Estella.[11]

It is thus suggested by Ayala that Trivet, a nephew of Sir Matthew Gournay, and Bertucat d'Albret, a Gascon soldier of fortune who had fought in Spain with the Black Prince, were the principal foreign knights employed by Charles II to defend his kingdom. Froissart goes into this question in much greater detail, naming a number of other foreigners recruited by the king. The records of the Navarrese treasury, which contain a mass of information about most aspects of the war, fully confirm what Froissart has to say on this particular matter (Castro 1954a and b) and substantiate his assertion that the principal task of the Navarrese forces in 1378, that of defending the capital against the besieging Castilians, was in fact carried out successfully by Roger-Bernart de Foix, vizconde de Castelbó.[12] Froissart also makes it clear that the English troops under Trivet were ordered to Navarre by Sir John Neville, the lieutenant of Aquitaine, in accordance with the recent treaty of alliance between Richard II and Charles II, and not recruited privately by Charles II, as Ayala's account implies. Navarrese documents seem, too, to support Froissart's assertion that Trivet wasted time interminably in Gascony instead of joining the forces of the Navarrese king. The first receipt by Trivet for payments made to him is dated 4 December 1378, long after the first disbursements to the other foreign defenders of Navarre.

Froissart's account of military operations, as seen from the Navarrese side, can also be substantially confirmed from Navarrese records. Thus his statement that Trivet, immediately on his arrival in the kingdom, was sent to defend the castle and town of Tudela, a key fortress on the Ebro, is correct. Froissart describes in detail a bold, large-scale raid into enemy territory undertaken by Trivet during the winter (after the Castilian army had withdrawn to winter quarters) which, he says, penetrated deep into enemy territory as far as the walls of Soria. The correctness of the chronicler's information is attested by contemporary Navarrese documents in which Charles II refers with considerable satisfaction to the recent 'raid against Soria'. It seems then that Froissart's account of the Navarrese war, the only detailed one we have, is reliable and may safely be used as a prime source for this campaign, though the chronicler once again goes to pieces when he describes the terms — highly unfavourable to Navarre — on which peace between the two countries was restored. The treaty of Briones (21 March 1379) turned Spanish Navarre into a military and political protectorate of Trastámaran Castile and therefore ruled out any future English attack on Castile over the Navarrese passes. The chronicler, rather characteristically, fails to point to these consequences.

How did Froissart acquire his information about the Navarrese campaign? He appears at first sight to provide an answer when he explains that, during his visit to Foix in 1388, he questioned veterans from whom 'fu-ge lors infourmé de grant foison de besongnes qui estoient avenues en Castille, *et en Navarre*, et en Portingal' (XII, 95). If his stay at Orthez in fact provided the material we have been discussing this would establish that Book II either was written after 1388, or had the account of the war in Navarre added to it subsequently. I think it difficult to believe that the chronicler contrived to secure such exact information about persons and events as he here offers after a passage of nearly ten years, though the possibility cannot be excluded. Perhaps the conclusion to be drawn is that we should not be over-ready to assume that Froissart was as totally dependent on his visit to Foix for information about Peninsular affairs in the 1380s and late 1370s as the passage quoted suggests.[13]

Towards the end of Book II Froissart first turns seriously to the role of Portugal in the Peninsular wars and to the history of John of Lancaster's attempt to exploit his theory that the *chemin de Portyngale* was the strategic route by which England could destroy the Trastámaran dynasty, break the Franco-Castilian alliance and place him and his Castilian princess on the throne of the latter's motherland. Structurally, Froissart's presentation of the three major episodes involved — Edmund of Cambridge's expedition to Portugal in 1381-2; the Castilian attempt to annex Portugal (1383-5); the expedition of Lancaster himself to the Peninsula (1386-7) — are presented in an extremely complicated way. The account of the Cambridge expedition is thus mainly contained in Book II (SHF, X) but Froissart picks up the subject again briefly at the beginning of Book III as a kind of introduction to his account of the Castilian attempt to take over Portugal. As already mentioned, the chronicler offers two different perspectives (probably more) on events involving that country. One, according to him, is that secured by interrogating veterans of these campaigns during his visit to Foix in 1388, where he found knights and squires able to tell him what he wanted to know 'des besongnes de Portingal et de Castille, et comment on s'i estoit porté le temps passé des guerres . . . que ces deux roys . . . ensamble avoient eu l'un contre l'autre' (XII, 118). He subsequently makes it clear, à propos of an anecdote about the count of Foix's clairvoyant gifts, that he secured his first long account of the battle of Aljubarrota at Orthez from an unnamed squire (XII, 170-1). Later the chronicler again rather unexpectedly returns to the origins of the war between Castile and Portugal (XII, 232-6) but then interrupts his narrative to explain that, after his return from Foix to Valenciennes, he encountered a difficulty about writing up the affairs of Castile and Portugal: 'Je . . . ne le povoie pas faire par avoir singulierement les parties de ceulx qui tiennent . . . l'opinion du roy de Castille.' Justice required that, before proceeding further, he must 'oïr otant bien parler les Portingalois comme je avoie fait les Gascons et Espaignols' (XII, 237-8). He then took himself off to Bruges and thence to Middelburg, where he was able to talk to a Portuguese knight, João Fernandes Pacheco (Jehan Ferrant Percok) who gave him full information about the Portuguese wars and Portuguese diplomatic relations with England etc. from the death of Ferdinand I (1383) to the day when João Fernandes himself left Portugal on the voyage during which the chronicler met him (1390). The whole history, already covered very fully, is then presented again according to the Portuguese knight's version of events, Froissart making no attempt to comment on or adjudicate between the two versions. The entire question is made more complicated because it now incorporates long and certainly fictitious conversations, mainly of a historical kind, which one of the Portuguese ambassadors in London, Lourenço Anes Fogaça, the chancellor of Portugal, had with Lancaster. These conversations again cover the story of events in Portugal since the departure of Edmund of Cambridge and include a second account of the battle of Aljubarrota. To complicate matters still further, João Fernandes Pacheco himself figures quite prominently in Fogaça's narrative to Lancaster! This interlacing narrative technique with use of multiple perspectives is reminiscent, perhaps not fortuitously, of the story-telling methods beloved of authors of romances of chivalry. It makes for difficult history — as does Froissart's refusal here to make any attempt to evaluate the source material his informants have supplied him with. One thinks regrettably, when confronted by these chapters, of the very different approach some decades later, of the

Portuguese chronicler, Fernão Lopes, who, confronted by a number of contradictory chronicle sources written by Portuguese about the events of the 1380s, determined to do his best, by using a historian's judgement, to establish where the truth lay.

There are, too, some reasons for doubting that the simple dichotomy between Franco-Castilian sources available in Orthez and the Anglo-Portuguese-orientated information supplied at Middelburg by João Fernandes Pacheco that Froissart suggests to his readers is really exact. He himself informs us, for example, that an English knight in the retinue of Lancaster was staying at the court of the count of Foix at Orthez during his own stay there.[14] Lancaster himself was, of course, also then in Gascony. Gascon knights were on hand there, too, and many Gascons had been in the ranks of Cambridge's army in 1381 and some had fought with the Portuguese at Aljubarrota. It seems plain to me that part of the information contained in Froissart's first ('Orthez') account of events in Portugal must, by its nature, have come from informants who had been on the Anglo-Portuguese side in these campaigns. Nor is the chronicler's suggestion that the second ('Middelburg') version of events in Portugal came wholly from Pacheco really defensible. The Portuguese knight, if that were the case, would have to know far more about the details of the negotiations and activities of John I of Portugal's ambassadors in London than we have any reason for supposing he possibly can have done. Froissart, it must be remembered, is even able, without hesitation, to supply the name of the hostelry in which they lodged there and the name of their landlord (XII, 294). The problem would be more easily resolved if we could establish that the chronicler had met Fogaça himself; Froissart does, after all, go out of his way to praise the excellence of the Portuguese chancellor's French. A Portuguese scholar, Salvador Dias Arnaut, has attempted to solve the conundrum by suggesting reasons why Fogaça might have been in Middelburg at the same time as Pacheco (and Froissart). But these reasons are unsubstantial and it is most unlikely that the chronicler, had he actually met the Portuguese chancellor, would have described Fogaça simply as a squire (above, n.5). All in all it looks more as if the chronicler, during his stay in Orthez, had been in contact with an informant very near Lancaster − perhaps even the ex-Pretender himself − to secure his information about the doings of the Portuguese envoys in London and their conversations with the then *soi-disant* king of Castile and León. For reasons of his own he chose to let it be thought that this material, too, had been given him by João Fernandes Pacheco.[15]

Froissart devotes substantial attention to Edmund of Cambridge's expedition to Portugal in 1381-2. Abundant documentary information concerning almost every aspect of this expedition is, however, available in English, Aragonese and Castilian archives, as I and others have shown. The subject is also discussed, with some important details not found elsewhere, by Pero López de Ayala in *D. Juan* (Rosell 1953b), and it is dealt with extensively and with great exactness by Fernão Lopes in his *Crónica de D. Fernando*. Lopes, in addition to Ayala's chronicle, had available to him some contemporary Portuguese narrative sources, only one of which has survived, that described the course of the expedition and the reasons for its failure (Machi 1975: 501, 533). Some use is also made by Fernão Lopes of documents then available to him in the chancery registers and other sections of the Portuguese royal archives, particularly to establish with exactness the itineraries of the king, Cambridge and the allied army. Given the existence of alternative contemporary sources of the high quality described, it is scarcely surprising that Froissart has relatively little to offer. It is not that the French chronicler has got things wrong — on the contrary, his account is, as far as it goes, unusually close to the attested facts; thus his lists of the principal English and Gascon knights who participated are, in the main, confirmed both by English muster lists and exchequer documents and by Fernão Lopes, while his topographical allusions are, for once, exact enough to make one wonder whether he had not, on this occasion, perhaps consulted a map. His account of the English army's troubles is confirmed not only by Lopes but by English documents which show that the mutinies in it led to proceedings against the ringleaders when they returned home. But Froissart's account, garnered at second-hand from an informant or informants who had taken part in this expedition under Cambridge's command — perhaps from some of the Gascons he met at Orthez — and filtered through his still narrow vision of what mattered in history — inevitably seems to lack depth and detail. The reason thought up by Froissart to explain why Ferdinand I of Portugal elected to ally himself with the English against Castile is thus absurd: the chronicler declares that the king acted out of a chivalrous desire to fight the usurping Castilian dynasty on behalf of Peter I's daughters! A long passage is devoted to an improbable story to the effect that the vessel carrying the Gascon knights from Plymouth to Lisbon was blown by a storm all the way to the North African coast where it remained for forty days in great peril from the Moors before returning — via Seville — to reach Lisbon. This is one of the occasions, referred to by Tucoo-Chala, when one suspects that Froissart has had his leg pulled by his informant: English records cited by Perroy (1933: 220, n.8) suggest that the ship carrying the Gascons left Plymouth a considerable time after the main fleet, which may be the origin of the tale. Froissart, rather surprisingly, seems to be unaware of the fact that Cambridge had to endure the final humiliation of being sent home, with the remnants of his army, not in English or Portuguese ships but in transports provided by the king of Castile (XII, 5).[16] But it is more the superiority of the competition, than any serious defects in this section of the *Chronicles*, that make it of scant value to historians today.

No such qualified praise can be accorded Froissart's account of the events in Portugal between 1383 and 1385 which made possible the Lancastrian invasion of 1386 and which he begins to relate at the beginning of Book III. Once again, the chronicler's account is inevitably put in the shade both by Ayala's long report on happenings in which he had been directly involved as diplomat and soldier and, even more so, by the monumental *Crónica de D. João I*, by Fernão Lopes, for whom the achievement of a very detailed description of this material, carefully scrutinised to achieve historical truth, was the principal purpose of his work as a chronicler.[17] But there is more to it than that: in both the first ('Orthez') version and the second ('Middelburg') one, Froissart has lost control of his material. His topographical references are again chaotic and his treatment of proper names often undecipherable. In a narrative largely concerned with the military movements of armies, his failure to discover what the distances between places even approximately were undermines whatever direct historical usefulness the recollections of his informants might have.[18] He is also wrong about some really major questions of fact, including the day of the week on which the battle of Aljubarrota took place. As might be expected, the second version, attributed mainly to his Portuguese informant, is marginally more unblemished than the first, but less so than we might expect. The Béarnais origins of the first version, proclaimed by the chronicler, are attested by a number of features of the text.[19] He himself states that he obtained his account of Aljubarrota, in particular, from a squire he met at Orthez (XII, 170-1). But it seems likely that he also may have attempted to inject into this version information secured from someone who had participated in the battle on the Anglo-Portuguese side, or pretended to have done so. Froissart, as has already been noted, makes no attempt to reconcile his two versions even when they are flagrantly contradictory. Thus, in the first version, he names three envoys whom, he says, John of Portugal sent to England to ask for military support immediately after his election as regent (XII, 13, 118).[20] We know, both from Fernão Lopes and from English records, the actual names of the envoys and these bear no relation to those given by Froissart. It is also claimed by him that both the constable and the marshal of the Castilian army besieging Lisbon were French (Olivier du Guesclin and Renaud de Solier respectively). There is no basis in fact for this claim, though French knights certainly served with the Castilian army there.

A notable feature of the action at Aljubarrota, as described in the first version, is the major role ascribed to three aged English squires, whom the chronicler calls 'Nortbery', 'Martebery' and 'Hugenin de Hartecele' (XII, 138, 146), and who had arrived with the 500 men-at-arms and archers the chronicler says here were sent from England to support the Portuguese.[21] According to the chronicler, the Portuguese king sent for the three squires in order to secure their advice about a suitable site for the imminent battle, advice which the king duly took. Since part of this included preparing field fortifications to hinder any Castilian attack from the flanks and to crowd the Castilian charge into a narrow space — measures which in reality contributed largely to the Portuguese success — Froissart is able to claim a major part in the victory for the 'sens et art' of the three English squires (XII, 157). This is clearly another occasion when the chronicler has been the victim of a tall story. Nothing is less likely than that two highly experienced campaigners like John of Aviz and Nun'Alvares, who had already used English-style tactics to great effect on other battlefields, would have put, or had any reason to put, the fate of Portugal in such hands. Another of the major errors in this account of the battle is that Froissart makes the enemy charge the Portuguese positions on horseback (XII, 157) though it is certain that they did so on foot — an error that does not occur in the second version (XII, 286). There is, however, one detail stressed in the first account of Aljubarrota which is not alluded to by the francophile Ayala, by Lopes or any other contemporary chronicle source but which nevertheless bears the stamp of probability. This is Froissart's stress on the anger felt by the Castilian nobles at the — very sensible — tendency of John I, like his father, to turn for tactical advice to the experienced French knights in his army (XII, 136-7, 152-4). But Froissart's ideas about good tactical advice are inspired by the ideas of chivalry rather than by those of prudent generalship for he makes the Frenchmen press the king to start the battle without waiting until a more favourable hour despite *Castilian* opposition to such a move. We know that, in fact, the exact reverse was the case. Was Froissart misinformed or could he not believe that the knights of France would advise postponing a battle against an enemy so inferior in numbers as were the Portuguese?[22]

The account of the action attributed to Pacheco, as has been mentioned earlier, perpetrates the mistake of reversing both the line of approach of each army to the battlefield and the movements of the Portuguese after the battle. Froissart may simply have muddled his notes (confused, perhaps, by the fact that each king was called 'John') or have misled himself because of the fact that the Portuguese army, originally facing north against the advancing Castilians, had had to undertake a short counter-march and then face south to defeat a move by the Castilians to take them in the rear. Despite this mistake, the description of the action, as indeed some of the political and diplomatic information contained in the whole of the 'Middelburg' version, is nearer the truth than Froissart's attempted recapitulation of what he was told at Foix.[23] It seems extraordinary to the modern reader that the chronicler could have been prepared to let both accounts stand but that is, perhaps, because we fail to grasp his attitude to history.

The section of the *Chronicles* devoted to the expedition of John of Lancaster to conquer his Castilian throne is Froissart's most ambitious contribution to the history of the English military interventions in the Iberian Peninsula in the second half of the fourteenth century. It ought to be, also, at least as far as Lancaster's campaigning in Galicia is concerned, potentially the most useful; this campaign is not well-documented in any other source — unlike the Anglo-Portuguese invasion of León, which was well-researched in the fifteenth century by Fernão Lopes and about which some useful documentary information is also available. Froissart claims that he got his information about the conquest of Galicia from 'chevaliers et escuiers d'Engleterre et de Portingal qui furent à tous les conquestes et par especial du gentil chevalier de Portingal [i.e. João Fernandes Pacheco] dont j'ay traitié cy dessus' (XIII, 53-4). Unhappily his chronicle has long been the despair of historians hoping to find in it a trustworthy account of what happened in north-western Spain during the year or more when that region, or most of it, was in the hands of Lancaster and Constance of Castile and when, after nearly two decades, the name of the assassinated Peter I could once more be officially praised on Castilian soil. Perroy's judgement was cited at the beginning of this essay. The best that León and Albert Mirot can find to say about it in their edition is that 'Froissart's information, although it is fanciful, ought not always to be rejected' (XIII, xi, n.2). Two factors contrive to destroy the chronicler's claim to be a serious historian of the campaign in Galicia. One is that, as already indicated, he confuses two quite separate zones in which the Lancastrian army carried out military operations — Galicia (and, perhaps, Asturias), and León. The first campaign, or campaigns, took place in the summer and autumn of 1386 and probably continued, on a small scale, when most of the Lancastrian army not needed for garrison duty in Galicia had been withdrawn south to the kingdom of León for combined operations with the Portuguese. Froissart presents us with a jumbled account of both. As if this were not enough, his ill-treatment of Iberian topography here achieves a new low; key towns and fortresses mentioned in his narrative are sometimes quite unidentifiable and he continuously shows, when he mentions places that we can recognise, that he has no idea of their locations or the distances between them.[24] There are various other important mistakes of fact. Thus he declares that the Lancastrian capital was established at Santiago de Compostela when, in fact, it was at Orense — at least by September 1386. While correctly recording that the Portuguese king displeased Lancaster by delaying his marriage to the duke's daughter Philippa, he asserts that this was because the king, fearing that England might be invaded and conquered by the French, did not want to commit himself too far to the Lancastrian cause. Once again the chronicler seems to have indulged in an over-slick piece of guess-work about causality. The delay was actually caused by the failure of the necessary papal dispensation for John's marriage to arrive, a delay brought about by the maladroit intervention of a Lancastrian agent at Urban VI's court. Anyway, as ought to have been obvious, John of Aviz had no hope of surviving if England were defeated by France.

Yet, when all has been said, historians cannot afford to ignore entirely what Froissart has to say about the Lancastrian occupation of Galicia. He mentions, sometimes identifiably, a great many places in the region where military operations took place and which he could not have known anything about unless his English informants had told him about them. Though his account of the occupation of Santiago de Compostela and the shrine of Spain's patron saint probably owes a great deal to his imagination, he is alone in pointing to the impact of such an event, not only in Spain but outside it. He dwells at some length on the grave losses the English army suffered in Galicia during the winter from the awful climate and from disease (KL XII, 308-10 etc.). This information is also correct. The shameful way in which the English army broke up and was deserted by its principal officers after the failure of the allied campaign in León is more or less correctly reported, as is the insouciant manner in which the duke took the apparent collapse of all his hopes in Castile; Froissart's informants could not know that Lancaster had achieved a settlement with John of Castile which left him with no further interest in making war. Confused and misleading as Froissart's account of these events is, information of value to scholars can thus be extracted from it and, in this case, the effort is worth making because of the absence of any alternative source which attempts to discuss the Galician campaign in detail.

How does Froissart emerge from a close scrutiny of his treatment of events in the Iberian Peninsula? While it is evident that, in general terms, these sections of the *Chronicles* cannot be used to defend him as a reliable historian of his times, each section needs to be judged separately; some are either more reliable than others or, *faute de mieux*, have to be used for whatever they can offer that is useful. However, only in the last case discussed, that of the Lancastrian campaign in Galicia, can it really be said that our knowledge of events would be significantly diminished if Froissart had not written about them at all, at least as far as the facts of history, and their causes, are concerned. Is the kind of history Froissart wrote about Peninsular affairs inevitable because he, with the one exception mentioned earlier in this essay, relied wholly on oral sources? The answer must be no. The Castilian chronicler, Pero López de Ayala, proclaimed, in his *Proemium* to *D. Pedro* (Rosell 1953a), a theory of history much the same as that of Froissart when he wrote, as many chroniclers in many countries might also then have done, that the purpose of history is to ensure that great deeds that have been performed by men should be preserved for posterity so that later generations shall know of them and draw from them good examples of how to behave well and to avoid evil. Ayala defines a chronicle primarily as a work concerned with deeds of war and chivalry with this exemplary purpose in mind. How does a chronicler go about his task? First he must report as truthfully as possible on the events which he himself saw. As for events which he did not see, he must rely on the testimony of 'nobles and knights and others worthy of trust and credence, from whom I heard about these matters, taking it down with the greatest care that I could'. This is very close to what Froissart has to say on a number of occasions about the object of his work and the methods he uses — for example when he turns to discuss Peninsular affairs in 1385 (XII, 237). Yet there is all the difference in the world between Ayala's orderly, motive-probing, controlled and critical presentation of events and causes and the way Froissart, starting with the same approach, writes history. The difference is not wholly accounted for by the fact that the Castilian chronicler knew at first-hand about many of the matters he wished to discuss. There is ample evidence that he sifted and weighed the evidence his informants gave him about things he had not been a party to before he accepted any of it. Froissart, on the other hand, seems to have believed that an eye-witness, by definition, was always worthy of belief, as long as he was a knight or squire. He appears to have interrogated his informants simply to secure information, never, at least as far as Peninsular affairs are concerned, to test their veracity. It is also obvious that his methods of recording what he was told were far from professional. He had evident difficulty in making sense of some of the notes he had taken. An unwillingness to criticise, to collate or to coordinate, sometimes frankly admitted, is a constant feature; nor does he seem prepared to employ obvious tools or sources that might have helped him to interpret what he had taken down from oral informants. But how far is it appropriate to complain because Froissart's programme as a historian is not what we would like it to have been? While he paid lip-service to a wider view of history, his real concern was plainly 'pour tous nobles coeurs encourager et eux montrer exemple en matière d'honneur' (KL I, i, 466). As long as this exemplary purpose is achieved by the tale he has to tell, the truth or exactness of the details does not matter all that much. The two versions of the battle of Aljubarrota cannot both be historically right but each is, from this point of view, a tale worth telling. There is much truth in Tucoo-Chala's assertion that Froissart should be viewed more as moralist than historian.[25] And, of course, his determination to see and interpret events so that they fitted into his view of a society dominated by chivalry implied imposing on history an aesthetic vision that also pulled him constantly towards the action-packed, incurious superficialities of romance, towards literature. Yet, as I have already suggested, his insistence on such a view of history may have its positive side if it reminds us that the ideology of chivalry, not only in Froissart's day but for a long time afterwards, was a force that could drive and give meaning to the lives of the nobles, knights and squires whom he so much admired and with whom he mixed whenever he got a chance. Chivalry may, as Huizinga claims, by then all have become an illusion, mere play-acting. Certainly, when we examine closely what went on in the Iberian Peninsula in the decades with which Froissart concerned himself, the underlying realities, and often the visible realities as well, were far removed from the world of chivalry. But the play, too, was often staged and it is useful to be reminded of this even if the cost is that we have to read, in the *Chronicles*, what is liable to seem now to be some rather bad history.

VII THE WAR IN THE LOW COUNTRIES *

J. van Herwaarden [1]

AS a native of Hainault, Froissart naturally enough showed a keen interest in the history of the Low Countries, an interest stimulated (we may well imagine) by the fact that his major patrons — Robert of Namur, Wenceslas of Brabant, and the house of Blois — either ruled in that area or had major territorial or dynastic concerns there. It is therefore scarcely surprising that events in the Low Countries, and in particular in Flanders, Brabant and Hainault, are a recurring theme running through the whole of the *Chronicles* from the very earliest chapters of Book I to the final page of Book IV.

But though Froissart had compelling reasons for wishing to include much of the history of the Low Countries, he rarely allowed his personal predilections or the interests of his patrons to dictate the overall shape of his work. He had one great theme to which all else was subordinated: the colossal struggle between Plantagenet and Valois for hegemony in western Europe which so overwhelmingly dominated the international scene throughout his lifetime. To this theme Froissart adhered with remarkable fidelity from beginning to end of his vast work. Anything which did not directly relate to this epic struggle, he ruthlessly discarded. Despite his slavish dependence upon the narrative of Jean le Bel for the period prior to 1362, for instance, Froissart jettisoned whole blocks of Le Bel's chapters devoted to the internal history of the Low Countries (Le Bel I, 220-44). No matter how important in their own right, the domestic events of the Low Countries were of no interest to Froissart unless they were relevant to the greater events of the war between England and France.

As a consequence, his attention to the affairs of the Low Countries is intermittent, episodic. The rulers of Brabant, Flanders, Hainault, Namur, Liège etc. make fleeting appearances throughout the narrative but are rarely on stage for any length of time. Only when the Low Countries itself became the focus of Anglo-French concern did Froissart fix his attention on the area for sufficiently long to make his narrative of first importance for historians of the Low Countries. He did so on three main occasions: between 1326-8, 1337-40 and 1379-85. Of these three, the last is by far the most sustained, complex and interesting piece of historical analysis.

The reasons are not far to seek. The two previous episodes, both recounted in Book I, are both derived from the *Chronicle* of Jean le Bel; and although Froissart made significant alterations and additions to the narrative of his predecessor — particularly in his account of the van Artevelde era —, the basic

* All references to the *Chronicles* are to volume and page of the Buchon edition (1840) unless otherwise stated.

structure and much of the detail of his version is taken from Le Bel. His account of the events of the years 1379-85 in Book II, however, is the work of a mature and independent historian. When he came to write this part of his *Chronicles*, Froissart had left his model behind him. He had reached a mature middle age, had had long experience of courts and politics, had written tens of thousands of words of history, and was writing about the events of his own adult lifetime which had taken place in an area with which he was personally familiar and had many possible sources of information. Any analysis of Froissart's presentation of the social, economic and political history of the Low Countries must therefore concentrate very heavily on this particular section of the *Chronicles*.

Despite its feudal dependence upon France, the county of Flanders had much closer economic ties with England,[2] a fact which was to colour its relationship to the two great powers throughout the course of their struggle. Froissart was well aware of this. Commenting upon the events of c.1370, he remarked (I, 547; Johnes I, 409): 'the commonalties of Flanders maintained the quarrel between the two kings to be more just on the part of England than of France', so it is understandable that the representatives of the three towns Bruges, Ghent and Ypres 'resolved that it was not for their advantage to be at war or to have any ill-will with the English, who were their neighbours and connected with them by commerce, on account of any quarrel of their count, nor would it be expedient for them to aid and support him.'

This attitude was formed slowly during the van Artevelde era (1338-45), when Flanders developed into one of the sheetanchors of Edward III's system of continental alliances during the early years of the Hundred Years War. Van Artevelde (Lucas 1933) and the Flemish towns felt justified in this attitude by the pro-French stance taken by their count, Louis of Nevers (1322-46). Originally intent only upon neutrality to protect their commerce, the Flemings were gradually driven into an alliance with Edward III by the combined effects of economic and political pressure exerted by the English king and the intransigence of Louis of Nevers.[3] Yet feudal loyalties were still strongly felt even by townsmen, and it was only after Edward III had received homage at Ghent as king of France in January 1340 — three years after the beginning of the war — that the Flemings lent him active support against the French.[4]

Successive versions of Book I of Froissart's *Chronicles* reveal an increasing appreciation of the importance of van Artevelde. His first edition does no more than copy the narrative of Jean le Bel, whereas the second and third editions focus much more sharply on van Artevelde and deal with his circumstances at greater length.[5] It may be doubted whether this is a reflection of Froissart's growing sympathy, since all versions recount the tale of van Artevelde's domestic tyranny which the chronicler had borrowed from Le Bel (I, 59-60; III, 454-8; Diller, 261-2, 270); but it undoubtedly reflects Froissart's growing awareness of the importance of van Artevelde's leadership in shaping events between 1338 and 1345, and in influencing the future role of Flanders in the Hundred Years War. The services of van Artevelde were remembered and applauded in the 1380s, as Froissart records in Book II (II, 144-6; *Cronyke*, 125-9).

Froissart also showed an appreciation of the stresses and strains which van Artevelde's policy produced within the urban communities of Flanders.

102

According to one of the versions of Book I, James van Artevelde was supported by the whole *communalty* of Ghent and a considerable part of the wealthier burghers, the *poorterie* (III, 454). In this way, Froissart suggests divisions within the *poorterie*, to which van Artevelde as a broker just failed to belong.[6] These disagreements probably concerned the extent to which the count's policy should be accepted or rejected. Van Artevelde and his supporters felt that the pro-French policy of the count was detrimental to the interests of Ghent and her trades, which required good relations with England.

Another aspect of the van Artevelde period with which Froissart deals, is the highly important question of the relationship between the towns of Flanders. He shows how van Artevelde co-operated with the towns of Bruges and Ypres in matters of general Flemish concern and even suggests that representatives of the (agrarian) Franc de Bruges were involved in these decisions (III, 471), though this seems to be a confusion with the situation under Louis of Male (1346-84).[7] However, the degree of harmony between the towns should not be exaggerated as Ghent dominated internal policies and people from Ghent were nominated as the real governors of the smaller towns in the Quarter of Ghent and even in Ypres.[8] The count had held such imperialist tendencies in check. In his absence, they could flourish.[9]

Froissart was aware, however, that van Artevelde did not have matters all his own way and that his situation was highly insecure. Opposition to the legitimate ruler was a risky course in the fourteenth century, and, according to Froissart, it was van Artevelde's appreciation of this fact and his efforts to compensate for it, which led to his death. The wish to recognise Edward as suzerain and the prince of Wales (the Black Prince) as *duke* of Flanders (I, 204; Diller, 633), in order to exclude completely both Louis of Nevers and his son Louis of Male, was suggested by him as 'he always mistrusted the Flemings because he thought them fickle' (Diller, 633). However, this plan challenged the powerful loyalties towards the lawful and natural ruler.

Moreover, according to Froissart, van Artevelde's policies aroused the distrust of the duke of Brabant, John III (1312-55), who had meanwhile been reconciled with Louis of Nevers (the count was even living in Brussels) and who feared that Ghent's example would inspire opposition from his own towns. John III considered the pro-English policies of the Flemings unfavourable for his territories, and he was considering a marriage between one of his daughters and the heir of Flanders, Louis of Male, which made those policies even less acceptable.

The duke of Brabant, according to Froissart's final version, was *cause de ceste aventure* with regard to Artevelde's death. He is said to have enabled the dean of the weavers to strike him down as a traitor, despite the fact that this dean had van Artevelde to thank for his post. Van Artevelde had been forced to support him in a power struggle between weavers and fullers, but is supposed to have tried to break this newly acquired power by means of the treaty with England — which meanwhile had probably been accepted by Bruges and Ypres.[10]

This story in the final version of Book I puts the murder of James van Artevelde in an entirely different light from that of the first version where, it is true, the English plan was also involved, but where van Artevelde's unpopularity is said to have been caused by his sending illegally acquired money over to England (I, 205) — a rumour that did not prevent Froissart, even in this version, from

FRIESLAND

HOLLAND

GUELDERS

ZEELAND

BRABANT

Rhine

Sluys
Bruges Damme
Veurne Ghent
Calais Roosebeke Louvain
Ypres Brussels
Courtrai Oudenaarde LIÈGE Liège
FLANDERS

Hesdin ARTOIS ＊ HAINAULT
Crécy OSTREVANT

Rouen Beauvais

Rheims

Seine Marne Chalons

Paris

Seine

Troyes

THE LOW COUNTRIES, c.1385.

regarding van Artevelde's murder as evidence of ingratitude on the part of the Flemings. The tale about money does not disappear in the final version, but here Froissart makes it clear that Edward had entered into financial obligations towards van Artevelde and Flanders (Diller, 449-51), in connection with which van Artevelde had sent three embassies to England.[11] This English debt to the Flemings would still play a part in the 1380s when Flemish ambassadors reminded Richard II of this outstanding Flemish claim. Had the Flemings, Froissart suggests, at that moment not acted in this way, Richard and the English would have come to their aid against the French (II, 219, 221; *Cronyke*, 225, 230).

Van Artevelde's death in 1345 did not bring an end to the Anglo-Flemish understanding,[12] nor did the death of the Flemish count, Louis of Nevers, at Crécy in 1346 (I, 240; Diller, 734) mean the end of his dynasty. Loyalty to the lawful and natural ruler was too strong; and by clever manoeuvring Louis of Male was able to make himself effective ruler of Flanders. In doing so, he rejected the idea of an English marriage, desired by the weavers' government of Ghent, thus making it easier for himself to remain neutral in the future.[13]

But of this, and of subsequent internal conflicts in Flanders, Froissart has almost nothing to say.[14] With the end of the dramatic phase of Anglo-French involvement in Flanders (1337-45), Froissart loses interest in Flanders until the eve of their equally dramatic involvement in the 1380s. Even the crucial marriage of Philip of Burgundy and Margaret of Male in 1369 receives only summary treatment (I, 573). His treatment of the affairs of Brabant and Hainault is equally sketchy. Something is said of the ambiguous attitude of Duke John III of Brabant[15] and of the vacillating policy of Count William II of Hainault, as William IV count of Holland and Zeeland (1337-45), who hesitated and only decided to sever his fealty to Philip VI after a French invasion of Hainault.[16] But thereafter Froissart has little to say about the Netherlands until he reaches the events of 1379. Until that date, his *Chronicles* are not an important source for events in the Low Countries and there is no need to concern ourselves with their scattered remarks.

A considerable part of the second book of Froissart's *Chronicles* is devoted to the upheavals in Flanders between 1379 and 1385.[17] His narrative is vivid and dramatic and although modern research has uncovered much more about the causes and consequences of these events,[18] Froissart himself has some shrewd insights to offer. For although he recorded his opinion that the persistent state of war in these years was the work of the devil, he did not allow this pious conclusion to prevent him from observing the faults and responsibilities of the parties involved.

Like others, Froissart extolled Flanders' prosperity (II, 65-6; *Cronyke*, 1, 2). The great towns, however, had financial problems; there was rivalry between these great towns, between them and the smaller towns, and between town and countryside (Nicholas 1971a). The policies of Louis of Male favoured the country-side to some extent, making it, for example, judicially more independent of the town courts by setting up a comital *Audiëntie* (Buntinx 1949). Froissart rightly points out that the count found his most loyal supporters in the Franc de Bruges (II, 133; *Cronyke*, 87). Louis wished to establish this as the fourth member of the estates of Flanders, alongside of Bruges, Ghent and Ypres, a policy later pushed through by Philip of Burgundy (Prevenier 1959, 1961b). Louis' currency manipulations had improved his income but disturbed the economy of the towns and social relations within them: the decline of the draperies was somewhat slowed down through a rise in exports due to the debasement, but the cost of living rose while wages — rigorously fixed — failed to keep pace.[19] Prosperity was unevenly spread; and compared with the rich *poorterie* and prosperous guilds such as the brokers, glasiers, butchers and fishmongers of Bruges (II, 208; *Cronyke*, 186), the other craft guilds and lesser trades were having a thin time.[20] These contrasts produced what was in fact a continuously revolutionary situation, in which a relatively unimportant matter might lead to the mobilisation of the many discontented.

Froissart begins his narrative with one such apparently trivial matter, the feud in Ghent between Jan Hyoens and Gijsbrecht Mayhuus, arising from a feud between two families from Damme to which both were related. Such private feuds could escalate considerably and become of much greater significance than a simple conflict between two families. For a number of years at the turn of the thirteenth century, Ghent was dominated by such a feud and the disturbances in Louvain around 1380 can also be traced back to a similar feud between two families. It was the chief function of the urban political system to keep such feuds in check and prevent them breaking out into open hostilities, but town governments were as yet not well enough equipped to do this successfully. Moreover, the basis of the urban community was the *coniuratio* of free men, and the *droit de vengeance* was precisely one of the prime elements of this freedom. Just how such a private feud could develop into a great conflict, whose origins can hardly be traced, is shown clearly in Froissart's narrative of this period. He repeatedly touches on this feud; and in recounting the reconciliation between Ghent and the count in 1385 he again refers back to this origin.

Such conflicts are indicative of a transitional phase in social developments: the break-up of the (agrarian) familial clan-solidarity through the growth of new forms of associations more marked by group solidarity. Firstly, there was the urban *coniuratio*, but this was sub-divided into smaller units: the craft-guilds or trades, and within these again the solidarity of various categories (masters, journeymen). To family ties were added *amicitia* ties with members of the group. Both these elements played a part in the formation of political factions; and neither family relationships nor group solidarity can be seen as the decisive criterion of party choice. Nor did economic criteria play a decisive role: the poor developed a dislike of the rich rather than any consciousness of their mutual solidarity.[21]

The feud in Ghent originated among the leaders of the shippers (Corryn 1944), but soon developed into a much broader conflict. Power in the town was completely taken over by one of the parties; the other was driven out or silenced (cf. Heers 1977: 41-2). The leaders were supported by armed fellow-citizens, the *White Hoods* (*Witte Kaproenen*), who, as in the time of James van Artevelde, formed a separate category, called a *secte* by Froissart, to distinguish them from the ordinary troops raised through parishes and trades.[22] The extent to which the *White Hoods* were a symbol of urban rebelliousness, and the far-reaching influence of events in Ghent, is shown by the fact that the *Cabochiens* in 1413 and the Norman rebels of the 1430s wore white hoods in memory of the Ghent rising.[23]

The count's permission to Bruges to dig a canal to the Lys (in Ghent's territory); Ghent's reaction to this by unleashing the *White Hoods* under Jan Hyoens; her refusal to accept a new comital tax (which had been accepted by Bruges); the arrest of a burgher of Ghent (a shipper) by a bailiff of the count in violation of the *ius de non evocando*; the killing of this bailiff by the people of Ghent; and finally the destruction of the count's castle of Wondelgem near Ghent by the *White Hoods* during negotiations for a settlement (II, 68-75; *Cronyke*, 3-36) – all this threatened an explosion of no mean proportions. The final outbreak could still be postponed by a reconciliation between ruler and subjects, arranged by Philip of Burgundy, but this was really more to save the hard-pressed knights besieged by Ghent at Oudenaarde than to bring peace with Ghent, as Froissart rightly observed.[24] The conflict broke out in all its severity once again after the relatives of the murdered bailiff, with the consent of the count, took a gruesome revenge on forty Ghent shippers, whose guild under the leadership of Jan Hyoens had been held chiefly responsible for the bailiff's murder (II, 88; *Cronyke*, 70).

When the conflict resumed in 1380, Louis of Male looked to other princes of the Netherlands for support, particularly to Albert of Bavaria, *ruwaard* of Holland, Zeeland and Hainault, and to the duke of Brabant, Wenceslas of Luxemburg: '. . . it is natural that great lords should support each other.'[25] Albert delivered up a number of Ghent leaders who had fled to Hainault to Louis of Male in 1380, and signed a treaty with him for the joint preservation of peace and order in both lands.[26] The three Flemish towns turned to the French king in that year to assure him that their actions were not directed against him as suzerain (II, 93; *Cronyke*, 85). The death of Charles V in 1380 was a disappointment for Ghent: 'The men of Ghent were much grieved at the death of the king of France, . . . for he had been very friendly to them during the war, loving but little the count of Flanders' (Johnes I, 618; II, 113-14).

In 1381 Louis of Male was almost able to force Ghent to surrender by means of a blockade on English wool and the help of Albert of Bavaria and Wenceslas of Brabant (II, 172-3, *Cronyke*, 149-50), but the towns of the latter two rulers opposed their policies and supported Ghent, which also received support and sympathy from the townspeople of Liège.[27] These princes together with the bishop of Liège were thus forced into a mediatory role.[28]

Froissart gives extensive treatment to the military expeditions sent by Ghent to extend or maintain its sphere of influence. At critical times Ghent was compelled to use large armed forces to forage for food to maintain the town's supplies. Here the unofficial support of Brabant, Liège, Holland and Zeeland becomes clear. A comparison with the town accounts of Ghent in this period shows how well Froissart portrayed these matters, not so much in his factual and chronological accuracy, as in their general tendencies.[29] Froissart's comments on steep price rises because of the shortages in Ghent (II, 196-7, 212; *Cronyke*, 149ff, 199), and on the low prices for forage and other goods in the Ghent army before Oudenaarde or the French army at Ypres in 1382 (II, 213, 243; *Cronyke*, 204, 304) similarly appear to be very accurate. The situation and the *faits et gestes* of Philip van Artevelde, who came to power in Ghent in January 1382, is extensively treated, and Froissart does not forget to mention that the memory of the earlier rule of James van Artevelde was so powerful that twelve of the conspirators against him who were still alive were executed.[30] He thus shows the extent to which grudges could survive over generations (cf. Mollat and Wolff 1973: 175).

In Froissart's view, urban society was not homogeneous. While he saw the disagreement between Bruges and Ghent as one of the causes of the rebellion of Ghent against the count (II, 68ff, III, 517; *Cronyke*, 1, 11ff), he also saw many divisions within Ghent itself and within other towns. It is notable here, that he blames the *poorterie* in Ghent, the most prominent burghers, for not taking sides as this was largely responsible for the catastrophic developments (II, 144, 339-40; *Cronyke*, 122-4, 515). They refused to accept the responsibility attached to their position and allowed demagogues to control policy. To Froissart this was an abdication of responsibility for he saw co-operation between ruler and the *poorterie* of his towns as the guarantee of prosperity, calm and peace. To him, the *poorterie* was 'the good people of Ghent who were the rich and industrious, and had wives, families and fortunes in the town and their goods and rents in the neighbourhood, and wished to live in an honourable way without danger'.[31] They were the pillars of the community. Or rather, they should have been.

But there was not only a division between the *poorterie*, mostly on the side of the count (cf. Pirenne 1908: 200), and the rest of the town population. The latter was by no means at one in its opposition to the social and economic élite of the towns. There were unexpected alliances between the *poorterie* and the lesser trades (due to patronage and financial interests) for example in Bruges, and not only were there conflicts between trades, but also within them as journeymen opposed masters – and this brought in an element of social conflict.[32]

Thus any idea that we are here confronted with proletarian rule is completely untenable. The lists of *schepenen* throughout the period of the revolt show the normal representation of the *poorterie* (three delegates), the weavers and the lesser trades (five delegates each). Although in December 1379 after the first rising and the reconciliation negotiated by Philip of Burgundy, the magistracy was replaced,[33] the categories remained the same and only the personnel were changed. A comital electoral college was involved in this intervention, which was bypassed in the following years but came into operation again after the settlement of 1385 (Vuylsteke 1893: 519-34).

Leaders such as Jan Hyoens and Philip van Artevelde did not ignore the *poorterie*, nor were the wealthier trades excluded, although the dean of the Ghent butchers, suspected of treason, was killed in 1382.[34] As might be expected, when in power each side confiscated its opponents' property and revenues, and it is notable that the lord of Herzele whose income had been taken away by the count, received a share of the confiscated comital revenues in Ghent 'to enable him the better to support his rank'.[35] This same lord of Herzele was later killed after he had accused one of the leaders of Ghent of too lax a defence of Oudenaarde in 1384.[36] Most of the initiatives towards a settlement with the count came from the higher social levels, and this cost the lives of two representatives of the *poorterie*; when they regarded the count's terms as reasonable, they were accused of treason and killed.[37]

In such a situation divisions proliferate and reactions become more extreme.

108

Moves towards a compromise were always doomed to failure. Within the towns, fear of the enemy led to internal terror, and dissidents feared to express their opinions (II, 143, 340; *Cronyke*, 121, 515). But the count too hardened his position as the struggle continued and was not inclined to leniency unless the town's leaders were first sacrificed.[38] This attitude helped the latter to keep the ranks closed: urban solidarity could not countenance the sacrifice of fellow-citizens for the sake of a settlement, although there were occasional grumbles that the sacrifice of a few could save the lives of many.[39]

In such circumstances, only a military victory seemed capable of bringing a decision. In Ghent, while many were close to despair, a final effort was decided on. At Philip van Artevelde's instigation all available resources were mobilised for an offensive to break out of their isolation. Ghent's forces advanced on Bruges where the count was staying and managed to defeat the troops of Bruges in a remarkable manner at Beverhoutsveld on 3 May 1382 and take the town; Louis of Male only just escaped (II, 201-8; *Cronyke*, 162-85). This victory for Ghent meant a fundamental change in both the domestic and foreign situation.

Domestically, it increased considerably the power of Ghent. The Flemish towns had traditionally sought to control large areas of the countryside outside their walls. After her victory, there was nothing left to oppose the ambitions of Ghent. The result was that Ghent, even more than in the 1340s, gained influence over the whole of Flanders. Everywhere men from Ghent or loyal to Ghent were placed in key positions, and Ghent commanders were the real rulers in the great towns, Bruges and Ypres, as well as in the castellanies. Philip van Artevelde regarded himself as *ruwaard* of all Flanders, took over comital prerogatives, and imposed taxes on the whole county (II, 211-12, 213; *Cronyke*, 194-200, 203-4).

However, this power, established by Beverhoutsveld, was destroyed after the defeat of the Flemings near West-Roosebeke on 27 November 1382. When the invading French army crossed the Lys and removed the castellanies from Ghent's sphere of influence, all the officials appointed there by Ghent suffered the fate of traitors: they were surrendered to the French, by the local inhabitants according to Froissart, and beheaded near Ypres. At that time there were suggestions of surrender in Bruges, but apprehension about the fate of the citizens of the town who were in the army of Philip van Artevelde, and especially of the five hundred prominent hostages, held the town back; moreover, a victory such as that at Courtrai in 1302 was not yet impossible. After Roosebeke the count's bailiffs acted harshly in the areas in which they had regained control towards the men from Ghent and their supporters. Froissart says little about this, but in the bailiffs' accounts numerous executions are recorded.[40]

The repercussions of these two battles were also felt, perhaps even more markedly, on the international scene. Until May 1382 both sides in Flanders had remained neutral with regard to France and England. After Beverhoutsveld this changed. Louis of Male had to flee his lands in shame and turn to France. Philip of Burgundy now took action. The aid sought from France was given, but not so much to the count as to protect the inheritance of Philip. The count of Flanders was only grudgingly accepted in the French army, as Froissart makes clear, although he fails to mention the count's Urbanist sympathies as one of the reasons for this (II, 243, 246; *Cronyke*, 303, 317). Philip van Artevelde had also first turned to the king of France, according to Froissart, in the hope that he would bring an end to the conflict, but his ambassador, sent without a safe-conduct, was arrested. Immediately, according to Froissart, Ghent turned to England.[41]

It is possible, however, that Froissart was exaggerating and that Ghent had tried to keep all her options open at this time. Precise information about Anglo-Flemish contacts in the spring of 1382 is lacking.[42] To assume that the elevation of Philip van Artevelde to the leadership of Ghent was a pro-English move would, in my opinion, be going too far. Ghent was in a difficult position at this point, even though the count's blockade on trade with England was not particularly effective.[43] The charisma of James van Artevelde reflected on his son and gave the inhabitants of Ghent a new élan. Peace proposals made through the mediation of Albert of Bavaria, Joan of Brabant and the bishop of Liège were rejected because they involved delivering their leaders into Louis' mercy (II, 199-202; Cronyke, 140-6, 159-61).

It is certainly not unlikely that contacts were made with England at the same time. They were, in fact, continuous, even if only through the Flemish colony in London or the English in, for example, Bruges; Froissart hints very clearly at such contacts via Bruges (II, 265-6; Cronyke, 355-6). It is understandable that these contacts reflected in content those of the period of James van Artevelde. Thus there may very well have been hints as to the recognition of Richard II as king of France, and even as count of Flanders, as spies informed Louis of Male on 22 April 1382. One of the informants of these spies was arrested and brought by the bailiff of Aalst, on or shortly before 5 May 1382, to Hesdin where Louis was encamped.[44]

At this time there was a reasonable chance of an agreement between France and England: a high-level conference was arranged for 1 June 1382. Events in Flanders thwarted these plans, although the English parliament still refused, in accordance with an earlier decision, on 7 May 1382 (thus after the battle of Beverhoutsveld) to agree to the sending of an English army of invasion to the continent.[45] Ghent's victory near Bruges encouraged England to favour the Flemings; Ghent protected foreign merchants and their goods better than Louis of Male; the blockade was lifted.[46]

English sources make it clear that English ambassadors were sent to Flanders and that contacts were maintained throughout the summer. Naval preparations might suggest plans for a joint effort. On 13 September 1382 an embassy from Ghent left for England, but only on 17 October 1382 did an official Flemish embassy set out for London. According to their brief, Richard II was to be recognised as king of England and France, and here Philip van Artevelde was following the example of his father.[47] French proposals for talks were rejected by the Flemings on 20 October 1382 (II, 224-4; Cronyke, 238-41).

The attitude of the English at this time was ambiguous. Despite the traditional English sympathy for Flanders whenever it turned against the French, there was no official English support before 27 November 1382, the date of the battle of Roosebeke. The handful of English archers in Philip van Artevelde's ranks had not been provided by Richard II but were mercenaries in search of gain (II, 218, 246; Cronyke, 223, 315). Vague English promises only arrived just before the battle, but at that point they no longer had any value (II, 240-1, 244; Cronyke, 294, 306).

This English reserve may have been determined by feelings which Froissart indicates in his account of the English response to the defeat of the Flemings: 'The nobles of England were not sorry on hearing it, for they said, that if the commonalty of Flanders had been victorious over the king of France, and his nobility had been slain, the pride of the common people would have been so great that all gentlemen would have had cause to lament it, for appearances of insurrections had been shown in England' (Johnes I, 749-50; II, 257; *Cronyke*, 348). Also the Commons were not without their doubts, and not merely on financial grounds. Since the 1340s there had been a structural change in the economic relations of the two countries. The growth of England's own cloth industry meant that the two countries were increasingly competing with each other and their economies were no longer as interdependent as they had once been (Miskimin 1975: 92-8).

The battle of Roosebeke was followed by the subjection of practically the whole of Flanders except Ghent to the king of France. The town sent ambassadors to Charles VI with a striking proposal: 'They declared ... that they would willingly put themselves under the obedience of the king and would form part of the domain of France, under the jurisdiction of Paris; but that they would never acknowledge for their lord Louis, because they would never love him for the great mischiefs he had done them' (Johnes I, 751; II, 258-9; *Cronyke*, 353). The French king, however, could not accept this offer: it would have meant betraying his vassal. Moreover, if Ghent's proposal had been accepted, this would have undermined the existing social hierarchy and set a dangerous precedent. Another source gives a list of Charles VI's demands on Ghent, which were refused probably chiefly because the concessions required included appeasing the count 'with red gold', i.e. blood (De Pauw 1909: 50-1). Louis of Male was restored as count, but the feud with Ghent was by no means over. French occupation troops were left behind (II, 259; *Cronyke*, 354).

Repeatedly after the battle of Roosebeke, the Flemish fear of the Bertoenen (Bretons) appears. Many fled from Bruges to Holland and Zeeland with their movable goods (II, 253; *Cronyke*, 336), while country people fled to Ghent.[48] The impression given by Froissart is confirmed by such prosaic sources as the bailiff's accounts of Bruges, where it is mentioned that a woman drowned herself for fear of the Bertoenen (De Pauw 1902: 67), or of Veurne, Courtrai and Oudenaarde, which give evidence of their lust for plunder and show that they were not averse to killing non-combattants, and where it is specifically mentioned when the Bretons killed combattants.[49] Only once in these bailiff's accounts is it reported that a Breton was executed at Dendermonde, for the murder of a woman (ibid., 547).

It is hardly surprising that after Roosebeke Louis of Male should have tried to prevent these troops taking Bruges. He succeeded through the good offices of Philip of Burgundy, and Bruges surrendered after having bought off the occupation of the town.[50] Another source, however, mentions misdemeanours and the cruelty of the Bretons in Bruges, who in consequence were executed (De Pauw 1909: 50). The Bretons nevertheless were outraged by the terms of Bruges' surrender 'for they thought to have had their share; and some of them said, when they heard peace had been made, that this war in Flanders was not worth anything, that they had gained too little pillage' (Johnes I, 743; II, 255; *Cronyke*,

111

341-2). They wished to seek compensation in Hainault, as its ruler, Albert of Bavaria, had withdrawn from the war against the Flemings. Froissart's patron, Guy of Blois, was able to prevent this happening (II, 255-6; *Cronyke*, 342-4).

The suppression of the Flemish revolt had its effect outside Flanders as well. Froissart saw a clear connection between the events in Flanders and unrest in France at this time.[51] A rising in Paris was prevented by Nicholas de Vlaming (!), through insisting in waiting for the outcome of the king's expedition in Flanders; the citizens agreed, but remained heavily armed and ready for revolt. Froissart calls the situation in France at this time — when the *vilains* at Reims, Châlons, along the Marne, in Orléans, Blois, Rouen and in the Beauvaisis were attacking knights and the estates of the nobility — worse than during the *Jacquerie*, though the two sides then had fought more fiercely than Christians and Saracens! Pointedly, and not without justification, Froissart follows the French victory at Roosebeke with an account of the suppression of the risings in France.[52]

The international repercussions of Roosebeke were no less marked. While the Flemish embassy was in London in the autumn of 1382, discussions had begun in parliament concerning the crusade against the followers of the French (Avignonese) pope, Clement VII, proposed by the Roman pope, Urban VI. The attraction of such an enterprise was that it could be directed against France, and especially that the consent of Urban VI to the levying of a tithe would reduce its cost, 'for it was well known that the nobles of England would not, for all the absolutions in the world, undertake any expedition, unless such were preceded by offers of money. Men at arms cannot live on pardons, nor do they pay much attention to them, except at the point of death' (Johnes I, 756; II, 266-7; *Cronyke*, 359-62).

According to Froissart two expeditions were considered, to Spain or to Flanders, the English nobles favouring the former and the townspeople the latter. This yet again reflects the English ambivalence with regard to Flanders. Possibly the suggestion that Flanders had become totally Clementist after Roosebeke (Van Asseldonk 1955: 68-9) played a part in the final decision of king and parliament to support a crusade for Urban VI to Flanders, led by Henry Despenser, the bishop of Norwich, but undoubtedly the financial spur by the pope's permission of levying tithes on ecclesiastical properties was one of the reasons why parliament, in February 1383, allowed a subsidy which had already been granted in the autumn of 1382 for a campaign on the continent to be used for this particular expedition.[53]

The count of Flanders, Louis of Male, as an Urbanist who had had to accept after Roosebeke that his defeated subjects had to become Clementist,[54] was placed in a difficult position by this expedition. The count persisted in his adherence to Urban VI and tried to free himself to some extent from French influence. After mediation attempts from the equally Urbanist bishop of Liège, Louis of Male agreed, in order to raise the siege of Ypres, to take part in alliance with Ghent on the Urbanist side in the struggle against the Clementists, and hence against the French. Ghent refused to trust the count and the siege continued (II, 276-7; *Cronyke*, 395-7). French action was necessary to rid Flanders of English troops. This episode was followed at the end of 1383 by Anglo-French negotiations, which again isolated Louis of Male; while he refused to include Ghent in the general truce, the others pushed it through (26 January

1384). A few days later the count died, to be succeeded by Philip of Burgundy.[55]

Despite the support of Ghent, the crusade had achieved nothing.[56] Even the truce was not fully accepted; and Froissart describes at some length the surprise of Oudenaarde by the lord of Schorisse, who refused to recognise the truce in his anger at the loss of his revenues, for which he blamed Ghent (II, 301-2; *Cronyke*, 452-7). The capture of Oudenaarde isolated Ghent; and she was in no way compensated for this loss by help from England. The only English aid to Ghent after 1383 was the dispatch of Sir John Bourchier, who acted as chief governor of the town from November 1384, and, a little later, of a handful of troops in July 1385 (II, 302, 343-4; *Cronyke*, 457, 530-2). The Despenser crusade, therefore, was little more than an incident in the great Anglo-French war, a remarkable intermezzo in Anglo-Flemish relations.

The year 1385 saw the establishment of the house of Burgundy in the Low Countries, a development described at some length by Froissart. He notes the frustration of the duke of Lancaster's efforts to combat Burgundian influence by the marriage of his daughter Philippa to William of Ostrevant and the subsequent double marriage between John of Nevers and Margaret of Bavaria and Margaret of Burgundy and William of Ostrevant (12 April 1385), marriages which laid the bases for the later expansion of Burgundian power in the Netherlands.[57]

He also relates at some length the way in which Ghent was reduced to obedience. Despite her military activities in the summer of 1385 — which saved England from a double invasion from Scotland and Flanders (II, 321; *Cronyke*, 492) — Ghent was unable to resist the weight of French resources thrown behind Philip of Burgundy. Charles VI himself was present at the final onslaught, signifying the importance that the Valois dynasty attached to the acquisition of Flanders by one of its scions (II, 316-17, 321-2, 325-7; *Cronyke*, 474-9, 492-6, 498-513). Ghent was forced to come to terms, and about the only advantage she was able to obtain was on the matter of religious obedience. In this, Philip was prepared to allow time to work in his favour.[58]

The submission of Ghent did not, however, put an end to the troubles in Flanders. Her problems had involved her neighbours, and England and France in particular were not prepared to cease fighting as soon as Ghent laid down its arms. The French were determined to use the military, strategic and naval resources of Flanders to deal England a crippling blow; and 1386 saw the concentration of a huge armada at Sluys, at immense cost to the French treasury and to the great loss of the Flemings who had the misfortune to live within twenty miles of this concentration and who suffered the depredations of the licentious French soldiers.[59] The only ones to gain were the shipowners of Holland and Zeeland, who hired out their craft at high rates without having in the end to put them in any danger (II, 498, 534).

The fiasco of 1386 was followed by another in 1387, when the Flemish fleet under its admiral Jan Bock was finally defeated by the English, an event greeted with unalloyed joy in Holland and Zeeland. The English, however, failed to capitalise on their victory by taking Sluys, as recommended by the Flemish exile Pieter van den Bossche; the capture of Sluys would possibly have paved the way for an English domination of Flanders, while there existed still a widespread discontent against the new ruler, Philip of Burgundy (II, 549-52).

Domestically the submission of Ghent failed to bring immediate peace.

Although the settlement of 1385 had not involved any revenge on the leaders of Ghent, one of them, Pieter van den Bossche, had thought it advisable to take refuge in England, not from fear of his new ruler, but because he feared the vengeance of his opponents in Ghent. The fate of the other great leader of Ghent shows how right he was: Francis Ackerman was killed in 1386 by a relative of one of the victims of the disputes within Ghent.[60]

The revolt of Flanders was, then, an event of international significance, as Froissart was well aware: 'This war, which Ghent had carried on against its lord the count Lewis of Flanders and the duke of Burgundy, had lasted near seven years; and it would be melancholy to relate all the various unfortunate events which it had caused. Turks, Saracens and Pagans would have been sorrowful on hearing them, for all commerce by sea was ruined. The sea-coasts from east to west, and all the north, suffered from it; for in truth the riches and merchandise of seventeen kingdoms were sent to Sluys, and the whole was unshipped at Damme or Bruges. Now consider, that if these distant countries suffered, still more bitterly must those nearer have felt it' (Johnes II, 58; II, 340; *Cronyke*, 516). As far as Holland and Zeeland are concerned, this period saw a boom in their trade, partly through greater familiarity with their English connections.[61]

After his extended treatment of events in Flanders between 1379 and 1385, Froissart deals only intermittently with the affairs of the Low Countries in Books III and IV, narrating only three episodes in any detail: the conflict between Guelders and Brabant (particularly in 1388) and its consequences (II, 648-745); the first expedition against the Frisians in 1396 (III, 231-55); and the debacle of Nicopolis in 1396 (III, 226-306) and its financial repercussions. While only the first of these events was at all directly related to the major theme of the *Chronicles* — the Anglo-French war — all three had a bearing upon the rise of Burgundian power in the Low Countries, a development of momentous importance for the future relations of England and France, as Froissart shrewdly observed.

As an ally of England, the duke of Guelders was a threat to Brabant, forcing the duchess Joan of Brabant to seek French support through the mediation of Philip of Burgundy. A large-scale French invasion, led by Charles VI in person, produced a settlement in 1388, implemented two years later.[62] It was a settlement entirely favourable to Philip of Burgundy, whose co-operation with the duchess of Brabant was bought by the promise of the succession to the duchy of one of his younger sons after Joan's death, thus confirming Philip's rights of inheritance through his mother-in-law, a younger sister of Joan of Brabant. On this, Froissart commented with considerable insight: 'He (Philip) was a great power by his marriage with the heiress of Flanders, and daily expecting to inherit Brabant also', adding 'if, therefore, in times to come, these countries should quarrel with France, and unite themselves, as they had formerly done, with England, they would be an overmatch for her' (III, 185; Johnes II, 558). These words look back to the alliance of 1338 but also forward to the treaty of Troyes of 1420.

It is noticeable that while Froissart does treat the expedition against the Frisians in 1396 — by which Albert of Bavaria tried to secure his title as lord of Friesland — in some detail, he totally ignores the domestic politics of Holland

and Zeeland which, among other things, led to a temporary rupture between Albert of Bavaria and his son, William of Ostrevant,[63] although Froissart does mention the differences of opinion between father and son (III, 93, 231). Froissart's remarks about William of Ostrevant show that he had a sympathy for this chivalrous prince. Perhaps he did not want to believe the rumours about William's activities against his father, particularly as he admired Albert of Bavaria too. The indifference of his patron, Guy of Blois, to the party struggles in Holland (despite his interests there) may also help to account for Froissart's lack of interest in the subject. Finally, these conflicts were against the Burgundian interest (with which Froissart sympathised at this time), since they threatened the inheritance of William of Ostrevant, son-in-law of the duke of Burgundy.

The reconciliation between father and son was sealed by William's participation in the expedition against the Frisians, though he had at first intended to join the Nicopolis expedition instead (III, 231). Both Richard II and (on the insistence of Philip of Burgundy) Charles VI sent troops to aid the expedition, despite some earlier disagreements between them over Hainault when William of Ostrevant had been awarded the Order of the Garter (III, 97-8). The expedition resulted in a victory, and another, two years later, in the conquest of Friesland (III, 253-5), though even this proved ephemeral.[64]

The report of the catastrophe of Nicopolis led to feverish activity, particularly by Philip of Burgundy whose son, John of Nevers, was led into captivity by the victorious sultan, Bayazid. Raising the ransom for John of Nevers forced Philip not only to pawn his valuables (III, 279) but also to appeal to his subjects in Burgundy, Artois and 'more especially those of Flanders, for they abounded in wealth, from their commerce and therefore the greater load was laid on them' (III, 303-4; Johnes II, 652); indeed, they agreed to an *aide*.[65] Nor was this the extent of their generosity. For when John of Nevers returned, he was fêted in Flanders according to Froissart, whose account is here confirmed by the town accounts of Bruges.[66] Having shown how Philip of Burgundy mastered his inheritance in the 1380s, Froissart thus concludes his account with a demonstration of the general, even enthusiastic acceptance of Burgundian rule towards the end of the century. The foundations of Burgundian influence in the Low Countries had been securely established by the time Froissart had completed the final book of his *Chronicles*.

Froissart's information about the Netherlands, especially Ghent and Flanders, shows that he was not simply the chronicler of a declining chivalry (Coulton 1930). Possibly the son of a money-broker, Froissart was clear that war and prosperity were incompatible. His conception of proper social order was peace, maintained by a just prince who watched over the general good, in harmony with his subjects (so too the — good — representatives of towns). Precisely that stratum of society from which Froissart himself came identified itself most with princely authority; the status he reached as a cleric changes nothing, for 'there cannot be a yolk of an egg without its white, nor a white without the yolk, so neither the clergy nor the lords can exist independently of each other' (Johnes II, 145; II, 458).

Froissart was not blind to the interest of the towns, but he saw them from a restricted viewpoint. Urban rivalry was a danger to peace in the land; internal disunity in the towns could be the nucleus of civil war and ruin. The revolt of Ghent and Flanders represented a great danger for traditional society and in one of the versions Froissart remarks that the battle of Roosebeke was won by the pillars of Christendom, knights and nobility, and that nothing more terrible could have happened in the Christian world than a victory for the rebels, who then could have realised their aims (*Cronyke*, 332-3). Yet Froissart saw in this antagonism no reason for implacable hostility: he believed that princes had a duty to take into account the interests of their urban subjects, who in their turn had to respect the existing order. In this respect Froissart was a defender of the *Society of Orders* (cf. Fourquin 1978: 38ff). The way in which Philip of Burgundy, who pushed through what he had planned (II, 325; *Cronyke*, 505), came finally to a reconciliation with Ghent received Froissart's approval: no revenge but an attempt to lay the foundations for a lasting peace.

War above all was Froissart's subject, but he reserved his highest praise for two princes who were also his patrons, Wenceslas of Brabant and Luxemburg and Guy of Blois, by writing that they lived without waging war or oppressing their subjects, they made no evil laws nor did they uphold evil customs (II, 654). This is the expression of the real antithesis, so brilliantly depicted in the fourteenth-century frescos in the town hall of Siena: that between *mal* and *bon governo*.

Froissart's *Chronicles* are not amenable to one single interpretation, and his account of events is not supported by a consistent view of society. He is hardly believable as an advocate of peace, given his great attention and respect for knightly *prowess* which without war could only be displayed in tournaments.[67] The peace which Froissart wished see retained was civil peace, whereby the prosperity of his subjects would allow the prince and his knights to carry out their function in just wars.

Froissart hardly took sides in the conflict of the knights. Whether they were French, English or other knights, the results of their actions remained the same, though in the course of the years, there are signs of a shift in sympathy from the English via the French to the Burgundian side: 'Froissart, l'enfant terrible de la chevalerie, nous raconte trahisons et cruautés sans fin, sans trop s'apercevoir de la contradiction entre ses conceptions générales et le contenu de son récit.'[68]

It is otherwise in his treatment of the conflict in Flanders and Ghent. Here Froissart chose the side neither of the count nor of his subjects: he chose moderation, *mesure*, personified in the actions of Philip of Burgundy. This made him an enemy of the rebels and a supporter of those who tried to bring an end to the conflict by negotiation. It was the Flemish *orgueil* which he condemned, which first led to rebelliousness, and then to the destruction of many. This did not blind him to the courage of those of Ghent and Flanders, but it was a courage which led to the unnecessary spilling of blood.

Froissart was influenced by fear of the overthrow of the established order.[69] He knew very well that armies of knights did not refrain from taking ecclesiastical as well as lay property; but such actions did not stem from any animosity to the existing social order. It was otherwise, however, with the attitude of the rebels in

England, France and Flanders. They turned in the first instance against the nobility and their property, but — although sometimes promises were made to spare the church's property (I, 408) — in the end nothing will be spared, not the church, not the clergy, not the rich people of all lands; even the towns would have been destroyed (I, 376, cf. II, 252; *Cronyke*, 332-3).

VIII   FROISSART DANS LE MIDI PYRENEEN *

Pierre Tucoo-Chala

FROISSART explique avec une grande clarté les raisons de son lointain voyage dans les Pyrénées, pendant l'hiver 1388-9, dans le prologue du livre III de ses *Chroniques*. Cette expédition le conduisit jusqu'en Béarn, à Orthez, à la cour de Gaston III Fébus (1343-91) seigneur de Foix-Béarn, dont l'action avait grandement contribué à la désagrégation de la Principauté d'Aquitaine crée par Edouard III pour son fils, le Prince Noir. Dans ce prologue Froissart dégage toute la philosophie de son oeuvre. Il veut s'assurer la renomée, contribuer à l'édification morale du monde chevaleresque ('car bien sçay que ou temps advenir, quant je seray mort et pourry, ceste haulte et noble hystoire sera en grant cours, et y prendront tous nobles et vaillans hommes plaisance et augmentation de bien') en faisant le récit de 'fais d'armes, prendre, embler et essillier chasteaulx et forteresses' (XII, 2, 1).

Pour parvenir à ce but le chroniqueur estime nécessaire de prendre deux précautions. En premier lieu il ne doit pas se consacrer exclusivement aux exploits accomplis dans les pays situés au nord de la Loire, mais également s'occuper des 'besoignes des lointaines marches'. Or comme la paix régnait en 1388 il pouvait quitter le service de Guy de Châtillon, comte de Blois, sans courrir le risque d'être privé du plaisir d'être témoin de quelque combat ('consideray en moy mesme que pas ne se failloit que grans fais d'armes en long temps advenissent en la marche de Picardie ne du pays de Flandres') pour se rendre près de la péninsule ibérique où des conflits faisaient rage en Castille et Portugal: 'car grandement m'anuioit à estre oiseux'. En second lieu, il estimait nécessaire de choisir judicieusement l'endroit le plus propice pour recueillir le plus facilement possible le maximum de renseignements. S'installer dans une cour recevant de multiples visiteurs apportant les nouvelles pouvait dispenser de bien des déplacements. Dans ce but il avait demandé à Guy de Châtillon des lettres d'introduction pour le comte de Foix: 'et bien savoie que se je povoie avoir l'aventure et la grace de venir en son hostel et là estre a loisir, je ne povoie mieulx ou monde escheir pour estre informé justement de toutes nouvelles, car là sont et retournent moult volentiers tous les chevaliers et escuiers estrangiers pour la haulte noblesse de lui' (XII, 2). Ce choix fait honneur à la sagacité de Froissart, car Fébus était effectivement en grande partie le maître du jeu politique dans la région pyrénéenne, et ses domaines confinaient à la péninsule ibérique. Sa cour était une plaque tournante, un remarquable lieu d'observation pour recueillir des informations sur les guerres passées d'Aquitaine, et sur les guerres présentes de Castille et du Portugal.

* All references to the *Chroniques* are to volume and page of the SHF edition.

Dans ce prologue Froissart explique donc bien sa démarche tout en révélant quelques unes de ses qualités maîtresses: le choix d'un sujet bien délimité, l'utilisation judicieuse des moyens pour atteindre l'objectif fixé. Notre propos est d'isoler dans la vaste fresque des *Chroniques* cet épisode, parfaitement délimité dans le temps et dans l'espace, pour analyser à travers lui ses méthodes de travail et son degré de véracité; mais auparavant il est indispensable de replacer le voyage dans le Midi pyrénéen dans un contexte plus général.

'Et tant travaillay et chevauchay, enquerant de tous costez nouvelles, que par la grace de Dieu, sans peril et sans dommaige je vins en son chastel à Ortays, ou pays de Berne, le jour Sainte Katherine que on compte pour lors en l'an de grace mil III^{C}IIII^{XX} et VIII' (XII, 2-3). Pour parvenir à Orthez le 25 novembre 1388 — il devait y rester jusqu'au début de l'année suivante — Froissart était probablement passé par la vallée du Rhône pour se trouver à Carcassonne vers la mi-novembre. Cette date du 28 octobre 1388 est la seule de son texte, mais des notations diverses permettent d'établir quand même une chronologie assez précise: 'Quant je eus sejourné en la cité de Paumiers trois jours'; 'pour quoy il nous convint retourner à Montesquieu, et disner et là estre tout le jour'. (XII, 20, 27). Son itinéraire est reporté sur une carte tenant également compte de la géo-politique du moment, avec indication particulière pour les lieux d'étape où Froissart passa au moins une nuit: Carcassonne, Pamiers, Montesquieu-Volvestre, Cazères-sur-Garonne, Saint-Gaudens, Tournay, Tarbes, Morlàas.

De Carcassonne, le 14 novembre 1388, il gagna Mazères où il pensait trouver Gaston III qui avait dans ce bourg sa résidence préférée quand il séjournait en pays de Foix. Par malchance, Febus était en Béarn; aussi notre chroniqueur poursuivit-il son chemin jusqu'à Pamiers espérant y rencontrer un compagnon de voyage capable de le mener en Béarn: Espan du Lion, un des familiers du seigneur de Foix-Béarn, retour d'une mission à la cour pontificale d'Avignon. Ils mirent huit jours pour couvrir les 250 kilomètres séparant Pamiers d'Orthez; mais la destruction d'un pont sur la Garonne leur fit perdre beaucoup de temps. En réalité, la moyenne journalière était d'une quarantaine de kilomètres, et Froissart pouvait couvrir des distances plus importantes, si nécessaire, dans une journée, comme les soixante kilomètres séparant Carcassonne de Pamiers.

Ce périple le long des Pyrénées avait l'avantage de se dérouler dans une zone sûre, à l'abri des attaques de toute bande de routiers car Espan du Lion fit suivre à son compagnon la route stratégique et commerciale placée sous la surveillance des garnisons de son maître. Si Froissart est peu attentif à l'aspect général du paysage (pas une seule fois il n'évoque le panorama sur la chaîne des Pyrénées, il se contente par exemple de noter que le Béarn est un pays très boisé, que les landes de Ger sont désolées), il sait parfaitement quand il quitte le Languedoc royal pour pénétrer dans les terres du comte de Foix: 'quant je me fus parti de Carcasonne je laissié le chemin de Thoulouse à la bonne main, et pris le chemin à la main senestre, à Montroial (Montréal), à Fougans (Fanjeaux), et puis à Belle (Belpech), la premiere ville fermée de la conté de Foeis, et de là à Maseres, et puis au chastel de Savredun (Saverdun), et puis arrivé à la belle et bonne cité de Paumiers, laquelle est toute au conte de Foies' (XII, 20).

Ne suivons pas l'itinéraire, la carte suffit en ce domaine, mais indiquons comment Fébus avait réussi à s'assurer le contrôle de cette route sous-pyrénéenne

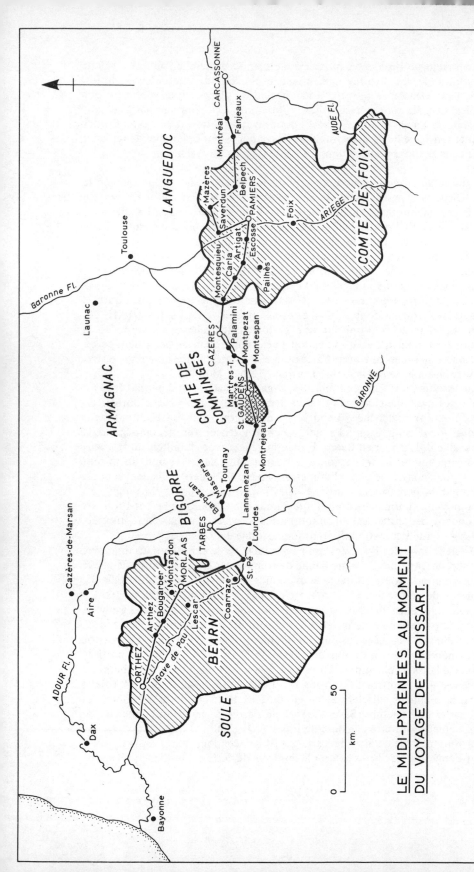

LE MIDI-PYRENEES AU MOMENT
DU VOYAGE DE FROISSART.

CARCASSONNE : Lieux d'étapes de Froissart.

Artigat : Lieux cités dans les chroniques.

Domaine des Foix-Béarn.

Occupation ou acquisitions par Fébus.

en fonction de laquelle se répartissaient les forces politiques dans la région. En 1343 il avait reçu en héritage un ensemble fort dispersé, dont les terres étaient réparties entre la zone de l'Aquitaine anglaise et le Languedoc royal. A l'Ouest il y avait les vicomtés de Béarn, Marsan et Gabardan, à l'Est le Pays de Foix avec des annexes comme le Lautrecois. A mi-chemin entre ces deux groupes, il possédait une partie du Nébouzan autour de Saint-Gaudens.

Profitant de la guerre de Cent ans, et des moments de paralysie des royaumes de France et d'Angleterre, Gaston Fébus avait mené à bien un ambitieux programme politique. Il avait réussi à transformer le Béarn en un pays qu'il ne tenait que 'de Dieu et de l'épée' (selon une formule recueillie par Froissart) face au Prince Noir et Jean II le Bon. Après avoir un moment éliminé la puissance de la grande famille seigneuriale rivale, celle des Armagnac, vaincue à Launac (1362), il avait absorbé une à une les seigneuries séparant le Béarn du Nébouzan, le Nébouzan du Foix, pour constituer un ensemble territorial homogène tout au long des Pyrénées. Tous les procédés avaient été bons pour y parvenir: des achats (Lannemezan en 1345, Tournay en 1365), des cessions par traité après une guerre victorieuse (Goudon, Mauvezin en 1377, Saint-Julien-sur-Garonne), des occupations sans droit ni titre par la volonté du plus fort (Soule, Bigorre, villages de la Garonne commingeoise entre Martres-Tolosanes et Saint-Martory).

Cette politique d'hégémonie se doublait d'un dessein économique. Le seigneur de Foix-Béarn n'avait que des ressources médiocres compte-tenu de la faible population de ses domaines et de leur activité. La guerre avait ravagé la vallée de la Garonne entre Toulouse et Bordeaux, rendant aléatoires les échanges entre la Méditerranée et l'Atlantique le long de cette voie habituelle. En contrôlant un itinéraire de remplacement des portes de Toulouse à celles de Bayonne, en y assurant la sécurité, et en éliminant par la force les concurrents, Gaston Fébus donnait une assiète complémentaire à son dessein politique. Les Béarnais jouaient le rôle de rouliers des Pyrénées; en dehors d'eux, seuls des marchands munis de sauf-conduits du châtelain d'Orthez pouvaient circuler en toute sécurité; les Béarnais commencèrent à mettre la main sur le trafic du pastel du Lauragais en direction de Bayonne.

Certes ces réalités économiques n'intéressent point Froissart, ni la vie rurale. Commerçants et paysans sont hors de son univers mental; mais il est attentif à la geste politique conduite par Fébus qui, avec un demi-siècle d'avance, annonçait la grande entreprise des Bourguignons: profiter de l'effacement du pouvoir monarchique pour constituer aux marges de la France une principauté indépendante en soudant des territoires disparates. La guerre et la diplomatie, la surveillance attentive des prolongements de la guerre de Cent ans dans la péninsule ibérique, des guerres civiles de Castille et du Portugal, avaient été à l'origine du succès de cette politique. Orthez était donc, a défaut de Mazères, le lieu idéal pour examiner de l'intérieur comment le comte avait tissé sa toile. Pour ces questions qui l'intéressent au plus haut point Froissart se révèle un enquêteur d'une habileté consommée et d'une énergie infatigable.

Pendant ses quatre mois de séjour près des Pyrénées le chroniqueur utilise des méthodes d'enquête rappelant, dans leur esprit, celle de nos modernes reporters travaillant pour la télévision: parler et faire parler très spontanément sans trop se soucier de réfléchir sur des documents écrits. Il manie l'interview avec une maîtrise remarquable, sait gagner la confiance des gens de rencontre, leur apporte lui-même beaucoup de nouvelles, ce qui les pousse d'autant plus à la confidence. Il a l'art de dénicher les compagnons de route capables de lui permettre de faire deux choses à la fois: voyager par le chemin le plus direct, recueillir des informations. Circuler seul est à la fois dangereux et une perte de temps. Au moment de quitter Pamiers avec Espan du Lion, il le note clairement: 'En cheminant, le gentil homme et bon chevalier, puis que il avoit dit au matin ses oroisons, jongloit le plus du jour à moy en demandant nouvelles. Je lui en demandoie aussi; il m'en disoit' (XII, 21). D'ailleurs ne s'était-il pas arrêté à Pamiers trois jours 'pour attendre compagnie'?

Pendant la route le dialogue est permanent. Comme Espan du Lion est un bavard impénitent, Froissart n'a guère, en général, de peine à le faire parler. La vue d'une cité ou d'un château fait fuser les questions. Par exemple devant le château d'Artigat tenu pendant cinq ans par Pierre d'Auchin: 'Et comment l'eust-il? dis-ge au chevalier' — 'Je le vous diray, dist-il' (XII, 21), ou bien devant un champ de bataille: 'Ha messire Jehan, que j'ay icy veu pluseurs fois de bonnes escarmuches et de dures et bonnes rencontres de Foiesois et d'Arminags' (XII, 31), constatation qui sert de prélude à l'étude de toute une large partie du conflit entre les maisons de Foix-Béarn et d'Armagnac.

Quand le trajet est terminé, la technique de l'interview demeure. Descendu à Orthez à l'hôtel de la Lune, Froissart, toujours aux aguets, remarque l'arrivée d'un personnage haut en couleur, menant grand train et au verbe haut. Se souvenant d'un récit d'Espan du Lion à propos d'un Basque ayant fait fortune par les armes, le chroniqueur demande tout de suite à ce même Espan: 'Et n'est-ce pas l'escuier qui se parti du chastel de Trigalet quant le duc d'Anjou sist devant Mauvoisin?' — 'Oïl respondi-il' (XII, 96); et Froissart d'attendre l'occasion la plus propice pour garnir son carnet de notes. Il préfère ne rien brusquer afin d'obtenir le maximum de confidences dans les meilleures conditions; les provoquer après un excellent repas, devant un bon feu, est une recette valable à toutes les époques: 'Une nuit après soupper, seans au feu et attendans la mie nuit, que le conte de Foies devoit soupper, son cousin le mist en voye de parler et de recorder de sa vie et des armes, où en son temps il avoit esté, tant de pertes que de prouffis, et trop bien lui en souvenoit. Si me demanda: 'Messire Jehan, avez vous point en vostre hystoire ce dont je vous parleray?' 'Je lui respondi: Je ne scay ai-ge ou non, di-ge. Faictes vostre compte, car je vous oy volentiers parler d'armes, et il ne me puet pas de tout souvenir, et aussi je ne puis pas avoir esté de tout infourmé' (XII, 96). Ceci est le point de départ d'une page admirable des *Chroniques* restituant à travers la vie du Bascot de Mauléon toute une aventure bien typique des soldats de fortune de la guerre de Cent ans. Froissart se contente d'intervenir discrètement pour orienter la conversation sur les épisodes qu'il ne connaît pas encore, car une fois lancé le Bascot est intarissable.

Cette enquête il la poursuit dans les rues d'Orthez, au château Moncade quand il rend visite à Fébus. Il peut se réjouir d'avoir si bien choisi cette cour pour son propos: 'Là vey chevaliers d'Arragon et Anglois, lesquels estoient de l'ostel au duc de Lancastre, qui pour ce temps se tenoit à Bourdiaux, ausquelz le conte de Foies fist bonne chiere et donna de biaulx dons. Je me accointay de ces chevaliers et par eulx fu-ge infourmé de grant foison de besongnes qui estoient avenues en Castille, et en Navarre et en Portingal' (XII, 95). Ainsi l'un des buts de la mission, exposé dans le prologue, s'informer sur les guerres dynastiques de Castille et du Portugal fut-il facilement rempli.

Dans des circonstances plus difficiles, Froissart fait preuve d'un acharnement remarquable pour parvenir à ses fins. Avant de partir pour le pays de Gaston de Foix-Béarn, il avait eu connaissance — comme toutes les cours — du drame qui s'était déroulé à Orthez au cours duquel le prince héritier était mort. Les uns parlaient de procès et d'exécution, les autres de meurtre. Bien entendu Froissart désirait d'autant plus susciter les confidences sur ce point que le sujet était brûlant, que les interlocuteurs se dérobaient. Regardons le au travail dans cette affaire délicate.

Il chevauche plusieurs jours avec Espan du Lion sans aborder ce sujet, et profite de la première occasion pour poser une question, en apparence innocente car il laisse supposer à son compagnon qu'il découvre brusquement une affaire dont il n'avait jamais entendu parler: près de Tarbes, Espan du Lion raconte comment Fébus avait mis en prison son héritier légitime, le vicomte de Castelbon, qu'il avait pris en haine. Et Froissart de saisir la balle au bond: 'Comment, sire, di-ge au chevalier, n'a dont le conte de Foies nulz enfans, que je vous oy dire que le visconte de Chasetelbon est son hiretier?' (XII, 62). Espan se contente de dire qu'il a eu deux fils bâtards. Froissart poursuit: 'Et ne fut-il oncques mariez?' — 'Si fu, respondi-il, et est encores; mais madame de Foies ne se tient point avec luy' — 'Et où se tient-elle? di-ge.' — 'Elle se tient en Navarre, respondi-il, car le roi de Navarre est son cousin, et fu fille jadis du roy Loys de Navarre.' — 'Et le conte de Foies n'en ot-il onques nulz enfans?' — 'Si eut, dist-il, ung biau filz' (XII, 63). Ceci dit, Espan du Lion profita de l'arrivée à Tarbes pour remettre à plus tard la suite de la discussion.

Le lendemain sur la route de Morlàas, Froissart revient sur le sujet non sans avoir préparé le terrain par une flatterie qui généralement réussissait auprès de tous ses interlocuteurs car il leur promettait la notoriété en les citant dans ses 'hystoires' lues par toute l'aristocratie d'Occident: 'Saincte Marie, sire, di-ge au chevalier, que vos paroles me son aggréables et que elles me font grant bien, tandis que vous me les comptés, et vous ne les perdez pas, car toutes seront mises en memoire et en ramenbrance et croniquiés en l'istoire que je poursieu . . . mais je suis courroucié d'une chose.' — 'De laquelle?' dist le chevalier. — 'Je vous le diray par ma foy, sire, que de si hault et si vaillant prince comme le conte de Foies est, il ne demeure nul hiretier de sa femme espousée' (XII, 70). Peine perdue car Espan se contente d'éluder encore la question en faisant entendre que l'héritier légitime était mort. Froissart laisse passer de longues heures et reprend son attaque aux portes mêmes de Morlàas: 'Mais encore de une chose si je la vous osoie requerre, je vous demanderoie volontiers: par quelle incidence le filz au conte de Foies, que est a present, morut?' — Lors pensa le chevalier et puis dist: 'La matiere est trop piteuse; si ne vous en vueil pas parler; quant vous venrez à Ortais, vous trouverez bien, se vous le demandez, qui le vous dira' (XII, 75).

Froissart se le tint pour dit et n'aborda plus le sujet avec Espan du Lion comprenant qu'il ne parlerait pas et refuserait même de continuer à l'aider sur tous les autres sujets en cas d'insistance maladroite. Bien entendu, à Orthez, il fit tout son possible pour percer ce mystère redoutable, et sa ténacité finit pas être récompensée: 'Je tendoie trop fort à demander et à savoir, pour tant que l'ostel de Foeis je veoie si large et si plantureux, que Gaston, le filz du conte estoit devenu, ne par quelle incidence il estoit mort, car messire Espaeng de Lion ne le m'avoit volu dire, et tant en enquis que ung escuier anciens et homme moult notable le me dist. Si commença son compte ainsi en disant et dist' (XII, 79). Sans donner le nom de cet homme âgé qui accepte enfin de parler, Froissart recueille le célèbre récit de la mort du prince héritier de Foix-Béarn et le termine par ces mots, dont on peut se demander s'ils ne constituent pas la conviction intime du chroniqueur: 'Son pere le occist voirement, mais le roy de Navarre li donna le cop de la mort' (XII, 89).

Ténacité, sens de la mesure, acuité d'esprit, tout concours à faire de Froissart un grand maître du reportage en milieu aristocratique. En 1388 sa notoriété est établie à travers tout le royaume de France et même hors de ses limites et c'est toujours avec une pointe de satisfaction qu'il promet à ses interlocuteurs de reproduire leurs paroles dans ses futurs écrits: 'Par ma foy, respondi-ge, oil et grant mercis, car à vos comptes oir ay-ge eu part autant bien que les autres et ilz ne sont pas perdus, car se Dieu me doint retourner en mon pays et en ma nacion, de ce que je vous ay oy dire et compter, et de tout ce que j'auray veu et trouvé sur mon voyage, qui appartiengne que je en face memoire en la noble et haulte hystoire, de laquelle le gentil conte Guy de Blois m'a ensonnié et ensomnie, je le croniqueray et escripray, afin que, avecques les autres besongnes dont j'ay parlé en la dicte hystoire et parleray et escripray par la grace de Dieu ensieuvant, il en soit memoire à tousjours' (XII, 115).

Cette enquête minutieuse, ce souci de la gloire future, ne conduit jamais Froissart à collecter le moindre document écrit, fragment de lettre ou traité par exemple. S'il évoque un moment le travail acharné du comte de Foix pour bien administrer ses Etats, il se contente de dire qu'il était capable de dicter plusieurs lettres en même temps à quatre secrétaires. Lacune essentielle qu'il ne chechait pas à combler au moment de la rédaction définitive.

C'était en effet une chose que de mener à bien toutes ces conversations, et une autre que de les enregistrer de façon sûre. Le chroniqueur passe une partie de ses nuits, ou se lève avant l'aube, pour tout transcrire car sa mémoire ne pourrait tout retenir. Ce travail inlassable est décrit de la façon suivante: 'Des paroles que messire Espaeng de Lyon me comptoit estoie tout rafreschi, car elles me venoient grandement à plaisance et toutes très bien les retenoie, et si tost que aux hostelz, sur le chemin que nous fesismes ensamble, descendu estoie, je les escripsoie, fust de soir ou de matin, pour avoir en tout temps advenir mieulx la memoire, car il n'est si juste retenue que cest d'escripture' (XII, 65).

On imagine facilement la masse de renseignements rapportés par Froissart après douze semaines de séjour à Orthez, sans compter tous ceux collectés pendant le voyage proprement dit. Il profita de son passage en Béarn pour s'y faire des amis qui continuèrent à l'informer après son retour en Flandres. En 1391 Froissart eut rapidement toutes les indications nécessaires sur la mort du 'gentil comte de Foix' et donna en quelque sorte une conclusion à son périple dans les pays pyrénéens en écrivant ses pages consacrées à la fin de Fébus, à ses obsèques, et aux problèmes politiques posés par sa disparition. En plus des documents qu'il obtenait lui même en se déplaçant le chroniqueur avait organisé un embryon de service chargé (par simple amitié, ou contre rémunération?) de lui procurer d'autres nouvelles.

Tout cette documentation il fallait maintenant la mettre en oeuvre. Aucun passage ne permet de savoir dans quelles conditions exactes Froissart fit le tri pour rédiger ses souvenirs relatifs à son aventure à la cour d'Orthez. Il réserva certains éléments pour son oeuvre poétique, en élimina d'autres, recomposa le tout pour donner à son récit une progression dramatique retenant l'attention de ses lecteurs. Dans quelle mesure son travail d'homme de lettres le conduisit-il à trahir sa documentation? Encore une question à laquelle il est impossible de répondre. La lecture de nombreux passages prouve cependant que Froissart, dans ce cas précis, a retranscrit mot à mot l'essentiel des notes consignant ses conversations avec Espan du Lion, ou avec le Bascot de Mauléon.

Bien entendu il se préoccupait des goûts de sa clientèle: l'aristocratie nobiliaire. Il concentre donc son attention sur les thèmes qui flattent ses lecteurs. Il privilégie tous les beaux faits d'armes; inutile de revenir sur ce point. Les cours étaient également friandes de ses histoires d'amour, bonnes ou mauvaises. Après la guerre décrite surtout à travers les prouesses chevaleresques, ce second thème est privilégié. Par exemple Froissart raconte comment le duc de Berry follement épris de Jeanne de Boulogne, pupille de Fébus, dut conclure avec ce dernier un étrange marché financier pour obtenir la main de cette toute jeune fille. Certaines histoires d'amour sont l'occasion d'aborder un troisième thème où se mêlent le tragique et le fantastique: celle de Pierre de Béarn et de Florence de Biscaye entre autres. Ce bâtard de Béarn était sujet à des crises terribles de somnanbulisme pendant lesquelles il frappait à tort et à travers avec une épée s'il parvenait à s'en saisir. Froissart savait par avance combien ses lecteurs adoraient toutes les histoires étranges confinant à la magie ou à la nécromancie. Le récit de la bataille d'Aljubarrota (15 août 1385) lui donne l'occasion de démontrer son talent de conteur dans ce domaine du fantastique.

Pour vider leur querelle dynastique les prétendants au trône du Portugal avaient enrôlé des chevaliers venus de tous les horizons. Malgré l'opposition de Fébus, pressentant que l'affaire finirait mal, et surtout peu soucieux de perdre une partie de ses meilleurs chevaliers, de nombreux Béarnais avaient décidé de tenter fortune dans cette aventure où les profits s'annonçaient gras. Ces Béarnais furent dans le mauvais camp le jour d'Aljubarrota, et bon nombre d'entre eux périrent. Or, selon un récit repris par Froissart, dès le 16 août le châtelain d'Orthez manifesta une grande inquiétude, prit un air sombre et confia à son frère, Guilhem-Arnaud de Morlanne: 'il est ainsi que je vous di, et briefvement nous orons nouvelles, mais oncques le pays de Berne ne perdi tant puis cent ans sus ung jour comme il a perdu à ceste fois en Portingal' (XII, 171). Et Froissart de s'étonner de la rapidité avec laquelle le comte de Foix était averti de tout ce qui se passait: ne fallait-il point y voir une sorte de magie: 'Dont il est divin, di-je, ou il a les messagiers qui chevauchent de nuit avecques le vent? Aucun art fault-il qu'il ait?' (XII, 172).

Froissart préférant la divination à une stricte organisation d'un service de renseignement supérieurement mis au point, en profite pour glisser le récit fantastique d'Orton, le génie familier du baron de Coarraze (XII, 181-3). Ce baron béarnais savait tout ce qui se passait en Europe, de façon quasi instantanée, grâce à un être mystérieux capable de se transporter en quelques secondes d'un point en un autre, à des distances considérables, même à Prague. Il venait la nuit tout raconter à son maître. La conclusion de ce long épisode qu'il est inutile de résumer pour notre propos est la suivante: 'Le conte de Foies est-il servy d'un tel messagier?' — Respondi l'escuier: 'En bonne vérité, c'est l'ymagination de pluseurs hommes en Berne que oil; car on ne fait riens ou pais ne ailleurs aussi, quant il met parfaictement sa cure, que il ne sache tantost' (XII, 180-1).

Cette société aristocratique a le goût de la violence et du meurtre. Voilà un dernier thème que Froissart privilégie volontiers. Sans revenir sur le drame d'Orthez, signalons par exemple l'épisode au cours duquel Fébus frappe à coup de dague son cousin Pierre-Arnaud de Béarn, le chef des Compagnons de Lourdes, avant de l'envoyer mourir dans une prison. Nous sommes ici déjà en plein romantisme médiéval avant la lettre, et ce d'autant plus que ce récit est controuvé.

En effet Froissart ne vérifie jamais la véracité des affirmations de ses interlocuteurs. Dans sa rédaction définitive, il se soucie peu de la véracité du récit, beaucoup plus de son effet littéraire que de son exactitude; manifestement il retranscrit mot à mot ce qu'il a entendu sans tenter de se livrer à une critique interne, sans s'informer sur la rectitude de certaines affirmations. C'est en particulier le cas pour ce meurtre de Pierre-Arnaud de Béarn, chef des Compagnons de Lourdes: cet exemple mérite un peu plus d'explication.

Des documents d'archives irréfutables prouvent que Pierre-Arnaud de Béarn, a qui le Prince Noir avait confié le château de Lourdes au lendemain du traité de Brétigny était devenu rapidement un pion manié sur l'échiquier méridional par Gaston III, d'autant plus qu'une grande partie de la garnison était d'origine béarnaise, comme son chef. La complicité entre Fébus et Pierre-Arnaud aboutit même à une manoeuvre, fort subtile, permettant au premier d'occuper la Bigorre. *Les Compagnons de Lourdes* exerçant une menace permanente sur les villages de Bigorre, leurs habitants n'eûrent d'autre ressource que de se tourner vers le seigneur de Béarn pour lui demander aide et protection. Celui-ci accepta d'envoyer des garnisons béarnaises chargées de les protéger contre les *Compagnons*, moyennant finances bien entendu. Tous les villages occupés, les attaques cessèrent comme par enchantement. La raison est simple, Fébus et Pierre-Arnaud étaient d'accord, le premier ristournant au second une partie de l'argent versé par les malheureux Bigourdans pour être protégés contre les routiers! Des documents d'archives irréfutables, en quantité, le démontrent de façon indiscutable.

Froissart a donné une tout autre version de l'affaire recueillie auprès d'Espan du Lion quand ils chevauchaient en Bigorre. En voici la trame. Le comte de Foix aurait convoqué son cousin bâtard pour lui demander de lui remettre le château de Lourdes. Pierre-Arnaud aurait refusé avec dignité alléguant qu'il ne pouvait trahir son honneur car il tenait la forteresse du roi d'Angleterre: 'Quant le comte de Foeis oy ceste response, si ly mua le sens en felonnie et en courroux, et dist en tirant hors une dague: 'Faulx traitre, as-tu dit ce mot de non faire? Par ceste teste, tu ne l'as pas dit pour neant'. Adont fery-il de sa dague sur le chevalier, par telle maniere que il le navra moult villainement en v lieux, ne il n'y avoit là baron ne chevalier qui osast aler au devant. Le chevalier disoit bien: 'Ha! monseigneur, vous ne faictes pas gentillesce. Vous m'avez mandé et si m'occiez'. Mais point n'arresta jusques à tant qu'il lue ot donné v colz d'une dague, et puis après commanda le conte qu'il fust mis en la fosse. Il y fut et là morut, car il fut povrement curez de ses playes' (XII, 62).

Admirable récit, faisant surgir à nos yeux la vision d'un Fébus hors de lui même, le poignard à la main, frappant à coups redoublés devant une assistance muette de terreur. A tout ceci un seul inconvénient: quelques années plus tard après la date de cet assassinat, Pierre-Arnaud attaquait avec ses hommes la région de Casteljaloux, essayait de recommencer — toujours pour le compte de Fébus — une opération identique à celle de Bigorre au détriment des sujets du comte d'Armagnac. Mieux encore Pierre-Arnaud figure dans la liste des personnes ayant assisté aux obsèques du comte de Foix en 1391! Avec un peu de chance Froissart aurait pu croiser ce mort dans les couloirs du château Moncade à Orthez. Tout cela n'est qu'une fable inventée par l'esprit fertile d'Espan du Lion et pieusement recueillie, sans le moindre esprit critique, par Froissart car elle correspondait trop bien à ce genre d'histoire que goûtaient tant ses lecteurs. Mais cette affaire de Pierre-Arnaud de Béarn n'est pas la seule gasconade gratifiée par Espan du Lion au malheureux Froissart.[1] Il y a même beaucoup plus fort comme mystification.

Au cours de leur périple Espan et Froissart passèrent par Cazères-sur-Garonne. Espan fit remarquer à son compagnon un pan de muraille 'plus neuf que les autres' (XII, 28) et lui donna l'explication suivante. Le sire de Béarn ayant vaincu l'an 1362, en la Saint Nicolas d'hiver, l'armée du comte Armagnac (effectivement cette victoire mémorable eut lieu le 5 décembre), fit prisonnier son adversaire ainsi que de nombreux autres chevaliers 'assez près du Mont de Marsen'. Sans aucune peine Froissart aurait pu apprendre que Launac, lieu de la bataille, cité dans un autre passage de ses récits, était en réalité fort loin de Mont-de-Marsan, aux portes de Toulouse. Libéré et désireux de se venger, le comte d'Armagnac reprit les hostilités. Après une rapide chevauchée, il s'empara de Cazères-sur-Garonne. Averti, Gaston III rassembla ses troupes au château de Pau, fonça et mit le siège autour de Cazères-sur-Garonne. Pris au piège, Armagnac accepta de négocier sa rédition et c'est alors que nous trouvons le fameux épisode de la brèche dans la muraille: 'On lui fist faire ung pertuis ou mur que ne fu pas trop grant, par lequel ung et ung ilz issoient, et là estoit sur le chemin le conte de Foies armé et toutes ses gens et en ordennance de bataille. Et ainsi que ceulx issoient, ilz trouvoeint qu'ilz les recueilloit et amenoit devers le conte' (XII, 30). Les prisonniers furent répartis dans divers châteaux et relachés contre de nouvelles rançons. Espan du Lion précise: 'y a environ x ans il en avint' (XII, 28), soit vers 1378.

La réalité est loin de cette fiction.[2] En septembre 1376, les hostilités effectivement rouvertes entre Foix et Armagnac, Gaston III dégagea le pays de Foix un moment attaqué par son ennemi, puis s'avança vers le coeur du pays d'Armagnac en assiégeant Barcelonne-du-Gers. Pour se dégager, le comte d'Armagnac prit par surprise Cazères-de-Marsan qui servait de base aux assaillants. Obligé de faire demi-tour, Fébus enferma les Armagnacs dans Cazères-de-Marsan. Louis d'Anjou, soucieux de rétablir la paix, intervint et ménagea une trève qui permit aux assiégés de sortir avec les honneurs de la guerre le 12 novembre 1376. Dans cette affaire, il semble exclu que Froissart ait mélangé deux récits distincts d'Espan du Lion, confondu Cazères-sur-Garonne avec Cazères-de-Marsan. La scène est trop réelle avec Espan arrêté devant les murs de Cazères-sur-Garonne, montrant du doigt à Froissart l'emplacement de la fameuse brèche par où seraient sortis les vaincus! Il semble également peu probable qu'Espan du Lion ait été à ce point brouillé avec la géographie. Il s'est tout simplement payé le plaisir de se moquer de ce célèbre écrivain venu de son lointain Hainaut, en mélangeant un peu de vrai, à beaucoup de faux, savourant par avance le fait que sa belle invention serait répercutée par le chroniqueur.

Il est donc bien établi que pendant son voyage en Béarn, Froissart n'a absolument pas cherché à vérifier ce qu'il entendait. Il était ainsi exposé à recueillir de belles fables au lieu d'histoires véridiques et, ceci est le point le plus grave à mettre au passif de sa crédibilité, ne se souciait pas au moment de la rédaction d'éliminer de telles fables. Il est enfin possible de discerner un dernier défaut en matière de véracité à côté de sa vision étroite du monde chevaleresque et de cette absence de vérification des affirmations les plus abracadabrantes. Froissart pouvait se laisser abuser par la flatterie; on peut même se demander parfois s'il n'est pas le complice objectif de ce procédé. Ceci met en cause son célèbre portrait du comte de Foix.

'Le gentil conte de Foeis' est au centre de toutes les pages écrites par Froissart sur son voyage dans le Midi pyrénéen. Ou bien il occupe le devant de la scène, ou bien son action est présente à travers les exploits racontés. Même s'il le charge de crimes qu'il n'a point commis, même s'il lui donne une dimension souvent inquiétante, sa personnalité étant entourée comme d'un halo de mystère, de gloire, de faste et de cruauté, le chroniqueur n'en donne pas moins un portrait d'ensemble particulièrement flatteur. Au total Fébus — et curieusement on ne trouve aucune allusion à ce surnom choisi pourtant par le comte lui même — est en quelque sorte le modèle de la chevalerie. Deux passages suffisent pour juger du ton général du récit: 'et vous di et aussi vous le direz, quant l'acointance et la coignoissance de li aurez, et oy parler vous l'arez, et l'estat et l'ordonnance de son hostel vous verrez, que il est aujourd'uy le plus saige prince qui vive et que nulz hauls sires, telz que le roy de France ou le roy d'Engleterre, courceroit le plus envies. De ses autres voisins, du roy d'Arragon ne du roy de Navarre ne fait-il compte, car il ne fineroit plus de gens d'armes, tant a-il acquis d'amis par ses dons et tant puet-il avoir par ses deniers, que ces deux roys ne feroient, et une fois ou deux je li ay oy dire que quant le roy de Cippre fu en son pays de Berne et il li remonstra le voyage du Saint Sepulcre, il l'en enamora si à faire ung grant conquest par delà, que se le roy de France et le roy d'Engleterre y feussent alez, après eulx ce eust esté le sire qui y eust mené le plus grant route et qui eust fait le greigneur fait' (XII, 46).

Certes ces paroles sortent de la bouche d'Espan du Lion; mais Froissart n'en ôte pas un mot et les prend finalement à son compte quand il donne lui même ses impressions sur son séjour à Orthez: 'Le conte de Foeis dont je parle, en ce temps que je fus devers luy, avoit environ cinquante neuf ans d'eage, et vous di que j'ay en mon temps veu moult de chevaliers, roys, princes et autres, mais je n'en vey oncques nul qui fust de si biaux membres, de si belle forme ne de si belle taille, viaire bel et rouvelent et riant, les yeux viers et amoureux, là où ly plaisoit son regard à asseir. De toutes choses il estoit si très parfait que on ne le pourroit trop loer' (XII, 76). 'Briefment et tout considéré, avant que je venisse en sa court, je avoie esté en moult de cours de roys, de ducs, de princes, de contes de haultes dames, mais je ne fus oncques en nulle qui mieulx me pleust, ne qui plus resjoye sur le fait d'armes estoit comme celle du conte de Foeis' (XII, 78).

Manifestement les deux hommes ont cherché à se séduire mutuellement.

Gaston III pressentait qu'il serait jugé à travers les siècles en fonction des écrits du célèbre chroniqueur. Il sut multiplier les prévenances qui vont droit au coeur, le traitant comme un familier de sa cour, et surtout discutant lettres et littérature avec lui. Il procura à Froissart le plaisir le plus raffiné pour un auteur en lui demandant de lire chaque soir, devant la cour, des passages de son *Meliador*, cet interminable poème vantant les exploits d'un chevalier, réprimant toute expression d'ennui ou d'indifférence chez les gens de sa suite! Ce sont des heures que la vanité d'un auteur ne saurait oublier. Fortement marqué par son séjour à Orthez, Froissart écrivit dans ses *Pastourelle* un *Dit du Florin* (le titre fait allusion à la dérisoire poignée de florins que lui donna Fébus avant de prendre congé de lui) où il chanta sans retenue la gloire de son hôte; seuls les rois de France et d'Angleterre le surpassaient en faste; il était en ce domaine l'égal de Berry et de Bourgogne.

L'historien n'a aucune peine à discerner une grande exagération dans tout ceci. Par exemple le château d'Orthez ne pouvait soutenir la comparaison avec les multiples résidences des ducs de Berry ou de Bourgogne. Il était si exigu sur son tertre que le comte ne pouvait y loger ses visiteurs obligés de peupler les auberges de la ville. Au lieu d'un homme généreux, distribuant à foison les dons (il ne remit que quatre-vingts florins à Froissart!) les documents d'archives révèlent un homme avant tout soucieux de ménager son trésor, devenant même d'une avarice sordide à la fin de ses jours. Il faut donc manier avec beaucoup de précaution tous ces passages dythirambiques et constater, une nouvelle fois, que Froissart a souvent restreint volontairement son champ de vision: il connaissait parfaitement l'amour de Fébus pour les chiens de chasse, puisqu'il lui avait amené à titre de présent quelques beaux lévriers, devait savoir qu'il avait écrit un *Livre des oraisons*, un *Livre de chasse* d'une très grande qualité; de celui-ci il ne souffle mot.

Manifestement, Froissart a voulu voir dans le comte de Foix le héros type après lequel il courrait depuis des années: vaillant chevalier, amoureux des arts, généreux et fastueux, mais en même temps soupçonneux, cruel. Est-ce à dire que toutes ces remarques doivent conduire l'historien à jeter aux orties toutes ces admirables pages du voyage dans le Midi pyrénéen? Nullement. Froissart abonde en détails, en scènes croquées sur le vif, par lui même, vérifiées jusque par le menu par divers documents d'archives. Prenons quelques exemples: l'ordonnance du souper de la Noël 1388 avec ses trois tables placées sous la surveillance d'Espan du Lion (XII, 116-7); sa description des cérémonies commémoratives de la victoire de Launac, avec une retraite aux flambeaux pendant laquelle on chantait, pour la plus grande gloire du comte, le psaume de David (XII, 94-5). Même si cela ne correspond pas à une préoccupation majeure de Froissart, il décrit au détour de son récit, avec une exactitude rigoureuse, comment le comte de Foix instaura un fouage permanent dans ses domaines (XII, 47). Bref ces pages des *Chroniques* fourmillent d'une masse considérable de faits authentiques, mais l'historien doit avoir toujours son attention aux aguets pour éliminer le faux, l'invraisemblable, l'exagéré de l'authentique, et pour résister au charme se dégageant de ces pages écrite par un homme au faîte de son talent.

Dans la vie de Froissart et ses *Chroniques*, ce lointain déplacement jusqu'au pied des Pyrénées occupe une place privilégié. Il précède son dernier grand voyage à la cour de Richard II, avant sa retraite studieuse à Chimay où la mort vint en 1410. Peut-être Froissart avait-il conscience qu'il s'agissait là de sa dernière grande aventure de reporter avant le moment inévitable, l'âge venant, de la stabilité? La place qu'il donne au Béarn dans son oeuvre poétique confirme la forte impression produite sur lui par le 'gentil conte de Foies'. Il garde les yeux fixés sur cette lointaine région, y conserve des informateurs. Quand Fébus meurt en 1391, les *Chroniques* consacrent à l'évènement et aux obsèques des pages admirables, extrêmement détaillées, sans que l'on puisse connaître sa source d'information et où, comme à l'accoutumée, il est fort difficile de séparer le bon grain de l'ivraie.[3] C'est l'occasion pour Froissart de dire un dernier adieu au châtelain d'Orthez dont il avait conservé un souvenir ému.

Toutes ces pages consacrées à Gaston Fébus ont lourdement pesé sur le destin posthume du sire de Foix-Béarn. Il n'avait pas eu tort de le choyer, de le flatter, se doutant que son image traverserait les siècles à travers la vision de Froissart. Parfois même Froissart a rendu un mauvais service à son héros car à partir du dix-neuvième siècle des romanciers se sont emparés du personnage, démarquant et pillant Froissart, sans jamais d'ailleurs l'égaler, ajoutant encore plus de fantastique et d'invraisemblable. Bien des erreurs trouvent leur source dans les *Chroniques*; même des auteurs en apparence sérieux continuent à prétendre que Fébus fut présent à la bataille de Crécy, sur une simple affirmation de Froissart, alors que le seigneur de Foix-Béarn évita soigneusement de répondre à toute convocation de Philippe VI et jeta les bases de l'indépendance du Béarn grâce à cette défaite française.

L'analyse du début du livre III des *Chroniques* permet de vérifier un certain nombre de faits bien connus à propos de Froissart. Il s'agit vraiment de l'ancêtre de nos grands reporters qui parcourent le monde afin de vivre du résultat de leurs enquêtes où le sensationnel, voire l'insolite, tiennent une place de choix pour retenir l'attention des lecteurs. Ce professionnel de la plume dut tenir compte du goût de sa clientèle d'alors, les milieux des cours occidentales. En conséquence, probablement aussi par inclination personnelle, il restreint son champ de vision faisant de lui, le plus souvent, une sorte d'amateur de la chronique mondaine, militaire et diplomatique. De tout ceci se dégage une vision étroite des faits. A travers les tournois (il n'en dit mot pendant son voyage en Béarn car Fébus ne pratiquait pas ce genre de divertissement), les banquets, les beaux coups d'épée, il cherche à donner aux générations futures une sorte de code moral de l'honneur, un 'Livre des faits d'armes et de chevalerie' et trouve le prototype du parfait chevalier sur les bords du gave de Pau, à Orthez.

Enfin Froissart est bien un miroir aux mille facettes. Malgré son art du récit, sa composition rigoureuse, il restitue la parole aux centaines de gens qu'il a eu l'occasion d'interroger. Le Bascot de Mauléon, Espan du Lion, pour reprendre les noms de ses deux principaux interlocuteurs pendant son voyage dans le Midi pyrénéen, demeurent pour nous des figures vivantes. Nul doute que les *Chroniques* ne nous transmettent fidèlement la teneur même de leurs paroles. Pour garder fraicheur et vivacité à son texte, Froissart a senti la nécessité de perpétuer pour le lecteur cette impression du direct, du vécu, de l'interview. Ce charme a ses limites, fort étroites pour l'historien. On ne saurait prendre pour argent comptant tout ce qui se trouve dans les *Chroniques*; cette source irremplaçable doit être critiquée pas à pas et son authenticité dépend finalement de la valeur des témoignages recueillis. Quand Espan du Lion se laisse aller à enfourcher les chevaux de l'imagination nous atteignons le sublime dans la fausseté, quand le Bascot de Mauléon décrit un épisode de la bataille de Poitiers nous sommes vraiment au coeur de la mêlée. Dans ces conditions porter un jugement d'ensemble sur la valeur des *Chroniques* me semble fort dangereux: à chaque épisode correspond un certain type de vérité, et dans chaque épisode tout dépend du degré de crédibilité des informateurs puisque Froissart a surtout voulu collecter des informations sans se livrer ensuite à un travail de réflexion critique approfondi sur elles.

IX FROISSART: ART MILITAIRE, PRATIQUE ET CONCEPTION DE LA GUERRE *

Philippe Contamine

À L'ÉVIDENCE, la guerre se situe au centre même de l'entreprise de Froissart chroniqueur, et cela même si, pour notre plaisir et notre instruction, il est loin d'être demeuré étroitement fidèle à son dessein primordial. Dessein qu'on trouve formulé dans le prologue, lorsqu'il déclare vouloir enregistrer et faire connaître à ses contemporains aussi bien qu'aux générations futures 'les grans merveilles et li biau fait d'armes, qui sont avenu par les grans guerres de France et d'Engleterre et des royaumes voisins' (I, 1).

Par un autre trait encore l'oeuvre de Froissart se différencie de la majorité des autres chroniques: l'abondance des développements consacrés à des épisodes, à des événements d'apparence tout à fait mineure. Froissart prend son temps, abandonne le chemin principal où devrait le conduire l'axe de son récit, n'hésite pas à s'enfoncer dans une voie de traverse pour conter une anecdote savoureuse: l'assaut d'une forteresse, le bon tour joué par un compagnon d'aventures, l' 'apertise d'armes' d'un jeune bachelier face aux barrières d'une cité.

Ce n'est pas cependant que l'art de Froissart soit désintéressé ni que son discours soit gratuit. L'écrivain ne se perd qu'en apparence dans les méandres d'une narration encombrée d'éléments adventices. Même lorsqu'il semble uniquement soucieux de divertir son public, subsiste, derrière le cliquetis des noms propres et l'entassement des formules imagées, une volonté latente ou affirmée de didactisme. Froissart entend fournir aux jeunes gentilshommes, aux écuyers débutant dans le métier des armes, qu'ils soient riches ou pauvres, 'matere et exemple', il veut leur procurer des modèles, des héros pour s'y référer ou s'y comparer. Les *Chroniques* sont et seront 'la memore des bons et li recors des preus'.[1] Car le public qu'il vise n'est pas seulement celui des rois, des princes et autres grands seigneurs, susceptibles d'acquérir ces coûteux manuscrits enluminés qui sont parvenus jusqu'à nous, mais aussi le commun de la classe chevaleresque, autrement dit le milieu social qui, organiquement, avait partie liée avec la guerre et aurait perdu un élément fondamental de son être en refusant les épreuves et les délices: 'Si com la busce ne poet ardoir sans feu, ne poet li gentilz homs venir à parfaite honneur ne à la glore dou monde, sans proèce' (I, 2).

Ne peut-on dire, à la limite, que, sous une forme plaisante, Froissart a voulu donner l'équivalent d'un manuel des études militaires, inspiré de l'expérience la plus contemporaine, la plus actuelle, et donc plus utile que le traité classique et démodé de Végèce, même dans ses versions en langue vulgaire? Chez Froissart,

* All references to the *Chroniques* are to volume and page of the SHF edition unless otherwise stated.

doit se manifester, au bout du compte, l'homme de guerre total, dans la plénitude de ses capacités et de ses responsabilités, en sorte que chacun puisse se mettre à l'école de 'cesti qui mist ceste cevaucie ou ceste armée sus, et qui ordonna ceste bataille si faiticement et le gouverna si sagement, et qui jousta de fier de glave si radement, et qui tresperça les conrois de ses ennemis par deus ou par trois fois, et qui se combati si vassaument ou qui entreprist ceste besongne si hardiement, et qui fu trouvés entre les mors et les bleciés navrés moult durement, et ne daigna onques fuir en place où il se trouvast' (I, 4).

Soucieux d'être le plus véridique possible, Froissart ne fit pas seulement usage de l'oeuvre de Jean le Bel, il ne consulta pas seulement des manuscrits de l'école historiographique de Saint-Denis, il ne se borna pas à insérer dans son texte diverses pièces officielles: il est redevable de l'essentiel de sa documentation au témoignage de très nombreux princes, seigneurs, chevaliers et écuyers, maréchaux et poursuivants d'armes, eux-mêmes témoins directs ou acteurs des événements qu'ils lui rapportèrent. Ces souvenirs, plus ou moins proches, plus ou moins fidèles, furent soigneusement notés par le chroniqueur, puis amalgamés, classifiés, ordonnés. De par la multiplicité même de ses informations, Froissart pouvait légitimement estimer avoir atteint un degré élevé de véracité et d'impartialité. 'Partout où je venois, je faisois enqueste aux anciens chevaliers et escuyers qui avoient esté en faits d'armes et qui proprement en savoient parler.' 'Si fus informé des deux parties et bien se concordoient les uns les autres.'[2]

De cette information prise aux bonnes sources donnons ici quelques exemples. À plusieurs reprises Jean Chandos l'entretint de la bataille manquée de Buironfosse, en 1339, où il avait été adoubé (I, 471). Froissart put connaître le déroulement de la rencontre de Nevill's Cross, en 1346, grâce à plusieurs chevaliers écossais interviewés lors de son séjour à la cour de David II d'Écosse, en 1365. Pour la bataille d'Auray, la distance entre l'événement et l'information fut spécialement réduite puisque cinq jours seulement après son déroulement, il put, alors qu'il se trouvait à Douvres en compagnie d'Édouard III, disposer de la missive adressée au roi d'Angleterre par Jean de Montfort, entendre un 'varlés poursievans d'armes' présent à l'affaire, tout cela complété ultérieurement par les témoignages de certains chevaliers appartenant à l'un et l'autre camps (VI, 173-4, 346).

Conscient de sa valeur en tant qu'écrivain, assuré d'autre part de la survie de son oeuvre,[3] Froissart, au terme de ses rédactions successives, pouvait se targuer d'avoir produit un récit ample, didactique, une 'juste et vraie histoire', résultat d'une 'juste enqueste' fondée 'sur title de verité'. Comment dès lors ne pas estimer que la façon dont il dépeint la guerre et dont il en évoque les protagonistes, quels que soient leur rang, leur rôle, leur nation, est bien le reflet aussi fidèle que possible de la réalité, en sorte que son témoignage mériterait d'être préféré à tous les autres?

Une première objection se présente. En dépit de ses voyages et de ses errances à travers une bonne partie de l'Occident, Froissart est loin d'avoir visité lui-même tous les pays où se déroulent les conflits dont il parle d'abondance: ainsi les guerres d'Espagne et de Portugal, le 'voyage de Barbarie' (1390), la croisade de Nicopolis (1396). De plus, ne serait-ce qu'en raison de son état de clerc, il ne semble pas que Froissart se soit jamais battu en personne. A-t-il connu d'expérience le poids de l'armure sur le corps? S'est-il jamais exercé au maniement de l'épée ou de la lance? Le courage et la peur ont-ils été pour lui autre chose que des abstractions? Mettre son corps, son honneur, sa chevance, tout, en aventure de mort ou de prison: a-t-il vécu la formule de l'intérieur, ou bien, pour en restituer l'épaisseur charnelle, s'est-il seulement fié aux ressources, indéniables il est vrai, de sa sensibilité et de son imagination?

Plus grave peut-être: s'il a pu, à coup sûr, observer le rassemblement de quelques armées, admirer des dizaines de villes fortifiées et de châteaux, constater *de visu* les ravages de la guerre sur le plat pays, s'il lui arriva d'être convié à des fêtes, à des noces princières, s'il goûta en connaisseur les fastes des joutes et des tournois, il ne paraît pas, en revanche, avoir jamais assisté à aucune bataille rangée ni même (sauf peut-être en 1383 lors de la campagne de Flandre, en supposant qu'il y ait accompagné son patron et seigneur Gui de Blois) à aucun siège en règle. C'est dire que son expérience directe de la guerre est inférieure à celle de chroniqueurs antérieurs comme Villehardouin et Robert de Clari, ou contemporains comme Jean le Bel, dont il rappelle comment il fut blessé d'une flèche, en 1327, lors d'une campagne en Écosse (I, 263), Jean, bâtard de Wavrin, présent aux journées d'Azincourt, de Cravant et de Verneuil, le héraut Chandos, témoin oculaire de la campagne d'Espagne menée par le Prince noir en 1367, le Religieux de Saint-Denis (sans doute Michel Pintoin[4]), dont on peut penser, pour le moins, qu'il accompagna Charles VI lors de la chevauchée du Mans de 1392, lors de la campagne de Berry de 1412 et lors du siège de Compiègne de 1414. On admettra malgré tout que la position de Froissart est plus assurée que celle, par exemple, du 'povre pelerin' picard Jean Cabaret d'Orreville lorsqu'il transcrit dans sa *Chronique du bon duc Loys de Bourbon* les souvenirs attendris et embrouillés du chevalier Jean de Châteaumorand, un demi-siècle *post eventum*.[5]

Donc, entre Froissart et la guerre, une certaine distance, un certain intervalle, où viennent s'insérer les témoignages de ses informateurs. Faut-il dès lors rendre ces derniers responsables des erreurs et des flottements qu'on n'a pas manqué de relever, spécialement dans les domaines de la géographie et de la chronologie? Campagnes antidatées, décalage de quelques jours dans la datation d'une bataille, absence de tout millésime dans les récits dont se régale notre chroniqueur: autant de travers qu'on ne peut ignorer depuis les érudites investigations d'un Siméon Luce, d'un F. Plaine, d'un Bertrandy.[6] De même que ne manquent ni les noms de lieux estropiés au point d'être devenus méconnaissables, ni les châteaux impossibles à identifier, ni les chevauchées difficiles à reporter sur la carte. L'examen du terrain ne permet guère de comprendre le dispositif du prince de Galles lors de la bataille de Poitiers (1356) tel que Froissart nous le rapporte: où situer le chemin 'forteffiet malement de haies et de buissons', à quoi peut correspondre la haie garnie d'archers, qu'on nous présente comme la seule voie d'accès aux 'batailles' anglo-gasconnes, si étroite que quatre hommes seulement pouvaient y chevaucher de front?[7] Autre exemple: pour la bataille de Cocherel, le texte de Froissart est trop vague pour qu'on puisse situer la 'montagne' surmontée d'un 'fort buisson espinerés' où vinrent s'installer les Anglo-Navarrais, au point qu'on peut hésiter entre la rive droite et la rive gauche de l'Eure (VI, 114-15).[8]

La critique historique s'est également attachée à souligner les grossières inexactitudes de Froissart dans son estimation des effectifs. À propos des chevauchées anglaises, Édouard Perroy écrit: 'Les gens du Moyen Age, brouillés avec les chiffres, nous ont donné ... des précisions numériques indignes de créance et que contredit toute la documentation administrative mise à jour par les érudits modernes' (1945: 74). Condamnation qui semble pouvoir s'appliquer à Froissart plus qu'à tout autre chroniqueur, ne serait-ce que parce que ses estimations varient sans raison objective d'un remaniement à l'autre de son oeuvre, et qu'il les assortit parfois de précisions telles que pendant longtemps elles emportèrent la conviction. À suivre par exemple le manuscrit d'Amiens, lors de la campagne de Buironfosse de 1339, l'ost du souverain Valois aurait compté quatre rois, cinq ducs, exactement 227 bannières et 2,705 chevaliers, et aussi, cette fois en chiffres ronds, 80,000 hommes d'armes et plus de 60,000 communiers (I, 472). En septembre 1340, les forces anglo-flamandes qui assiégeaient Tournai se seraient élevées à 120,000 hommes d'armes. Des effectifs de 100,000 hommes se rencontrent aussi bien en 1346, aux côtés de Jean, duc de Normandie, qu'en 1379 lorsque les Flamands tentèrent de s'emparer d'Audenarde, en 1385 lors du siège de Damme par Charles VI. 100,000 hommes encore dans les armées françaises du 'voyage de la mer' (1386) et du 'voyage d'Allemagne' (1388). Pour l'armée ottomane de Nicopolis, l'estimation grimpe à 200,000 combattants. Et pour l'ost de Bourbourg de 1383 à 300,000 chevaux — un record! — quitte à ce que, dans un autre endroit de son récit, Froissart fournisse des chiffres sensiblement différents, quoique toujours par trop généreux: 'Fu par les hiraus nombrés li nombres des chevaliers, que li rois [Charles VI] eut devant Bourbourc, à noef mille et set chens chevaliers, et estoient en toute somme vint et quatre mille hommes d'armes, chevaliers et escuiers, et cinc cens' (XI, 134-5).

Dans le même ordre d'idée, on a jugé et on juge encore très exagérés, invraisemblables, les chiffres des pertes, du moins du côté des vaincus: à Montiel (1369), jusqu'à 30,000 morts dans l'armée de Pierre le Cruel, à Roosebeke (1382), 26,000 tués chez les Flamands de Philippe van Artevelde, sans compter les massacres lors de la poursuite; à Crécy (1346), pas moins de 31,291 victimes dans le camp de Philippe de Valois, selon le 'juste rapport' des chevaliers qu'Édouard III chargea officiellement de recenser les cadavres (III, 190).

L'exubérance statistique de Froissart est apparue d'autant plus trompeuse qu'elle n'est pas uniforme et que, pour les besoins de la cause, il lui est arrivé de grossir sans retenue les effectifs de l'un des protagonistes tout en maintenant ceux de l'adversaire dans des limites raisonnables. Du coup, le déroulement et le dénouement de la bataille se transforment en énigme historique. Comment expliquer la victoire du prince de Galles à Poitiers quand on oppose 14,000 Anglo-Gascons à 60,000 Français? Comment rendre compte de l'issue de Montiel si l'on admet que le vainqueur Henri de Trastamare se battit à un contre six?[9] À Crécy, le manuscrit de Rome exalte la victoire de 16,000 Anglais sur 100,000 Français: là aussi, un rapport d'un contre six (III, 404).

La suspicion s'étend encore à l'étendue relative des pertes. On admettra difficilement le bien-fondé du rapport établi par les quatre chevaliers et les quatre hérauts envoyés sur le champ de bataille de Nájera par le Prince noir, après sa victoire: quatre chevaliers, vingt archers et quarante soudoyers tués chez les vainqueurs, contre 5,060 hommes d'armes et 7,500 communiers (plus les noyés) chez les vaincus. À Crécy, pertes anglaises limitées à trois chevaliers et vingt archers.

La critique de Froissart chroniqueur des guerres de son temps ne s'étend pas au seul domaine quantitatif ni même aux erreurs matérielles flagrantes. On peut aussi s'interroger sur la véracité de son discours dans la mesure où il paraît souvent s'enfermer à l'intérieur d'un nombre relativement restreint de schémas tout faits, stéréotypés, à caractère répétitif. Il est facile d'épingler, presque d'un bout à l'autre des *Chroniques*, toute une foule de menus épisodes construits selon un modèle uniforme: deux troupes se surprennent, s'affrontent, bannières déployées et pennons au vent, jusqu'à ce que l'une d'elles soit défaite. D'un récit à l'autre, les mêmes expressions se rencontrent, que Froissart n'avait qu'à décrocher dans les réserves de sa 'forge' de Chimay ou de Valenciennes: 'Là eut dur hustin et fort et bien combatu, et pluisseurs reverssés d'un lés et de l'autre' (VII, 338). Ou encore: 'Là se combatirent li François et li Englès un grant temps . . . et y eut fait maintes grans apertises d'armes' (VII, 204). Le combat achevé, allégresse chez les vainqueurs, qui ont accru leur honneur et se sont enrichis de bonnes prises, courroux, douleur et mélancolie chez les vaincus, 'mais pour cette fois ils ne le peurent amender'. Et le chroniqueur de conclure: 'Une fois perdoient et l'autre gaegnoient, ensi que les aventures aviennent en telz fais d'armes et en samblables' (VII, 119).[10]

Le même caractère répétitif se rencontre lorsqu'il s'agit d'évoquer l'assaut d'une forteresse: c'est d'abord l'arrivée des combattants, qui examinent le lieu, se mettent en bonne ordonnance, disposent leurs gens de trait, entassent toutes sortes de matériaux pour combler les fossés. Les assaillants s'avancent alors, et, à l'abri de leurs targes et de leurs pavois, s'approchent de la muraille, pics à la main, pour établir une brèche. Naturellement, ceux du dedans résistent de leur mieux: pluie de flèches, jets de pierres. L'issue est variable: tantôt, découragés, les attaquants se retirent, tantôt une négotiation intervient, qui permettra aux assiégés de s'en aller librement, tantôt au contraire la place est emportée d'un seul élan, et il n'est pas rare, alors, que les vaincus soient passés au fil de l'épée, sous un prétexte quelconque.

Il n'est pas jusqu'aux amples récits des 'batailles mortelles' qui n'obéissent, en dépit de leur rareté, à des règles assez strictement définies. Cela commence par l'énumération détaillée des forces en présence, jointe à la mention nominale des principaux seigneurs. Puis on passe à l'ordonnance des deux armées, leur arroi, leur disposition en conrois et en 'batailles'. Une place est faite aux rites qui précèdent toute rencontre digne de ce nom: confessions, messes et communions, harangues que les chefs adressent à leurs troupes pour les stimuler, rappeler leur bon droit, leur 'juste querelle', promotion des 'chevaliers nouveaux' qui viennent ensuite se placer, de préférence, à l'avant-garde, là où ils auront l'occasion de déployer leur jeune valeur. Un dernier coup d'oeil, le plus souvent admiratif: 'Si vous di que c'estoit moult belle cose à veoir et à considerer, car on y veoit banières, pennons parés et armoiiés de tous costés moult richement' (VI, 157). Les chefs peuvent alors faire avancer leurs troupes 'bellement le pas', 'cescun sires en son arroi et entre ses gens, et sa banniere ou son pennon devant lui', en ordre si serré — point capital — qu'on ne pourrait jeter en l'air une pomme, une plume, une balle, une prune, qu'elle ne retombe sur un bassinet ou sur une lance. Vient l'affrontement, 'bataille' contre 'bataille', 'grans bouteis et esteceis de lances', 'fort estour et dur', tandis que l'intervention des gens de trait risque d'entraîner la rupture du dispositif. Tout cela dans le fracas des armes et des armures qui s'entrechoquent, au milieu des huées, des cris de guerre qui se répondent d'une bannière à l'autre. Car la guerre chez Froissart est bruit tout autant que fureur.[11] La lutte se prolonge en une sorte de poussée continue et confuse (on songe à la mêlée de deux équipes de rugby) jusqu'à ce que chez l'un des protagonistes un corps de bataille en vienne à reculer, à se 'desroier', à se rompre, à s'ouvrir, 'branler ou desclore'. Des drapeaux sont alors jetés à terre, déchirés. Froissart insiste sur l'effet de panique, si contagieux que tous les efforts de ralliement sont incapables de l'enrayer. La masse des combattants, naguère soudée, s'effiloche, s'éparpille, ou encore, prise comme dans un étau, elle s'effondre sur elle-même. 'Au voir dire, quant une desconfiture vient, li desconfi se desconfisent et esbahissent de trop peu, et sus un cheu, il en chiet trois, et sus trois, dix, et sus dix, trente, et pour dix, se il s'enfuient, il s'enfuient cent' (VI, 166). Tantôt les vainqueurs demeurent sur place, raflant les prisonniers, accumulant les redditions individuelles ou collectives, tantôt ils sont autorisés à poursuivre à cheval les fuyards. Telle est la 'chasse', qui peut durer plusieurs heures et s'étendre sur un rayon de plusieurs lieues. Tôt ou tard, les troupes victorieuses se retrouvent sur le champ de bataille, y campent, après avoir rendu grâces à Dieu pour avoir fait pencher sa balance du côté des justes et des preux. Pendant des rites initiaux: les rites terminaux, recensement et enterrement des morts, mise à rançon des prisonniers, ramassage des dépouilles et partage du butin.

Autrement dit, Froissart fait défiler trop mécaniquement une succession de tableaux, succession certes logique, tableaux à coup sûr vigoureux, mais qui perdent une partie de leur puissance d'évocation, à force d'être sans cesse réutilisés. Son 'montage' (comme on parle du montage d'un cinéaste) tourne parfois à la routine. Son évocation des scènes de guerre fait la part trop belle à l'imagerie, au détriment de la réflexion et de l'analyse.

On peut encore reprocher aux *Chroniques* d'être relativement mal informées des décisions d'état-major, des projets et des objectifs du commandement. C'est la guerre vécue par l'homme d'armes moyen, par le combattant ordinaire (à condition qu'il soit d'origine noble) qui est surtout mise en valeur, plutôt que celle que les chefs s'efforcent de maîtriser, de penser et de conduire. D'où une certaine myopie, un manque relatif de recul et de perspective. Il n'arrive que rarement à Froissart de consigner des renseignements précis et sûrs dans le domaine de la stratégie d'ensemble. Une exception: la campagne de Flandre de 1382, à l'occasion de laquelle le chroniqueur reproduit, comme s'il s'agissait de l'exacte transcription d'un document d'état-major, l'ordre de marche en neuf points de l'armée de Charles VI, élaboré au terme d'un véritable conseil de guerre sous la présidence du connétable de France Olivier de Clisson et transmis ensuite, pour information et exécution, aux moindres seigneurs et barons qui n'avaient pas été convoqués (XI, 5-7).

Enfin, on est en droit de s'interroger sur les déformations que, prisonnier de son idéologie chevaleresque, Froissart a immanquablement fait subir à la réalité. Sa guerre serait trop riche en passes d'armes individuelles (X, 35-7), en descriptions d'armoiries et de bannières, elle compterait trop de joutes et de tournois, de trompettes et de ménestrels. Décor factice, en trompe-l'oeil. Trop de place accordée au fade cerémonial de la courtoisie. La guerre parée de couleurs prestigieuses mais fausses. Bref Froissart coupable à la fois d'idéalisme et d'anachronisme, et d'autant plus trompeur qu'il met au service de ses préjugés son talent de plume, le charme indéniable de sa langue 'patoisante',[12] de sa vive et brillante imagination. Il a fourni à son public le discours sur la guerre que celui-ci attendait, parce que ce discours le flattait, le rassurait, lui donnait bonne conscience, procurait du style et du panache à des actions sauvages, à des comportements sordides, métamorphosait en preux des bandits de grand chemin.

Que Froissart ait ses limites, ses oeillères, qu'il prenne souvent de grandes libertés avec les faits, les noms, les dates, rien de moins contestable. Il est et il sera toujours nécessaire de confronter son témoignage avec celui d'auteurs de sentiments plus populaires (Jean de Venette, l'auteur anonyme de la *Chronique des quatre premiers Valois*), ou dont la position est plus officielle (les *Chroniques de Saint-Denis*) et de vérifier ses dires au moyen des archives publiques et des documents administratifs, surtout de nature financière. Et cependant la tâche n'est pas impossible de montrer que les fautes commises par Froissart à l'égard de la vérité historique sont souvent vénielles, ne conduisent pas en tout cas à des contresens fondamentaux, que son discours est moins univoque qu'on ne l'a parfois soutenu, enfin qu'on trouve chez lui, dans le domaine de la guerre, bien des données essentielles que les autres sources nous livrent avec plus de parcimonie.

Peut-être d'ailleurs les erreurs de fait paraissent-elles moins graves à l'historien d'aujourd'hui, adepte de la longue durée, du 'sériel', de la 'pesée globale', soucieux avant tout de dégager les structures et les mentalités, qu'à l'historien d'hier, singulièrement attaché à la critique ponctuelle des événements et des faits. Qu'importe par exemple que Froissart ait daté du 9 octobre 1364 (et non du 29 septembre) la bataille d'Auray, qu'importe qu'il ait raccourci de quelques jours la durée de tel siège, allongé de quelques semaines la durée de telle campagne? Qu'importe même que la tactique de l' 'Amourath Bacquin' à la bataille de Nicopolis ait bien été celle que Froissart décrit: le plus intéressant ici n'est-il pas que pour notre auteur une manoeuvre d'encerclement — et donc l'existence d'un plan de bataille — sont tout à fait compatibles avec l'idée que lui-même et le public informé, spécialisé, auquel il s'adresse se font d'une bataille livrée selon les règles?[13] Qu'importe encore qu'avant la rencontre de Roosebeke la reconnaissance des positions flamandes ait été effectuée, selon Froissart, par le connétable de France assisté de l'amiral Jean de Vienne et de Guillaume de Poitiers, alors que le Religieux de Saint-Denis, ici plus fiable, confie cette tâche, dans sa chronique, à douze éclaireurs connaissant le flamand, sous les ordres de Guillaume de Poitiers?[14] On doit surtout retenir, en l'occurrence, que Froissart a estimé plausible qu'un chef d'état-major accomplisse en personne une mission qu'à l'époque de Louis XIV ou de Napoléon on aurait confiée à un officier subalterne.

Même dans le domaine quantitatif (évaluation des effectifs et des pertes), Froissart est peut-être moins grossièrement inexact que ne le pensaient Hans Delbrück (1923) et Ferdinand Lot (1946). Au début de la guerre de Cent ans, des effectifs considérables, s'élevant à des dizaines de milliers de combattants, furent bel et bien réunis, il est vrai pour de courtes périodes, tant du côté de Philippe VI que du côté d'Édouard III et de ses alliés continentaux (Contamine 1972: 70, 73). De nouveau, à la fin du quatorzième siècle, les 'osts' de Charles VI se situèrent à un niveau nullement dérisoire, surtout si l'on inclut les auxiliaires, serviteurs ou valets d'armes, dont toute 'lance' était nécessairement pourvue.[15]

Substantiellement, Froissart n'est pas non plus dans l'erreur lorsqu'il mentionne, à différentes reprises, la disparité des forces en présence et la victoire des moins nombreux. Même si l'on n'accepte pas les proportions qui ressortent de ses chiffres, il faut bien admettre d'une part que les Français furent régulièrement battus par un adversaire numériquement très inférieur, d'autre part que la tactique utilisée sur le terrain permet de rendre compte de ce paradoxe. Dieu donnant la victoire au petit nombre: ce n'était pas là seulement un thème cher à bien des clercs, qui l'illustraient d'exemples bibliques, mais une des possibilités que tout chef de guerre devait envisager. On comprend à la limite que le duc de Bourgogne, en 1369, ait refusé, selon Froissart, d'affronter les Anglais, en dépit d'une supériorité numérique de sept contre un, faute d'avoir obtenu la permission de son frère Charles V (VI, 166). D'autant plus que l'avantage, toujours à suivre Froissart, était à peu près régulièrement aux attaquants, car, quatre fois sur cinq, les 'requerans' l'emportent sur les 'non requerans', et 'on est par nature plus fort et mieulx encoragé en assaillant que on n'est en deffendant' (XII, 143).

Il n'est pas jusqu'au contraste entre les pertes des vaincus et des vainqueurs qu'on ne puisse admettre, à la limite. Une poignée de tués d'un côté, des milliers de victimes de l'autre: ne voyons pas là, nécessairement, le résultat de la propagande des vainqueurs qui, maîtres du terrain, étaient matériellement les seuls en mesure de recenser les cadavres et psychologiquement les mieux placés pour diffuser les nouvelles. Les conditions mêmes de la tactique médiévale peuvent aussi bien rendre compte du phénomène. En effet, elle consistait avant tout 'soit à rompre et à désorganiser le dispositif adverse, soit à l'encercler. Dans le premier cas, la percée entraîne presque toujours la débandade de l'ennemi, qui se laisse en général occire sans résistance au cours de la poursuite qui s'ensuit; dans le second, on assiste au massacre de l'armée, prise dans un étau et incapable de manoeuvre' (Gaier 1968: 74).[16] Ajoutons que, plus souvent qu'on ne s'imagine, les principes de la guerre courtoise étaient délibérément mis de côté et que l''occision' l'emportait alors sur la rançon. Mais même lorsqu'on admettait de faire des prisonniers, il était préférable pour les vaincus de demeurer sur place, de négocier et de faire reconnaître leur reddition, car la 'chasse' s'accompagnait trop facilement de la mise à mort des fuyards. Là encore, les recherches des spécialistes ne font que confirmer Froissart, quand il écrit que 'c'est une rieule general, que le grosse pertes se traient sus les desconfitures' (XIV, 165-6) et ajoute ailleurs que dans la fuite 'avient que il y a plus de perilz que il n'a ou plus fort de la bataille, car en fuiant on chace, on fiert, on tue' (XII, 160).

Si les *Chroniques* souffrent de leur aspect répétitif, il ne faudrait pas croire trop vite à un pastiche pur et simple, d'un épisode à l'autre. Prenons les développements copieux consacrés aux six grandes chevauchées anglaises entre 1359 et 1380. Certes on y retrouve toujours un peu la même atmosphère, les mêmes problèmes, les mêmes dispositifs. À plusieurs reprises (ainsi en 1359 et en 1373) on note les moulins à bras pour moudre le blé, les fours portatifs pour cuire le pain; face à ces invasions successives, l'attitude de la monarchie française, des villes et des populations du plat pays demeure presque identique. Deux fois, pour 1373 (VIII, 168) et pour 1380 (IX, 240), Froissart expose les trois points que les chefs de l'expédition doivent, avant leur départ, s'engager par serment, sous peine de perdre leur honneur, à respecter: (1) mettre tout leur pouvoir à accomplir le voyage dont ils sont chargés; (2) garder un secret inviolable sur leurs projets, (3) ne jamais traiter avec l'ennemi à l'insu ou contre la volonté du roi et de son conseil. Tout cela au point que Roland Delachenal a pu émettre quelque doute sur la solidité du récit de Froissart quant à la chevauchée de Buckingham, en 1380: 'Froissart a indiqué avec une extrême précision les étapes de sa route, la durée des haltes et des séjours, mais sans ajouter quelques dates qui eussent été, pour le lecteur, d'utiles points de repère. ... La précision dont se pique le chroniqueur ne doit pas nous en imposer. Il n'a vraisemblablement pas eu un journal de marche sous les yeux, mais il connaissait bien une partie du pays traversé par l'armée de Buckingham et il lui était facile de paraître minutieusement informé. ... En lisant le récit détaillé de la campagne de 1380, on a le sentiment très net de quelque chose de déjà vu' (1931: 370). Il est permis malgré tout d'être moins sévère et moins sceptique que le rigoureux historien de Charles V. Reportés sur la carte, les déplacements des Anglais demeurent très vraisemblables; on peut, à de rares exceptions près, les dater avec précision, et quand le recoupement est possible grâce à d'autres documents (ainsi lors de la halte sous la cité de Troyes, où se trouvent rassemblées les forces françaises du duc de Bourgogne), Froissart, pour une fois, est pris en flagrant délit d'exactitude: on peut supposer qu'il a recueilli et transmis, en l'occurrence, le témoignage précis de quelque seigneur ou chevalier ayant lui-même effectué la chevauchée.[17]

Un autre de ses mérites est de mettre en relief, avec une grande puissance d'évocation, les conditions concrètes de la guerre, sur lesquelles d'autres narrations, plus sèches, plus impersonnelles, ne daignent pas s'appesantir. Relevons ici quelques exemples de ce souci manifeste de réalisme.

Le climat. Voici l'interminable pluie écossaise qui, en 1327, pourrit le harnois des montures anglaises, transperce les hauquetons, éteint les feux (I, 60). Voici encore le célèbre orage qui éclata à Gallardon, accablant l'armée d'Édouard III, alors qu'elle marchait vers Chartres (VI, 5). Ou encore ces hommes d'armes français qui, en novembre 1382, pataugeaient allègrement dans les marais de Comines, la boue jusqu'aux chevilles. Une prouesse que Froissart nous demande d'admirer: 'Regardés et considerés le paine qu'il eurent et le grant vaillance d'eux, quant à ces longues nuis d'ivier, un mois devant calandes ou environ, toute nuit anuitie en leurs armeures estans sous leur piés, les bachinès en leurs testes, il furent là sans boire et sans mengier' (XI, 18).

Tout autant que le froid et la pluie, Froissart, homme du Nord, semble avoir redouté pour les gens de guerre qu'il met en scène l'excessive chaleur. D'où son appréciation peu flatteuse du climat espagnol ou africain: soleil brûlant, soif ardente que ne peuvent étancher les vins du Midi, trop secs et trop chauds, facilité avec laquelle on tombe 'en fievre et en chaulde maladie', surtout lorsqu'on est de complexion française ou anglaise.[18]

Le lancinant problème des vivres, du ravitaillement, ne se posait pas seulement à une place assiégée, mais aussi à un corps expéditionnaire, selon qu'il se déplaçait en un pays 'apovris', 'exilliés', ou en une 'marche grasse et plainne de tous vivres', dans laquelle il était possible, en garantissant aux villages de ne pas les brûler, d'obtenir en suffisance 'vins et sas de pain et bues et moutons' (VIII, 155). Même en terre amie, nourrir une troupe de quelque importance nécessitait toujours une certaine organisation.

C'est ainsi que Froissart raconte qu'en 1327, l'armée du jeune Édouard III, campée entre l'Écosse et l'Angleterre, à onze lieues de Carlisle et à quatorze lieues de Newcastle-upon-Tyne, connut pénurie et disette. D'où l'envoi de messagers et de bêtes de somme afin d'obtenir des vivres qui seraient payés 'tout sec'. Et de fait, attirés par la perspective d'un profit immédiat et rassurés par la promesse d'un sauf-conduit, les marchands de Newcastle apportèrent, sur des petits chevaux et des mulets, du 'pain mal cuit, en paniers' et du 'povre vin, en grans barilz'. Mais tout cela en trop faible quantité pour prévenir la montée des prix: les *Chroniques* parlent d'un pain vendu quatre esterlins alors qu'il n'aurait dû valoir qu'un parisis, et d'un gallon de vin acheté vingt-quatre esterlins, contre quatre en temps normal. Contre-coup au niveau de la discipline: des 'hustins' et des 'debats' survenaient entre les compagnons affamés (I, 60).

À lire le récit que Froissart a laissé du projet de débarquement en Angleterre (1386), on ne peut manquer d'être frappé par l'importance des questions de ravitaillement, qui apparaissent régulièrement dans la narration. Rassemblons ces données éparses. Durant tout l'été, sur l'ordre de Charles VI, on fit moudre de la farine et cuire du 'pain biscuit' à Tournai, à Lille, à Douai, à Arras, à Béthune, à Saint-Omer, à destination de L'Écluse, port d'embarquement prévu. Vin, chair salée, avoine et sel affluèrent en Flandre, et l'on commença à charger les nefs. De leur côté, les Anglais, qui craignaient que l'expédition ne se muât en une tentative pour prendre Calais, garnirent la place en grains, viande et poisson salés, en vin et en cervoise. À mesure des arrivées, les effectifs français devinrent si nombreux à L'Écluse et tout autour que l'administration royale fut incapable de suffire à la demande. Les grands seigneurs achetaient leurs denrées quatre fois plus cher qu'en temps normal, tandis que les 'petis compaignons, chevaliers et escuiers' étaient dans l'obligation de vendre leur équipement et devaient se défaire pour des sommes dérisoires d'armures achetées naguère au prix fort. Une fois l'expédition décommandée, sur intervention du duc de Berry, il fut ordonné de stocker les vivres qui pouvaient se conserver d'une année sur l'autre et d'écouler au mieux les denrées périssables.[19]

L'argent. Tout autant que la volonté de puissance, ou l'orgueil, ou la quête de la gloire et de l'honneur, tout autant que le goût des aventures, c'est bien l'argent, sous la forme du profit matériel le plus immédiat et le plus tangible, qui se trouve au coeur de la conception de la guerre selon Froissart. Rançons, butins, appatis, sont présentés comme les motivations habituelles chez les combattants de tout rang. Les *Chroniques* font également mention des soldes et des gages régulièrement versés. Elles évoquent, en 1359, l'afflux des 'compagnons d'estragnes pays' à Calais, auprès d'Édouard III, dans la perspective de se faire enrôler et 'pour l'esperance d'avoir monnoie'. Il est vrai qu'après quelques jours d'attente, le roi d'Angleterre leur fait dire que son trésor est insuffisant et que s'il consent à ce qu'ils suivent sa chevauchée pour leur propre compte, à leurs risques et périls, ils ne doivent rien espérer de lui 'pour leurs gages ne pour chevaux perdus ne pour despens ne dommages' (V, 194-5). En 1373 comme en 1380, il est fait référence à l'avance habituelle de trois ou six mois de gages consentie par le gouvernement anglais aux soldats de son corps expéditionnaire. En 1386, pour le 'voyage de la mer', Froissart, se faisant sans doute l'écho de doléances qui lui furent faites, oppose les grands seigneurs, 'bien payez et delivrez de leurs gaiges et sauldées', aux petits compagnons dont l'arriéré de solde ne cessait de croître. Avec son sens aigu du dialogue, il met en scène le trésorier des guerres s'efforçant de calmer les récriminations: 'Attendez jusques à la sepmaine, vous serez delivrez de tous poins'. Et le chroniqueur d'ajouter: 'Ainsi estoient-ilz delaiez de sepmaine en sepmaine, et quant on leur fist ung paiement, il ne fu que d'un mois, et on leur devoit de VI sepmaines'.[20]

Les déplacements. Dans ce domaine aussi Froissart est incomparable, sinon irremplaçable. Son oeuvre est pleine de charrois et de sommiers, de rivières franchies à gué, de landes désertiques traversées d'une traite, de plantureux pays parcourus à petites étapes, par des troupes qui font halte tôt dans la journée, a 'haute none'. En diverses occasions, se trouve mentionnée l'existence de pionniers chargés d'ouvrir la voie au gros des troupes: ainsi en 1359, lors de la chevauchée d'Édouard III où, pour permettre la progression régulière des 6,000 chariots de l'armée anglaise, 500 valets sont placés à l'avant-garde, avec pelles et cognées, pour aplanir les chemins, couper les épines et les buissons. Pour l'ost de Flandre de 1382, une mission identique aurait été confiée à 1,760 ouvriers. Six ans plus tard, lors du 'voyage d'Allemagne', il est parlé de 2,500 tailleurs de haies et de buissons pour faciliter la traversée des Ardennes.[21] Le récit très circonstancié de l'expédition de Buckingham, en 1380, laisse apercevoir d'autres aspects: la construction d'un pont de fortune lorsque les Français ont rompu les passages; le logis des troupes, chaque soir, non pas dans un camp, mais en rase campagne, ou dans une forêt (ainsi celles de Marchenoir et de Coulommiers), ou dans un monastère: Vaucelles, Origny-Sainte-Benoite, Cîteaux près de Vendôme, Vertus en Champagne; les montres d'armes à l'occasion desquelles les effectifs sont recensés, les équipements et les montures inspectés, le complément de solde distribué; les hérauts d'armes qui ne sont pas seulement chargés de porter les messages, mais de négocier (avec participation aux bénéfices) le rachat des forts, des villages et des récoltes.

Quant aux techniques de la guerre de siège, elles se trouvent exposées avec suffisamment d'abondance pour qu'on puisse en saisir le mécanisme. Les mines et les contremines, le tir des trébuchets, l'érection de bastides en bois pour clore la place assiégée: on trouve dans Froissart des exemples concrets de tous ces procédés, de même que la description de quelques grandes machines de guerre dont la représentation figurée doit être cherchée dans les miniatures ainsi que dans les manuscrits d'ingénieurs militaires, tels que le quinzième siècle les verra se multiplier. C'est, au siège d'Audenarde de 1382, la mise en place par les Flamands d'un 'engin' de vingt pieds de large, quarante de long et vingt de haut, pour jeter des pierres sur la ville; en 1385, il s'agit d'un engin sur quatre roues, appelé 'passe avant', muni de trois étages avec vingt arbalétriers en poste à chaque étage; en 1387, pour la prise de Ribadavia, en Galice, les Anglais poussent un engin, lui aussi sur roues, comportant des 'manteaulx' recouverts de cuir, à l'abri desquels il est loisible aux assaillants d'attaquer la muraille à coups de pics.[22]

On a parfois accusé Froissart de se référer, tout au long des quelque quatre-vingts ans que couvrent les *Chroniques*, à un art militaire immobile et intangible, en sorte qu'il n'aurait pas su rendre compte de l'assez grande évolution qu'ont connue, dans les faits, la pratique de la guerre et l'organisation des armées, entre le début et la fin du quatorzième siècle. Reproche mal fondé. Une étude précise de son vocabulaire militaire montre l'apparition de nouveaux types de combattants, l'adoption de nouveaux usages guerriers. L'expression 'armures de fer', fréquente jusqu'aux années 1360, s'efface progressivement au profit de l'expression 'hommes d'armes'. À propos d'une expédition de Philippe de Valois, en 1346, le manuscrit de Rome, du début du quinzième siècle, mentionne des 'hommes as lances et as pavais', mais pour ajouter: 'les quels on nomme pour le temps present gros varlès' (III, 327). Cette fidélité au réel, on la retrouve encore dans la place que Froissart accorde, à côté des machines de jet traditionnelles, à l'artillerie nouvelle, à poudre. C'est en 1340 que les premiers canons font leur apparition dans les *Chroniques*: 'Cil dou Kesnoi descliquèrent canons et bombardes qui jettoient grans quariaus' (II, 14). Et certes il est possible que Froissart, à l'échelle de l'Occident, soit en retard d'une vingtaine d'années par rapport aux faits. Mais en ce qui concerne la France c'est bel et bien autour de 1338-40 qu'on relève les premiers documents d'archives concernant l'emploi de cette arme (Finó 1977: 275-6). Froissart, dans sa seconde rédaction, s'accorde avec Villani pour attester la présence de bombardes anglaises à Crécy (III, lii-iii). Il n'a pas ignoré la mutation des années 1370-80, à la fois quant au nombre de pièces disponibles et quant à leur calibre: lors du siège de Saint-Malo de 1378, il parle (sans doute trop généreusement) de quatre cents canons du côté anglais et d'un grand nombre de pièces du côté français.[23] En 1380, il mentionne une bombarde de cinquante-trois pouces de diamètre, jetant des 'quarreaulx' si grands, si gros, si pesants que lors du tir l'explosion s'entendait jusqu'à cinq lieues le jour et dix la nuit.[24] Deux ans plus tard, il montre fort bien l'intervention des canons tout au début des batailles de Beverhoutsveld (X, 224, 147) et de Roosebeke (XI, 50): une salve initiale, et puis l'artillerie n'intervient plus pendant le reste de l'action. On trouve chez lui mention des canons sur les bateaux (KL XIV, 221). Il est l'un des premiers chroniqueurs à citer par leur nom propre les victimes, parfois notables, de l'arme nouvelle.[25]

Enfin, le moindre intérêt de Froissart analyste de la guerre n'est pas d'offrir une série de développements, tantôt épars, tantôt regroupés, sur les usages militaires des peuples, de nous proposer une ethnographie de la guerre, à la manière d'un Hérodote décrivant les armées de Darius. Songeons aux remarques très critiques sur les pratiques discourtoises auxquelles les Allemands, mus par une cupidité de mauvais aloi, ont recours vis-à-vis de leurs prisonniers,[26] à l'évocation haute en couleur des campagnes écossaises, dans les premières pages des *Chroniques*. Voici les Sarrasins, avec leurs armures souples (KL XIV, 230), leurs targes faites de cuir bouilli de Cappadoce, les communiers de Galice, 'mal armez et de povre couraige' (XIII, 260), les gentilshommes de Castille, bons au premier assaut mais prompts à se retirer si l'adversaire résiste, car 'si très tost comme ilz ont laissié et fait voler deux ou trois dardes et donné un cop d'espée, et ilz veent que leurs ennemis ne se desconfissent point, ilz se doubtent et retournent les frains de leurs chevaulx' (XII, 164). Il y a dans les *Chroniques* une guerre exotique (celle des Turcs, des Infidèles), une guerre sauvage (celle des Irlandais, dans le secret de leurs repaires: KL XV, 169-70), une guerre populaire (celle du franc peuple frison: KL XV, 288), à côté de la guerre courtoise, civilisée, des chevaliers de France et d'Angleterre, celle, bien sûr, qui a les faveurs de Froissart.

Dans le traité sur la chevalerie (oeuvre littérairement assez médiocre mais historiquement suggestive) que Geoffroi de Charny, 'le plus preudomme et le plus vaillant de tous les aultres' (KL V, 412) composa au milieu du quatorzième siècle, se trouve tracé le programme idéal de l'apprenti aux armes. D'abord la joute et le tournoi, qualifiés de faits d'armes de paix, puis les faits d'armes de guerre: successivement comment entreprendre une chevauchée, courir à l'ennemi, régler l'ordonnance des gens d'armes et de pied, procéder à l'attaque et à la défense d'une place, y mettre en oeuvre les différents engins; enfin ce plus noble des faits d'armes que constitue la bataille rangée (KL I, ii, 463-533). On admettra que notre jouvencel aurait trouvé chez Froissart de quoi réussir pleinement aux 'épreuves théoriques' du métier d'armes. Car le chroniqueur de Valenciennes parvient à suppléer grâce à la vivacité de son imagination et à l'étendue de sa curiosité les lacunes de son information ainsi que son manque d'expérience directe de la guerre. Il faut ajouter que son mérite (dû peut-être à son honnêteté, à sa naïve bonne conscience) fut aussi de dépasser le conformisme social qu'il affectait. Quoi qu'il en soit de son ton détaché, mondain, de ses évidents snobismes, c'est une image plurielle de la guerre qui nous est offerte, vigoureuse, contrastée, éloignée aussi bien de la démystification décapante que de l'hagiographie complaisante.

X FROISSART: PATRONS AND TEXTS *

George T. Diller [1]

> En si grande et si noble histoire, comme ceste est, dont je, sire Jehan
> Froissart, qui en ay esté augmenteur et traicteur depuis le commancement
> jusques à maintenant par la grace et vertu que Dieu m'a donné de si
> longuement vivre, que j'ay en mon temps veu toutes ces choses d'abondance
> et de bonne voulenté . . . (XIII, 121).

FROISSART'S career has been traced many times, most recently by F. S. Shears
(1930), whose study provides an elegant and enthusiastic summary of our
knowledge of Froissart and his works as well as a balanced defence of the
chronicler as a skilful prose writer and as an historian who eclipsed his model,
Jean le Bel, as he advanced in his work. However, by the very general nature of
his study, Shears could only suggest the many uncertainties and problems
produced by the numerous successive versions of the vast *Chronicles* as preserved
for us in more than one hundred manuscripts. Little has been done to examine
how Froissart's relationships with his patrons affect his treatment and analysis of
certain figures and events in his saga of the Hundred Years War. Little consideration has been given to the role that scribes and copyists may have played in the
elaboration of the four books of this huge prose work. We know that Froissart's
chronology and statements are at times fanciful and internally inconsistent. But
may it not be the case that his re-ordering of events, his factual deformations,
reflect another level of historical reality, that of beliefs generally held among his
noble patrons? In some cases, fictional reconstruction in the *Chronicles* may
even correspond to a particular method employed by the chronicler for explaining
historical causality.

Within the framework of this short essay, the rich, complex and often
troubling relationships between the writer, his texts and his patrons may best be
illustrated by two textual probes: the death scene of William I, count of Hainault
and the role of John III, the 'Triumphant', duke of Brabant. Both examples are
taken from Book I of the *Chronicles*.

Three versions of the death, 7 June 1337, of William I, count of Hainault,
conveniently present many of the complex and possibly inextricable textual
problems that have attended every modern reader and editor of the *Chronicles*.
We reproduce below these three versions in order of their composition as
established by Simon Luce in 1869 and later accepted by Shears in 1930.

---

* All references to the *Chronicles* are to volume and page of the SHF edition
unless otherwise stated.

I Et li rois leur renvoioit grant or et grant argent, pour paiier leurs frais, et pour departir à ces signeurs d'Alemagne, qui ne convoitoient aultre cose.

En ce temps, trespassa de ce siècle li gentilz contes Guillaumes de Haynau, sept jours ou mois de juing, l'an de grasce mil trois cens trente sept. Si fu ensepelis as Cordeliers, à Valenciènes; et li fist on là son obsèque. Et chanta le messe li evesques Guillaumes de Cambrai. Si y eut grant fuison de dus, de contes et de barons, ce fu bien raisons, car il estoit grandement amé et renommés de tous. Apriès son trespas, se traist à le conté de Haynau, de Hollandes et de Zelandes, messires Guillaumes, ses filz, qui eut à femme la fille au duch Jehan de Braibant. Et fu ceste dame, qui s'appelloit Jehane, doée de le terre de Binch, qui est un moult biaus hiretages et pourfitables. Et ma dame Jehane de Vallois, sa mère, s'en vint demorer à Fontenielles sus Escaut, et là usa sa vie comme bonne et devote en le ditte abbeye, et y fist moult de biens.

De toutes ces devises et ces ordenances, ensi com elles se portoient et estendoient, et des confors et des alliances que li rois englès acqueroit par deça le mer, tant en l'Empire comme ailleurs, estoit li rois Phelippes tous infourmés . . . (I, 131-2).

II La vint messires Robiers d'Artois et toutte se route, et i basti le siege fort et fier, et dist qu'il ne s'en partiroit jammais se l'aroit a se vollenté.

En ce meysme tamps et en ceste propre annee, ou mois de juing, l'an mil CCC.XXXVII trespassa de ce siecle le bons comtes Guillaumme de Haynnau en l'ostel de Hollandez a Vallenchienne et fu ensepelis en l'eglise des Cordeliers en ceste meysme ville. De le mort dou comte furent pluiseur coer courouchié, car il fu larges, noblez, preux hardis, courtois, humbles, piteux et debonnaires a touttez gens. Si le plaindirent moult si enfans, messires Guillaummes ses filz, li roynne d'Allemaigne, li roynne d'Engleterre, li comtesse de Jullers, medamme Ysabiel, se maisnee fille, qui depuis eut monseigneur Robert de Namur espouset, et trop li plaindi et regreta messires Jehans de Haynnau ses biaux frerez, car il y perdi grant comfort et grant amour, car moult amoient l'un l'autre. Apriés le trespas dou comte dessus dist, prist messires Guillaummes ses filz le possession del comtet de Haynnau, de Hollandez et de Zellandes, et li fissent li noble des trois pays, li prelat et les bonnes villes foy et sierement et hoummaige, et il leur jura a tenir as us et as coustummes anchiennes. Medamme se mere Jehanne de Vallois eult devotion de li traire a Fontenellez, si comme elle fist, une abbeie de dammez dallez Valenchiennes, et la usa se vie.

Or dist li comtes, quant messires Robiers d'Artois eult assegiet le castiel de Saint Malquaire et juret qu'il ne s'en partiroit se l'aroit a se vollenté, il le fist assaillir vighereusement d'enghiens et ossi de compaignons archiers, qui tampre et tart y livroient merveilleusement grans assaux . . . (BM Amiens MS 486, fo. 25a-b).

III Jaques d'Artevelle faisoit semer paroles aval le pais et dire que qant il vodroit bien, acertes li pas seroit delivrés, et l'euist juret li contes de Flandres et tout chil qui l'en vodroient aidier.

En ce temps, trespassa de ce siecle li gentils Guillaumes de Hainnau, vint jours ou mois de jun le jour de la Pentecouste, en l'an de grasce Nostre Signeur mille. CCC.XXXVII. Et fu et est ensepvelis en l'eglise des Cordeliers en la ville de Valenchiennes. Et la fu fais son obseque tres reveraument, et chanta la messe Guillaumes de Cambrai. Et ot a che dit sene grant fuisson de dus, de contes et de barons. Apriés le trespas dou gentil conte, se traist a l'iretage de Hainnau, de Hollandes et de Zellandes messires Guillaumes de Hainnau son fil. Qant li rois d'Engleterre et la roine furent segnefiiet de la mort dou conte, lor signeur de pere, si en furent grandement courouchié, mais passer lor convint. Et s'en vestirent de noir; et li fissent faire son obseque en Engleterre, ens ou chastiel de Windesore, la ou il se tenoient. Madame Jehane de Valois, qui fenme avoit esté au conte de Hainnau, assés tos apriés le trespas de son dit signeur, se ordonna a demorer en l'abeie de Fontenelles dalés Valenchiennes, en cause de devotion, et la persevera et usa le demorant de sa vie.

Vous savés conment li contes de Flandres avoit mis et establi garnison de gens d'armes en l'ille Gagant, liquel fissent pluisseurs destourbiers et grans anois a ceuls qui voloient par mer venir prendre port a l'Escluse, et tant que tous li pais de Flandres s'en contentoit malement . . . (Diller 271-3).

For convenience, we shall refer to these texts of Book I as the 'first' (SHF), the 'second' (Amiens) and the 'third' (Rome) texts.

The alert reader must at once wonder why we have not reproduced Jean le Bel's account of this scene. After all, Count William was the brother of John of Hainault, one of Jean le Bel's principal patrons. Curiously enough, the canon of Saint-Lambert makes only the barest passing mention of William's death (Le Bel, I, 140). This circumstance, of course, serves well our immediate purpose. Here we can analyse a text whose varying forms, unlike so many other passages in Book I directly derived from Jean le Bel, cannot be attributed to the canon of Chimay's ambition to liberate his work from an early tutelage. In a moment, we will return to some of the reasons which may have induced Froissart to rewrite this passage at least three times, but first let us compare the content of each version.

Aside from the identity of person and place, it is immediately apparent that each of the three texts adds, suppresses and varies statements and details throughout. The differing dates assigned to William's death in each version constitutes a most startling inconsistency: only the first text gives the correct, precise historical date. If, as S. Luce believed, Froissart composed these three versions in the order we have reproduced them, this kind of variation would appear inexplicable. The other differences, though less shocking, are hardly less significant. The first version alone names Count William II's wife, Joan of Brabant, who, by her second marriage to Wenceslas of Bohemia in 1347, was later to become one of Froissart's main patrons. The presence of Joan of Brabant in the first text is all the more peculiar when we observe that the second text, while omitting Joan of Brabant, is at the same time the only one of the three to name Robert of Namur as the future husband of William I's youngest daughter, 'Ysabiel' (error for Elizabeth: I, ccix). This near juxtaposition of Joan of Brabant and Robert of Namur seemingly contradicts S. Luce's opinion that Froissart wrote his first version of the *Chronicles* under the patronage of the pro-English Robert of Namur while composing his second version under the patronage of the pro-French Guy of Blois and Wenceslas of Bohemia.[2] The third text, finally, omits any mention of either Joan or Robert while, in their place, giving special attention to a third child of the deceased William I, Philippa of Hainault, wife of King Edward III, and to a description of that royal couple's mourning at Windsor Castle.

The second text contains a great number of details absent from the other two texts: the exact place of the count's death, the virtues of the deceased count and a description of the investiture of his son.

Further, the difference between the three texts is not limited to their content: their widely varied positions in the surrounding narrative matrix is no less striking. This aspect is directly apparent from the preceding and following sentences which we have purposely appended to each text. A more extended reading of each version reveals that in the first text, the count's death occurred *before* Louis of Nevers, count of Flanders, sent a garrison to occupy the isle of Cadsand, whereas the opposite is true in the third text. The position of the second text has nothing in common with the other two texts: here the count's death falls in the middle of an unrelated episode, unique to the Amiens manuscript, where Froissart relates an English expedition to Gascony led by the contumacious French knight, Robert of Artois.[3] This highly fanciful expedition, along with many other similarly romanesque episodes, renders the Amiens text profoundly different from all other versions of the first book of the *Chronicles*.

The diversity of content and composition illustrated by this example is typical of a great number of episodes in the first book. Both in terms of Froissart's personal ties and in terms of the central subject of his *Chronicles*, the Anglo-French conflict, we can well understand why Froissart could not omit Count William I's death from any of his versions of Book I. Father-in-law of both the king of England (Edward III) and the German emperor (Louis of Bavaria), and brother-in-law of the king of France (Phillip VI), William had by matrimonial alliances tied the three main powers of northern Europe to himself (Lucas 1929: 93). As a fellow citizen of Valenciennes and respectively as the father and twice as the father-in-law of three of Froissart's most considerable patrons, Philippa of Hainault, Robert of Namur and Joan of Brabant, Count William more than deserved the chronicler's final testimonial in each of his versions of Book I.

But while the space which Froissart allocates to this episode may in some way reflect his relations with his patrons, these relationships cannot in themselves explain the singular textual variations from one version to another. For it is abundantly clear that not one of these highly divergent texts can derive *textually* from the other two. Each is patently an independent composition owing nothing to its immediate predecessor. The importance of this observation cannot be too strongly emphasised. In this instance, at least, we must evidently discard the accepted view that Froissart produced each of his editions by 'revising' the text of the preceding version.

But if he did not work in this manner, how *did* Froissart set about composing the various versions of his vast *Chronicles*? Some clues to his technique may perhaps be uncovered by a scrutiny of his personal interventions in his narrative and by a consideration of his own descriptions of the methods he employed to construct and compose his work.

Though Froissart — unlike other well-known medieval French historiographers such as Robert of Clari, Villehardouin, Joinville and Commynes — did not generally write his *Chronicles* in the form of a personal memoir, he does, as did all medieval writers, constantly intervene in his narration. In certain better-known sections of the *Chronicles*, he does indeed describe his personal activities. Examples of such autobiographical sections are recurrent passages where he recalls his early visit to England and Scotland and where later, in Book IV, he partially deals with his last visit to England in 1395.[4] All of these passages are very short and intermittent. Even the famous journal he has left us in Book III of his journey to Orthez in the fall of 1388 occupies little more than about the first 150 pages out of what may be conservatively estimated as a total of around 5,000 pages for all four books. On the other hand, Froissart's brief personal interventions in the form of incises, exclamatory address and transitional formulas are to be encountered on practically every page. It is these short interventions, where Froissart seems almost to share his judgements of the events at hand and his task as writer with the reader that create a special bond of allegiance between the reader and the chronicler, a bond rarely attained in medieval French prose.

A partial inventory and examination of these interventions leads us to distinguish two main categories among them. The first category includes all those passages where Froissart personally participates in the events he describes such as is the case during the account of his trip to Orthez with Espan du Lion. The verbs in narration of this type are always in the past tense. By contrast, in the second category, where, as we have said, Froissart only briefly intervenes as author in his narration, the verbs are always found in the present tense.

At first sight, we would expect to find among the 'objective' texts of the first — autobiographical — type of intervention the most concrete information about how Froissart composed the texts preserved by the existing manuscripts. In fact, Alfred Jeanroy and later Shears did use passages of this category to illustrate (though to support, let it be said in passing, opposite conclusions) the chronicler's techniques of composition.[5] In one such text for instance, Froissart speaks of the use he made of his béarnais travel companion's accounts:

> Des paroles que messire Espaeng de Lyon me comptoit estoie tout rafreschi, car elles me venoient grandement à plaisance et toutes très bien les retenoie et si tost que aux hostelz, sur le chemin que nous fesismes ensemble, descendu estoie, je les escripsoie, fust de soir ou de matin, pour avoir en tou[t] temps advenir mieulx la memoire, car il n'est si juste retenue que cest d'escripture ...
> (XII, 65; cf XV, 181).

That Froissart assiduously maintained a travel journal, nothing could be more normal for a writer of his profession. But as to how exactly the chronicler actually employed his notes when later he undertook the composition of the texts conserved by our manuscripts, on this critical point, such a passage is of no assistance. And yet, without even considering the way Froissart disperses select portions of Espan du Lion's accounts among tens of other sources in the third book, it is perfectly evident that a major transformation separates his travel notes from the text of the *Chronicles*. The same is true in every case where the chronicler seemingly discusses his methods of composition: none of these passages go beyond a description of his methods of gathering information and his repeated affirmation of the superior value of the written record.[6] Never does Froissart tell the reader how he went about arranging and producing the text

149

that he left for posterity. So it is that we learn that in 1389, the chronicler spent six days at Middelburg in Holland in the company of João Fernandes Pacheco, where:

> Cil m'endita et informa de toutes les besongnes avenues entre le royaume de Castille et le royaume de Portingal, depuis la mort du roy Ferrant jusques au jour que il estoit yssi hors du dit royaume. Et si bellement le me comptoit et si arreement et tant volontiers, que je prendoie grant plaisir à l'oïr et à l'escripre . . .

> Or retournay depuis a Bruges et en mon pays, si ouvray sus les paroles et relations faites du gentil chevalier . . . et cronisay tout ce que de Portingal et de Castille est avenu jusques à l'an de grace MCCCIIII^{XX} et X (XII, 238-9; cf 227).

The verb 'enditer' here could even indicate that Froissart often took direct dictation from his informants. In any case, the last sentence of this passage leaves no doubt as to the substantial transformations to which the writer subjected his primary written records before entering them into the *Chronicles*. But this last sentence from the above passage intrigues us even more for another reason, and that is because of his use of the verb 'croniser', a verb which recurs a good twenty times throughout the third book.[7] Often the verbs 'historier' and 'escripre' accompany this verb 'croniser'. Yet, in every case, Froissart uses these verbs, which denote aspects of written redaction, in the past tense. Thus, unless these verbs have a special formulaic value, what Froissart designates by such retrospective references to his activity as a writer cannot be the redaction of the texts he left to posterity. 'Historier', 'croniser' and 'escripre' appear to refer almost exclusively to the initial preparation and organisation of primary sources, be these notes, documents or other written texts at his disposition.

The second category of interventions — those where the chronicler directly but briefly addresses the reader in the present tense — should logically offer a good opportunity to grasp at first-hand the compositional techniques that resulted in the numerous and independent redactions of the manuscripts. For the moment, we eliminate from among this huge pool of expressions all interventions governed by the pronoun 'vous', that is all direct address to the reader of the type 'si poés et devés bien croire que . . .' (V, 20), 'vous avés bien oy compter chi dessus comment . . .' (V, 29), 'si sachiés bien qui estoit . . .' (V, 39), 'or regardés se ce ne fu mies . . .' (V, 270). All such expressions, however characteristic of Froissart's congenial style, along with certain others in the third person, such as 'si com il est contenu ci dessus en ce livre' (VI, 53) and 'or dist l'histoire' (XII, 239, XV, 28) may well be tributary to literary formulas. Many are to be found in effect — though less frequently and in less varied forms — in Jean le Bel's *Chronicle*; others bear resemblance to the formulas of Arthurian romances which Froissart read with predilection.[8]

In contrast with those interventions governed by the second or third person, others governed by the author's first person pronoun, 'je' or 'nous', should more closely approach the direct and spontaneous presence of the writer in his narration. Two aspects of these 'personal' interventions immediately catch the reader's attention. First, in their very great majority, Froissart employs these expressions, not to judge the men and actions he is describing, but rather to introduce transitions and brief halts in his narration. Secondly, we observe that the verbs employed by Froissart to intervene personally in his text designate oral gestures. The following sampling is typical of such:

Si voel jou parler au plus justement que je porai selonch ce que j'en fui depuis enfourmés . . . (V, 48).

Si com je vous en parleray quant temps et lieus seront . . . (VI, 17; cf 243).

Nous parlerons dou prince de Galles et aprocerons son voyage et vous compterons . . . (VI, 228).

Les parolles que je vous ay pronunciées . . . (XIV, 179).

Je vous di, si com je oy depuis recorder ceulz qui y furent d'un costé et d'autre, que . . . (VI, 128).

. . . Il ne peult mies dou tout souvenir; et toutteffois de chiaux dont il me souvient et sui enfourmés, parole jou vollentiers (Amiens, fo. 42c).

Similar expressions — encountered constantly thoughout Froissart's entire prose work and which thus mark moments of repose and transition — may well point toward a dictated text. Two things intrigue anyone who starts making an inventory of this sort of intervention. On the one hand, the chronicler constantly employs the verbs 'dire', 'parler', 'oir' and 'recorder'. At the same time, he always uses these verbs in either the present, future or immediate past (i.e. 'passé composé', which has the virtual value of a present). By contrast, he practically never uses the verbs 'écrire' and 'ditier' ('to compose') in any tense except the past definte (preterit).[9]

The general weight of evidence suggests then that Froissart reserved the verb 'écrire' to designate the already redacted text on the sheet in opposition to the present, continuous transformation that constitutes oral composition by dictation.

Certain other aspects of the chronicler's texts appear to result from oral composition. There exists, for example, another type of intervention where Froissart allows himself to be carried away by the drama of his own account. Thus, after having described in Book II the victory of the rebellious citizens of Ghent over the men of Bruges in 1382, Froissart exclaims:

Or se gardent de eulz enorgueillir et leurs cappitaines ossi! Mais non feront: il s'enorgueilliront tellement que Dieu s'en courroucera et leur remonstrera leur orgueil avant que l'an soit oultre, sicomme vous recorderons en l'istoire . . . (X, 236; cf X, 239, 243; XI, 14).

With its imperatives and future tenses, we can nearly visualise Froissart raising his voice with emotion and shaking a warning finger before his scribe as he declaims this text. Further along, this time in Book III, Froissart returns to the wars of Brittany which far back in Book I had set John of Montfort against Charles of Blois. Of a sudden, the chronicler recalls that he had inopportunely left Charles of Blois's sons, John and Guy, in an English prison:

. . . car je ne les ay pas mis encoires hors de la prison et dangier du roy d'Engleterre où leur pere saint Charles de Blois les ot mis [!] (XIII, 122; cf I, 401, 425; VIII, 226, 243).

Such passages possess the charm of transporting the reader into the presence of the author's voice. Their spontaneous quality may well represent the directly exclaimed and faithfully recorded words of Froissart.

Without denying the provisory and fragmentary nature of this evidence of oral composition, as such it does lead us to propose a technique of writing which may explain many of the otherwise imponderable divergences between the different versions of the *Chronicles*. At the same time, the notion of oral composition can help us to better grasp certain literary and historical dimensions of these texts.

Let us first propose a brief synthesis of our survey of the methods Froissart used to produce his manuscripts. At the outset he himself was responsible for the preliminary tasks of documentation. These consisted of voyages for information, interviews, writing up notes and assembling various texts and documents. Once he had collected these materials, he may well have drawn up a chronological sketch. We might call this first step the preparatory written redaction stage. Then the chronicler was ready to dictate to his scribe the finished version which we read today. The intimate collaboration between the author and his scribe may be in great part responsible for the mobility of the chronicler's texts, a mobility which Paul Zumthor has recently defined as the essential trait of the medieval text (1972: 71). Moreover, it is quite legitimate to suppose, especially in the case of texts several times rewritten, that the scribe played a considerable role in the elaboration of the text. In the case, for instance, where the chronicler considered certain episodes to be satisfactorily composed in a previous redaction, he may have simply requested the scribe to incorporate intact such passages into the new version; frequently he must have completely set aside previous redactions before dictating anew; at other moments, pressed for time or perhaps engaged in simultaneous redactions, instead of dictating word for word, Froissart could well have given his scribe general instructions, while leaving to him the responsibility for elaborating the final *mise en page*, much in the same way that illustration and illumination of luxury manuscripts was delegated to specialised artists. In modern terms, not giving proper credit to each collaborator of a written work falls within the category of plagiarism. Such obviously not being the case for the medieval writer, renders our task of classifying Froissart's manuscripts a most arduous if not vain task. Successive copyists of course compounded the 'degradation' of Froissart's texts which by the public nature of their historical subject would constantly tempt each new scribe to interpolate the text in accordance with the interests of his particular patrons and his own regional, political background.

More optimistically, this technique of oral composition, once envisaged, opens several paths to a better interpretation and appreciation of the literary and historical values of the *Chronicles*. Composing by dictation did, after all, give to the chronicler the occasion to retell all the tales and accounts that the heralds and knights had previously recited to him. Composing aloud corresponds *par excellence* to the method of the story teller who enjoys above all recounting and improving his tale with each new telling. Like a good teller of tales, Froissart, indeed, seems to have had a special predilection for superimposed accounts. In Book III, for example, he reports the account of João Fernandes Pacheco who related in turn Lourenço Fogaça's narrative and how Fogaça had described the events of the battle of Aljubarrota (1385) to the duke of Lancaster (XII,

278ff). Might there not have been for Froissart, between his pleasure in telling anew each of his informants' episodic accounts and his indefatigable taste for recommencing the great recitation of the *Chronicles*, a solution of deep creative continuity?

When viewed as the work of a perpetual teller of tales, the *Chronicles* have often and understandably appeared as a highly unreliable source of historical information. In the texts relating the death of William I of Hainault, we noted a sort of substitution phenomenon that governs each successive version. In the second text, Robert of Namur replaced Joan of Brabant, with Philippa of Hainault effectively taking the place of Robert in the third text. Each version is as it were a quasi-independent renewal of the previous one rather than a textual derivative. Such absence of critical, internal control constitutes a basic characteristic of the work. A striking example of this phenomenon are the accounts of the battle of Aljubarrota. Froissart first relates this battle on the basis of accounts given to him by French knights in 1388-9 at the court of Gaston of Foix in Orthez (XII, §§37-9). At the end of 1389, he made, as we have seen, a trip to Middelburg expressly for the purpose of obtaining the Anglo-Portuguese version of the battle. Yet nowhere does he make any attempt to compare his two often-contradictory relations of the events. Symptomatic of this 'add-on' quality of his narrative is the ever-recurrent formula 'si comme je fui depuis enfourmés' (VI, 198). Alfred Coville summed up well this dimension of the *Chronicles* when he wrote that Froissart is 'plus soucieux d'interroger et de raconter que de vérifier' (1949: 346). However naive such a narrative procedure may at times appear to us coming from an author who proclaimed himself to be a historian and not a simple chronicler (XIII, 222), his method does in fact have the real advantage of communicating directly to us the voices and emotions of his century, an advantage which would have been lost had he carefully filtered his accounts by means of a critical, comparative and synthetic method. And as we shall see in the case of Duke John III of Brabant, his accounts often are far less unmindful than the preceding considerations would suggest.

Finally, we must not neglect one important literary aspect of Froissart's narrative interventions. The constant presence of the author/narrator in the form of apostrophes to the reader, such as 'si poés et devés bien croire que' (V, 20) and 'creés fermenent que' (V, 44), tend to create a climate in which we are brought to feel that the work itself takes the place of history. Thus do we regret somewhat that Daniel Poirion declares of Froissart's work, 'ce ne sont pas des *mémoires,* mais une narration objective, en ce sens que [Froissart] n'y figure que comme le témoin épisodique' (1971: 200). For though it is true that Froissart is but rarely the personal witness to the events he recounts, he is nevertheless the omnipresent witness to his own narration, so much so that it is the act of narrating itself, and not the events, which in the final analysis constitutes historical destiny in the *Chronicles*. Jules Michelet's formula, 'L'histoire, l'historien se mêlent en ce regard' (1876: ix) applies quite appropriately to his distant predecessor and spiritual parent.

This technique of oral composition linked to frequent intervention in the narrative tends to suggest a work of spontaneous candor in which the narrator's voice so dominates as to give the illusion that his telling possesses greater reality than the events recounted. Yet it would appear that such dramatic and literary virtues are often obtained at the cost of fragmentation and non-sequential retelling of events with, in addition, the superficiality attendant upon such headlong narrative that never turns back on itself. Indeed, the varied texts of Book I are 'new' versions, never corrected revisions, and we observe in this respect that nowhere in any text of Book I does there exist any reference to another version.[10] Hence it comes as a pleasurable surprise to the reader when he discovers that despite the breathless pace of his narrative, Froissart is quite capable of developing searching and penetrating portraits and analyses of men and their motives. In this respect, he certainly merits greater esteem than he has been accorded.[11] His treatment of Gaston of Foix's politics of independence, or of King Charles V's defensive strategy against the English invaders, and his penetration of the political realities behind the Great Schism are good examples of Froissart's acute historical perception.

Among his accounts, that of the role of Duke John III of Brabant, during the preliminary years of the Anglo-French struggle, reveals well Froissart's capacity to comprehend the importance of intriguing and calculating individual conduct in determining the outcome of historical events. This account goes well beyond the outward appearances of knightly prowess and deeds by the sword for which Froissart is rather unjustly renowned. There is no need to retrace in detail here the capital role of this astute prince in the Low Countries, a role which has been amply verified by modern historians and above all by H. S. Lucas (1929) to whose study we shall frequently refer in the following pages.[12] Let us first briefly recall the duke's strategic geographic position and his close blood relationships to the governing nobility and to Froissart's patrons Wenceslas and the duchess of Brabant. By his mother, Margaret, King Edward II's sister, John III was a first cousin of King Edward III. And, indeed, King Edward III made enormous payments to his cousin in an attempt to gain John's critically-needed support for the English offensive alliance with the Low Countries, and the German principalities in 1338-40. However, John, by his wife, Mary of Evreux, grand-daughter of a previous French king, Philip III, was tied equally closely to French royalty. Need it be recalled that in addition the duchy of Brabant, lying as it did in the centre of the Low Countries, played at the time a pivotal role between France and England. Set, then, squarely in the middle of the great politico-dynastic struggle of the century, the duke extracted with consummate skill every advantage from his two great neighbours' rivalry: 'Throughout the entire period, the duke of Brabant displayed a most remarkable cunning . . . (Lucas 1929: 579). . . . [He] was withal determined to maintain his traditional aloofness and to extract the greatest possible benefit from the troubles of his neighbours' (586).

With this essential framework in mind, let us examine how Froissart deals, in the three major versions of Book I, with the astute father-in-law of his chivalrous patron, Wenceslas of Bohemia.

The period of Duke John's influence that interests us corresponds to that of King Edward's first two expeditions on the continent, the first extending from July 1338 to February 1340, and the second from June to November 1340. To these two periods we will annex two other related events in which the duke's role caught Froissart's attention: the assassination of James van Artevelde on 17 July 1345, and the marriage of the young count of Flanders to John's second daughter, Margaret (celebrated 2 July 1347).

Aside from two titles gained — vicar of the Empire on 5 September 1338 and 'king of France' on 26 January 1340 — Edward's first venture in the Low Countries amounted to little more than a drawn out series of delays, an unsuccessful siege (Cambrai 25 September — 8 October 1339), an unproductive stand-off with King Philip's armies (Buironfosse 23-4 October 1339), and a crushing accumulation of debts owed to his less than disinterested allies. In the course of about a half dozen scenes and events, Froissart established John's heavy, if not predominant responsibility for this long series of unproductive efforts undertaken by King Edward in his attempt to further his political and dynastic ambitions. These events would merit critical historical review; however, within the scope of our essay, let them suffice to illustrate Froissart's manner of placing an exceptional individual's less than chivalrous conduct at the centre of historical causality.

All three of Froissart's versions plus Jean le Bel's account harmonise generally as to the events in question, though differing always in their ordering of them.[13] In general, Jean le Bel's text and Froissart's first text (SHF) give the briefest account, while Froissart's second version (Amiens) gives the most expansive descriptions. But it is Froissart's third text (Rome) which portrays most dramatically and insistently the influential and devious dimension of Duke John's manoeuvring. In this text, the chronicler returns repeatedly to the first duke's scheming, manipulating conduct. Although first cousin of the English king, John, '. . . se faindoit ils de li aider, ensi que faire deuist, et estoit moult pesans a esmouvoir' (Diller 292: cf 288; SHF I, 140). In order to keep his presence with the English as inconspicuous as possible, John then insisted on holding the allies' assembled meeting in the tiny village of Herkes. Here again, Froissart writes that John '. . . se voloit dissimuler de ces besongnes et ordonna et i trouva une cautelle nouvelle . . .' (Diller 293; cf Le Bel I, 148; SHF I, 149; Amiens fo. 32c), obviously downgrading his association with Edward. Again, during the winter of 1338-9, John lodged Edward at his castle at Louvain (Antwerp, according to Lucas 1929, 300), but his motives were far from candid: 'Encores se dissimuloit ce qu'il pooit li dus de Braibant, quel amour ne compagnie que il fesist ne monstrast au roi d'Engleterre son cousin' (Diller 297; cf Le Bel I, 150; SHF I, 151; Amiens fos. 31a, 33a). Again, throughout the long months of 1338 and 1339, the allies 'prendoient piet sus le duch' for they knew full well about his agent Leo of Cranehem, and how John '. . se dissimuloit et se portoit de ces besongnes assés froidement . . .' (Diller 298).

At last, Edward made two determined efforts to put an end to his cousin's delaying, fence-sitting tactics. First he attempted to oblige him to sign letters of defiance to Philip VI with the other princes, immediately prior to the siege of Cambrai. In the Rome text, Froissart uses dialogues and direct discourse characteristic of this version to highlight John's stubborn, intriguing neutrality. Next, at Brussels, when Edward accused his cousin before the assembled princes of 'defaute et dissimulation', John 'se hontoia' and agreed to leading an army before Cambrai, but only when he should learn that Edward had arrived there before him (Diller 299-300, 308-9; cf Le Bel I, 153, 159; SHF I, 154, 159; Amiens fo. 33b).

The Rome text's version of John's conduct during the siege of Cambrai (25 September — 8 October 1339) differs substantially from all the other versions.

155

Here (Diller 314), upon his arrival at the siege, Duke John at first refused to uphold his promise to defy King Philip VI and asserted that he should do so only when he saw that the English king intended to advance from the Empire into the territory of the French kingdom. By this renewed refusal, John managed to prolong his outward appearance of neutrality still a few more days. Yet at winter's approach and with it dwindling hopes for the capture of Cambrai, the allies decided to coerce Duke John into acts of war and defiance. They summoned him to the king's tent, where, before the assembled lords, Edward proclaimed an offensive into France in four days and then challenged John to make good his oft-made but ill-kept promise to defy the Valois king (Diller 317). So, at last, John, who 'plus ne pooit requler ne faire nulle dissimulation' (Diller 318), agreed, sent his letter of defiance to Philip and provoked in so doing the public shaming and consequential death of his loyal agent, Leo of Cranehem. Where, in other texts, the duke's final submission and Cranehem's death occupy but a few lines (Le Bel I, 158-9; SHF I, 166, Amiens fo. 33c), in the Rome text, the chronicler expands and dwells insistently upon the duke of Brabant's wanton behaviour over some five pages (Diller 314-19). In no version, despite his submission to Edward's coercion, does John play any more than a titular role in the military operations around Cambrai, in the Vendômois and at Buironfosse.

If anything at all, his conduct becomes even more scheming and deceitful at Buironfosse: 'Et par especial li dus de Braibant s'en dissimuloit et dissimula couvertement trop' (Diller 334). Here, the divergence between the Rome text and the two others becomes even greater for, whereas in the other versions John becomes the leading partisan of an aggressive English stance — 'c'estoit bien ses accors que dou combattre, car aultrement à leur honneur il ne s'en pooient partir' (I, 175; cf Amiens, fo. 34d) — Froissart informs us in the Rome version, that the English dislodged first from Buironfosse, persuaded by the dukes of Brabant and Guelders and by the count of Juliers that the French forces were overwhelmingly superior (Diller 335).[14]

In another revealing passage unique to the Rome text and taken from the subsequent period of Edward's residence at Brussels near the end of 1339, Froissart concentrates responsibility for the English monarch's military and political failures on the duke's all-pervasive cunning. Here we read of how the French mocked Edward III whom they judged a simple victim of the greed of his allies, and especially of Duke John's manipulations: '... Il le mainne et pourmainne ... Il ne le soustient pour aultre cose que pour le pourfit' (Diller 337).[15] Adding to the realistic evaluation of John's conduct, this pecuniary dimension though already suggested earlier during the negotiations of 1337 (Diller 257; SHF I, 125) becomes markedly more persistent as the narrative advances in the Rome text.

Froissart next describes a trip that Count William II of Hainault made to England during the spring of 1340 in quest of English aid in resisting the duke of Normandy's invasion of his lands. Though all of Froissart's texts contain this episode which Lucas considers to be a 'pure fiction' (1929: 391), the Rome text alone recounts William's visit to Duke John and the duke's cynical response to his son-in-law's complaints about the French incursions: 'Aussi, biaus fils, respondi li dus, lor en avés vous fait ...' (Diller 363). How striking and shrewd this brief, indirect, commentary on the Anglo-French conflict! Exaggerated and fictional passages in the *Chronicles* appear often thus highly instructive. They represent the chronicler's efforts to go beyond the simple recording of information, to penetrate the surface of events, to interpret men and their actions.

Shortly before the battle of Sluys (24 June 1340), a confrontation occurred between the French troups under John of Normandy besieging Thun-l'Evêque and the forces under John of Hainault. Though characteristically the Rome text alone specifies that Duke John was the last prince to join John of Hainault's army (Diller 400), it is the Amiens text which gives the most extensive account of the duke of Brabant's role in this engagement (fos. 43d-44d). The Scheldt River lay between John of Hainault's army and the besieged city thus preventing him from attacking the French and coming to the aid of the city. After repeated refusals from the French to agree to a suitable place to do battle, John of Hainault asked for Duke John's counsel. John advised retreat, observing that to combat the French in the absence of King Edward would be to disregard solemn agreements made with the English king. Yet, however well chosen for the circumstances the duke's advice may appear, nothing in this passage connects such counsel with the duke's own personal opportunistic political goals. In a sense, the Amiens text reduces the individual to a simple mouthpiece of historical destiny. The chronicler could, almost indifferently, have assigned this counsel of retreat to any one of the numerous princes in the company of John of Hainault. By contrast, the Rome text suggests on nearly every occasion that the course of events results from the duke's personal and calculating ambition to out-manoeuvre those around him.

Though all of Froissart's texts signal Duke John's presence at the siege of Tournai (II, 45; Amiens, fo. 45c; Diller 417, 449), it is John's total non-participation in the extensively recounted raids and attacks on the towns and villages surrounding Tournai which is most striking. Clearly John's ambition and influence would have been poorly served by a decisive battle between the opposing forces. Yet the Rome text alone presents John in his true colours as a behind the scenes peacemaker during the negotiations which culminated in the truce of Esplechin (25 September 1340):

> Comsiderés le peuple qui la estoit assamblés, tant pour l'un roi que pour l'autre, car li rois d'Engleterre, parmi les Flamens, avoit plus de cent. M. honmes. Grant ocision et grande mortalité de peuple i euist esté, se par bataille il fuissent venu ensamble. On en fu sus le point, mais li dus de Braibant . . . brisoit et brisa toutdis couvertement la bataille . . . (Diller 454).

In the ensuing description of the peace negotiations, Froissart develops a searching portrait and assessment of the duke of Brabant's dominant and devious role. Though Edward III was the leader and paymaster of the coalition, it was his first cousin who 'desus tous . . . avoit la grignor vois et audiense' (Diller 455). John pretended ('monstra par couvreture') to support peace in deference to Joan of Valois, mother of Count William, and to Edward's wife, Phillipa. He alleged the unfavourable approaching long and cold winter nights, asserted that 'pour celle saison, on en avoit assés fait' (Diller 455). He even promised to his royal cousin that by the terms of the treaty, he, Edward, would gain possession of a great part of the French kingdom, including at least 'toute la ducee de Normendie' (Diller 457). It is as though no terms can satisfy the chronicler in his desire to magnify Duke John's duplicity.

> Ces proumesses ou la environ et encores plus grandes que li dus de Braibant remonstroit a son cousin le roi d'Engleterre l'apaisoient grandement et li brisoient ses abusions ... et s'accorda assés doucement a la trieuve (Diller 457).[16]

As Froissart coldly observes, still young, Edward was no match for this crafty lord: '... pas ne congnissoit encores le malisce et pratique dou monde' (Diller 455).

Later in his account of John of Montfort's voyage to England in 1341 (also an event of doubtful historical reality), Froissart returns to the duke of Brabant's preponderant role in the costly and unsuccessful campaigns of 1338-40. Here we learn why the royal council received so favourably Montfort's request to become an English ally by giving homage to the king for his disputed duchy of Brittany:

> ... Li dus de Braibant ses cousins germains, li dus de Gerlles son serouge et les Alemans l'avoient [Edward III] mené et pourmené ja par deus saisons et fait despendre son argent si grandement que encores il s'en trouvoit derriere et veroit un lonch temps, et si n'avoit riens fait fors que travailliet son corps et ses gens, et courut une petite escroe dou roiaume de France, et tenu sieges devant Cambrai et Tournai ... (Diller 480-1; cf SHF II, 101, where, in a much briefer passage, Duke John is not mentioned).

This vigorous piece of analysis is borne out in the main by modern historical interpretation of the role of the duke of Brabant. It is, therefore, important to note that later in the Rome text the chronicler's persistent desire to make of the duke a master shaping-force of events remains so constant that it leads Froissart to depart very seriously from historical truth. Let us briefly retrace his explanation of the chain of events which led to the duke's alliance with King Philip of France and to the marriage of his second daughter to the young count of Flanders, Louis of Male (2 July 1347).

In 1345, when John perceived that his ambitions for a matrimonial alliance with Louis of Male were menaced by James van Artevelde's attempt to persuade Edward III to establish his son, the prince of Wales, in Flanders, as its duke, he '... avisa que il i meteroit un tel touel que il romperoit et briseroit tout' (Diller 637). As a result, the 'soubtieus' (Diller 637) duke not only became the sinister master mind behind the assassination of Van Artevelde on 17 (or 22) July 1345 (Lucas 1929: 524), but, by another series of extravagant promises — this time to the French king — he achieved his agreement to the marriage of his daughter, Margaret, to the count of Flanders and in so doing dashed Edward III's plans to marry his own daughter, Isabella, to the young count (Diller 797-9, 808-9, 878-9). Now however disappointing it is to learn from Lucas (1929: 526-7) that this account of the final series of triumphant manoeuvres by the duke must be dismissed as largely 'worthless', the chronicler's lively tale of intrigue is, from one point of view, more informative than a more 'factual' account could be. How Froissart's contemporaries interpreted events — and perhaps acted on their interpretations — is assuredly as significant as the 'real' historical events. Taken as a whole and within the framework of a work whose avowed purpose is to give example ('exempliier': Diller 36, for example) to the reader, John of Brabant's life illustrates how a lesser prince by virtue of adroit cunning and skill managed to preserve his independence by continuously out-manoeuvring his two powerful royal neighbours. In many respects, John of Brabant's success resembles that of Count Gaston of Foix, who expertly and proudly preserved his independence in Béarn between the two warring royalties. Jacqueline Picoche states the relationship between the *Chronicles* and their public in slightly different terms: '. . . Le succès de son oeuvre . . . prouve que ses contemporains se sont reconnus dans le portrait qu'il leur présentait d'eux-mêmes' (1976: 9). And were not in fact the majority of Froissart's patrons — Wenceslas, Guy of Blois, Albert of Bavaria, Béraut of Auvergne, and even King David of Scotland, to name but a few — all lesser princes who would find comfort in the example of a John of Brabant? Though Shears (1930: 104), to illustrate the chronicler's integrity as a historian, concludes,

> If Froissart had wished to hide unpleasant truths for personal reasons he would not have called attention so insistently to the breach of faith of the duke of Brabant who was father of Jeanne, wife of his patron Wenceslas . . .

it is most probable that Joan saw in the accounts of the duke's duplicity not 'unpleasant truths' but rather flattering testimony to her father's high intelligence and political astuteness. Again, could Joan have taken umbrage against her historiographer because Froissart places her first marriage with William II of Hainault in 1337, three years after the 'true' date of 1334 (Le Bel I, 227 n.2), when she read the gracious portrait of her the chronicler committed to posterity '. . . La plus belle, la plus gente, la plus frice et mieuls aians toutes nobles manieres que nulle jone dame dont on euist la congnissance . . .' (Diller 267)? Paradoxically, had fourteenth-century French nobility truly read the *Chronicles* as was the writer's intent, how, after so many repeated passages demonstrating the superiority of the long-bow, could the catastrophe of Agincourt have been possible?

Indeed, this short essay leaves many problems unanswered, above all that of Froissart's manuscripts which strike us more and more in their unpredictable make-up as similar to the different redactions of the earlier *chansons de geste*, but without even the advantage of rhyme, metre or epic formulae to guide the author's memory from one 'recital' to the next.

Compared to other contemporary chronicles or annals, such as the *Chronique des quatre premiers Valois*, the *Chronique normande du XIVe siècle* or the *Grandes chroniques de France*, the overwhelming superiority of Froissart's prose work becomes immediately manifest. A total absence of historical perspective characterises such impersonal, cumulative, annalistic texts. Meteors, the passing of stars and comets, unusual weather, abundance and famine, variations of prices and currencies mingle indiscriminately in such works along with political and military events. Valuable though such works may be for primary information, they entirely lack the personal perspective and global outlook of the *Chronicles* where men and their actions are always set at a critical distance and seen in a constant interplay with the totality of society. In the best of his texts, such as the Rome text and many parts of books three and four, Froissart integrates vast sequences of far-ranging events into close-linked causal patterns which, however severely criticised by twentieth-century historians, transmit to us a forceful interpretation of events which was widely accepted among the governing classes of fourteenth-century Europe.

NOTES

Introduction

1 Luce 1890: 247-59; KL I, i, 387; Palmer 1978: 161-2.
2 For Dickens and Thackeray, see Stonehouse 1935: 49, 157. Hazlitt's recommendation is in his essay 'On Reading Old Books'.
3 Two trial pages of the projected Kelmscott edition were, in fact, run off in 1897, the year after Morris' death.
4 He mooted a revision of Berners edition (he was scornful of Johnes'), and thought Southey the ideal man for the job, though he realised that he would have to settle for someone less eminent to do the hackwork under his own supervision. While he dithered, however, he was anticipated by the reissue of Berners by Utterson in 1812 (Grierson 1932: 169, 402).
5 Voltaire's *Essai sur les moeurs* was published in 1756. A little over a year later (Jan. 1758), he was inquiring whether Froissart was the source of an anecdote about Charles VII and Agnes Sorel (Besterman 1958: 44)!
6 Chateaubriand's main borrowings from Froissart are to be found in vols. 6-8 of his complete works (Paris, 1836), the reference to Froissart as the Herodotus of his age occurring at p.345 of vol. 8. For the similar statements of Merimée (1803-70) and Wallon (1812-1904), see *Mémoires de l'Academie des Inscriptions et Belles-lettres*, vol. 20 (1861), 268, 277; and for the statement of Taine (1828-93), his *Essai sur Tite-Live* (1856), p.334.
7 Sainte-Beuve (1804-69), *Causeries du Lundi*, IX (Paris, n.d.), p.120. For the editions of Froissart in this period — far too numerous to itemise — see the catalogues of the BL, BN, and above all of the Library of Congress; and, for English translations, see Thomas 1948.
8 The first two letters of Bertrandy's *Étude sur les Chroniques de Froissart: Guerre de Guienne, 1345-1346. Lettres addressées à M. Léon Lacabane* were published in the *Revue d'Aquitaine* for 1867-8. The complete work was published in book form in 1870.

I Book I (1325-1378) and its Sources

1 See for instance the voluminous notes to the editions of SHF and KL and the works of Bertrandy and Plaine listed in the bibliography.
2 See below, notably the chapter by Michael Jones.
3 KL II, 425; III, 187. SHF I, ccxii for identification of St Venant.
4 There are several passages where Froissart records his collection of materials in the 1360s, notably in relation to the battle of Auray (VI, 162), to Scottish events (KL II, 290), and in the famous passage in the penultimate chapter of Book IV of the *Chronicles* where he records his presence at the birth of the

future Richard II, an event he was told to record. The record duly appears in Book I (below, n. 12). See also the essay below by Barber p. 27.

5   The entire structure and presentation of the Rome version has clearly been affected by the deposition and death of Richard II and so must have been conceived after January 1400.

6   The B MSS are the basis of the SHF edition and the Amiens MS that of KL; the epitome is published in KL XVII; and the Rome MS by Diller. Despite the fact that there are many times more manuscripts of the A text than of all the others put together, and despite the fact that the A MSS have been recognised as the first edition of Book I for the past century, no edition of these manuscripts has been published, though variants from them are included in both the SHF and KL editions. Anyone who has tried to use the A text — particularly for the 1370s — will be aware that this is a very unsatisfactory state of affairs. The edition of the Amiens MS by KL is defective in many important respects and a new edition — being prepared by G. T. Diller — is much needed.

7   Although I shall refer throughout this paper to the Amiens MS as though it were the sole MS of its family, there is also an incomplete version of this same family in BM Valenciennes MS 638. This is an intriguing manuscript, the work of a literary forger (Palmer 1978: 157-8), a fact which in view of the hypothesis to be advanced later in this paper may well be highly significant. A critical edition of the Valenciennes MS would be worthwhile.

8   The relationship of B6 to the other versions of Book I, though, is an interesting question in its own right and deserves investigation. Its attribution to Froissart has been disputed (Molinier 1904: 12) but see below n. 34 for arguments in favour of Froissart's authorship. The view that B6 is an abridgement of the A and B MSS is wrong: the author has drawn on the Amiens MS as well. A critical edition of this text would be worthwhile.

9   The text of the A MSS for these years deserves publication. It was inexplicably omitted from the SHF edition and has to be read from the variants given by KL, which give no indication of just how much of the text is published or whether it is reproduced *seriatim*. (Lettenhove had an unfortunate habit of printing parts of his MSS where he thought they should have occurred rather than where they actually were in his manuscripts.)

10   Paris 1836-8, and Delachenal 1910-20. An analysis of the textual relationship of the A MSS of Book I and the various manuscripts of the *Grandes chroniques* might well throw some interesting light on both works. Neither Lacabane 1840-1, Farley 1969 nor Spiegel 1978 throw any light on this topic.

11   By Saenger 1975: 15-26, who has produced interesting new evidence that one at least of the B MSS is very much later than Luce supposed and must be dated c.1391. See also the chapter by Barber below.

12   SHF VII, 1, 259; Johnes I, 357; BL Royal MS 14 D III, fo. 202v; Add. MS 38659, fo. 120; BN MS Fr. 86, fo. 410; MS Fr. 2634, fo. 305v; MS Fr. 2640, fo. 263; MS Fr. 2649, fo. 306; MS Fr. 2651, fo. 269v; MS Fr. 2655, fo. 273v; MS Fr. 2674, fo. 225; MS Fr. 6474, fo. 301v; MS Fr. 20356, fo. 286v.

13   SHF V, 134, 351; Johnes I, 252; BL Royal MS 14 D III, fo. 70; Add. MS 38659, fo. 40v; Arundel MS 67, fo. 212v; BN MS Fr. 86, fo. 301v; MS Fr. 2634, fo. 235v; MS Fr. 2640, fo. 196; MS Fr. 2649, fo. 218; MS Fr. 2651, fo. 228v; MS Fr. 2655, fo. 202v; MS Fr. 2674, fo. 160; MS Fr. 6474, 211; MS Fr. 20356, fo. 212; BM Arras MS 175, fo. 253.

14   For further details see Palmer 1981. Saenger 1975: 15-26 supports this conclusion so far as the B MSS are concerned. This argument does not, of

course, mean that no part of Book I was *composed* before the 1390s. Evidence that Froissart was working on Book I much earlier than this has been given earlier in this essay. But none of the surviving manuscripts can have been completed before the 1390s, and their evidence indicates that the text of Book I did not achieve its final form until then.

15 There is not much doubt about this but if further proof were required it is supplied by BL Arundel MS 67. This is an A MS and contains the standard A text for the years 1350-6; but at the end of the manuscript the scribe has added at a later date − after the table of contents had been compiled − the B version of the years 1350-6.

16 Le Bel I, 93-4; SHF I, 84-7; KL II, 216-22; Diller 177-80; cf. Philippeau 1936 for Froissart and Le Bel.

17 Le Bel I, 323-33; SHF II, 157-69; KL IV, 62-91; Diller 536-49.

18 For the allies: Le Bel I, 119-28; SHF I, 114-26; KL II, 320-84; Diller 228-60; for van Artevelde: Le Bel I, 128-34; SHF I, 126-38; KL II, 361-437; Diller 261-79; for Brittany: Le Bel I, 245-55; SHF II, 86-96; KL III, 323-52; Diller 462-6; for Philip VI: Le Bel I, 260-3; SHF II, 102-5; KL III, 381-6; Diller 483-8; for Mauny: Le Bel I, 323-33; SHF II, 157-69; KL IV, 62-91; Diller 536-49; and for the countess of Salisbury and Edward III: Le Bel I, 290-4, II, 1-4, 30-3; SHF II, 135, 340-2, III, 1-4, 198-203; KL III, 446-69, IV, 122-6, 273-4; Diller 562-4. Most of what Froissart has to say about Brittany in the 1340s is derived from Le Bel in the A/B MSS but rewritten in Amiens (below pp.67-70).

19 Le Bel I, 89-93; SHF I, 83-4; KL II, 211-15; Diller 173-6.

20 Le Bel I, 95-100; SHF I, 100-3; KL II, 297-303; Diller 196-201.

21 Le Bel I, 319-23; SHF II, 154-7; KL IV, 50-62; Diller 530-7.

22 Le Bel I, 21-5; SHF I, 29-32; KL II, 75-82; Diller 80-6.

23 Le Bel II, 100-6; SHF III, 168-89; KL V, 30-57; Diller 717-38; cf. Rigollot 1840 and Manyon 1926.

24 See especially the passages in KL V, 31-2, 37-40, 46-7.

25 Such sentences and phrases occur at Diller 717, 718, 723-34, 736-8. The corresponding passages in the A/B MSS are in SHF III, 168, 169, 173-81, 187-9.

26 For Queen Isabella: Le Bel I, 8-12; SHF I, 12-18; KL II, 20-40; Diller 47-57; for the Scottish campaign: Le Bel I, 63-75; SHF I, 63-72; KL II, 160-82; Diller 141-51; for the aftermath of Sluys: Le Bel I, 182; SHF II, 43; KL III, 215; for Normandy: Le Bel II, 75-86; SHF III, 136-49; KL IV, 394-420; Diller 681-99; for Poitiers: Le Bel II, 229-38; SHF V, 1-69; KL V, 382-465; and for 1359: Le Bel II, 290-313; SHF V, 197-234; KL VI, 216-69.

27 The best edition of the text is Tyson 1975 but see also Pope and Lodge 1910 for a very useful introduction and notes. Palmer 1981 offers further analysis of points discussed above.

28 For Edward's homage: SHF I, 96-100; Diller 191-5; for the earl of Derby: Le Bel II, 40-1; SHF III, 58-84; KL IV, 237-87; Diller 610-27; for van Artevelde: Le Bel II, 36-8; SHF III, 96-105; KL IV, 310-24; Diller 633-41; and for Aiguillon: Le Bel II, 56-64; SHF III, 120-8; KL IV, 355-62; Diller 359-71.

29 E.g. Le Bel I, 166-7; SHF I, 185-6; KL III, 62; Diller 339-40. Other examples could be cited. Cases where the transition: Le Bel-Amiens-MSS A and B occur are even more frequent and are scattered through much of the text of Book I.

30 Le Bel I, 166-8; KL III, 62-4 (SHF I, 184-6; Diller 337-40); Le Bel I, 169-70; KL III, 73 (SHF I, 188-9; Diller 344-5); Le Bel I, 171-2; KL III, 98-111 (SHF I, 199-205; Diller 357-64).

31   It would require another essay of equal length to demonstrate which parts of these manuscripts are 'first' and which 'second' edition compositions. The situation is complex, for the first and second edition elements are not (generally speaking) grouped in unbroken blocks.

32   KL II, 425-7, III, 187, 231, 323, V, 432, VI, 381, VII, 65, 297; SHF VI, 92.

33   See above. These features recur so frequently that it is superfluous to cite individual instances.

34   Which would also tend to confirm that the epitome itself is the work of Froissart: see above, n.8.

35   KL IV, 386; Diller 677 (cf. SHF III, 133).

36   E.g. I, 46 (cf. Le Bel I, 44-5; KL II, 116-17; Diller 117-18). Many other examples could be cited.

37   Again, examples can be found scattered throughout Book I. See, e.g. KL IV, 62-91; Diller 536-49 (cf. Le Bel I, 323-33; SHF II, 157-69).

38   Two examples among many which could be cited must suffice: (1) the capture of Auray and Vannes: KL IV, 109-20; cf. Le Bel I, 339-42; SHF II, 177-81; Diller 555-61; and (2) Auberoche: KL IV, 239-57; cf. SHF III, 59-73; Diller 611-22.

39   Le Bel II, 234-5; KL V, 424-35; SHF V, 35-62.

40   KL VI, 276-7; SHF VI, 108-33 (KL VI, 409-27); KL VII, 93, 116; SHF VI, 93-8 (KL VI, 387-94).

41   SHF VII, 239-55; KL VIII, 24-44. Among other differences, the A/B MSS state that the townsfolk could not negotiate with the Black Prince because of the French garrison in the town, whereas the Amiens version omits this and states that Prince Edward simply refused to grant terms.

42   Among other examples which could be cited, the accounts in MSS A and B of Edward III's homage (I, 96-100), of brigandage (IV, 67-70), of Espagnols-sur-Mer (IV, 88-90), and of the Flagellants (100-2) do not appear in Amiens.

43   In particular, most of the text of KL II, 393-429.

44   Le Bel I, 109-18; SHF I, 107-14; KL II, 261-320; Diller 216-27.

45   Le Bel I, 119-28; SHF I, 114-26; KL II, 320-84; Diller 228-60.

46   KL II, 361-3, 409-25; cf. Le Bel I, 128-31; SHF I, 126-9; Diller 261-3.

47   Le Bel II, 71-4; SHF III, 133-6; KL IV, 386-9; Chandos Herald, lines 145-70.

48   It is perhaps significant that the changes produced by the use of the *Life of the Black Prince* have made the Amiens version very markedly more favourable to the French than any of the other versions of Book I, a characteristic of the Amiens MS discussed above. If these changes were the work of Froissart and introduced for this motive alone, we would have yet further cause to lower our estimate of his qualities as an historian.

II Jean Froissart and Edward the Black Prince

1   KL I, i, 36; Scheler 1872: 5, 7 (*Cour de May*: 134, 190).

2   XIV, 4. The last six words are a variant.

3   I can find no support for Lettenhove's assertion that he was formally appointed a clerk, except in the tenor of the letters of introduction to the king of Scotland (SHF I, 269).

4   There is a similar passage at IV, 235-6. The passages only occur in the

Rome MS, like the full account of his travels with Edward Despenser.

5 In a lecture to the twelfth International Arthurian Congress, Regensburg, August 1979.

6 The argument for a date before 1373 (summarised by Shears 1930: 35) rests on the assumption that the first version of the *Chronicles* must antedate *Le joli buisson de joenece*; but there is no reason why Robert of Namur should not have first patronised Froissart *after* that date, which then becomes a *terminus a quo* for the version naming him, which is not necessarily the first. For further discussion of the date of the composition of Book I see pp.11-12.

7 Pinchart 1855: 45-6, 68.

8 The treaty of Brétigny is an exception: the whole document appears in MSS A and B (VI, 27-33), but not in the Amiens version, and an associated text is in both versions (VII, 87-91, 321-2). The text of Edward III's letter recognising that his homage to Philip VI was liege also appears in the A and B MSS (I, 97-9) and in Rome (Diller 193-5) but not in Amiens.

9 E.g. *DNB* VI, 514, Emerson 1976: 168; Harvey 1976: 103; Dupuy 1970: 195-6.

10 VII, 66-79, 84-99, 109-13, 305-11, 319-25, 332-5. Much of the text exists in three versions: A/B, Amiens and MS B6 (KL XVII).

11 Pinchart 1855: 45, 68.

12 VII, 250. The Amiens MS gives a much shorter version, but repeats the charge of a civilian massacre.

III The Age of Charles V

1 These words are the subtitle of Tuchman 1978, a work that makes considerable use of Froissart and has been criticised for over-stressing disasters like plague, famine and violence. Had the critics worked closely with French documents, particularly for the thirty years after 1348, they would have found it difficult to charge this author with exaggeration.

2 KL I, i, 35-370 for one editor's account of Froissart's career and itinerary, but see the comments below at nn.15-16. Thompson 1966: 11, is rightly more circumspect about the chronicler's early itinerary. On his first departures from Le Bel, see SHF I, 210, and V, i, n.1; KL I, ii, 54-5.

3 See Thompson 1966: 12-13. The subject of his patrons is dealt with in Chapter 11. Shifts of emphasis to please actual or potential patrons, once considered something of a blot on Froissart's reputation, may now be appreciated as an early form of 'grantsmanship', as American scholars call the technique of seeking support from funding agencies.

4 In treating the crisis of 1356-8 (Henneman 1976: 17-83), I have found the most useful of modern works to be Avout 1960, Cazelles 1965 and Faral 1945. For the classic detailed account (still very useful), see Delachenal 1909a: 251-432.

5 Delachenal 1900: 18-19; Delachenal 1910: 76-80; Douët d'Arcq 1840-1: 382-3; Faral 1945; Delachenal 1909a: 251-2 and notes.

6 *Ord.* III, 124-46. See Cazelles 1962-3: 92. For the events of 1356-7, see Henneman 1976: 26-45 and notes (many of which refer to works cited above, nn.4-5).

7   The three main sources (discussed Henneman 1976: 26, and especially by
    Faral 1945) are *Journal des états* (Delachenal 1900), *Chron. Jean II*
    (Delachenal 1910) and 'Acte d'accusation' (Douët d'Arcq 1840-1).
8   SHF V, 72, 95-9, and notes on xxvii-viii; KL VI, 1-5, 37-44; Johnes I, 231,
    239; and Berners I, 389.
9   SHF V, 79; KL VI, 12; Johnes I, 233; and Berners I, 392 for the supposed
    regency of the dauphin in 1356. For modern views on the critical events of
    February and March 1358, see Avout 1960: 148-65; Delachenal 1909a:
    356-78; Henneman 1976: 66-70.
10 SHF V, 99-103, 317-24; KL VI, 47-55; Johnes I, 240-1.
11 For example, Luce states (V, xix, n. 1) that the eleven clergy, six nobles, and
    seventeen bourgeois representatives named in Douët d'Arcq 1840-1: 382-3
    were the commission named by the Estates in October 1356 which Froissart/
    Le Bel thought consisted of twelve men from each Estate. These individuals
    are now understood to have been only those members of the commission
    who were regarded as particular enemies by the royal officials whose views
    appear in the 'Acte d'accusation' (Douët d'Arcq 1840-1).
12 Thompson 1966: xvii. As Luce pointed out (SHF I, cxxiii), of contemporary
    chroniclers, the *Chronique des quatre premiers Valois* (Luce 1862) appears
    most accurate when compared with official documents.
13 *Ord*. III, 433-42. For the foregoing discussion of 1358-60, see Henneman
    1976: 84-120 and notes.
14 For these events and the appropriate sources, see Henneman 1976: 154-60,
    171-92, 206-32. For Froissart's treatment of the battle of Cocherel, see
    SHF VI, 110-30, 295-310; KL VI, 416-43; Berners II, 114-17; Johnes I,
    317-21.
15 SHF VI, 59-74, 256-69; KL VI, 336-58; Berners II, 82-7; Johnes I, 293-7.
    For Kervyn de Lettenhove's discussion of Froissart's supposed trip to the
    Midi, see KL I, i, 61-74.
16 SHF VI, notes on xix-xxxii. Froissart departs in some respects from his
    predecessor in describing these years, but at the cost of less, rather than more,
    accuracy. See Le Bel II, 321-3, where the capture of Pont-Saint-Esprit is
    dated properly.
17 On the battle of Cocherel, see above, note 14. The earlier battle, Brignais
    (VI, 260-5; KL VI, 336-45; Johnes I, 294-7) offers a nice example of the
    routiers as tacticians. Froissart unaccountably fails to mention the chief
    French commander at Brignais, the count of Tancarville, who had been
    given extensive powers over a large region precisely to coordinate efforts
    against the *routiers*. See Guigue 1886: 59-60.
18 KL I, i, 126: Auberchicourt, one of the leading *routier* captain, was an
    acquaintance and countryman of Froissart's, from Hainault.
19 VI, 34-6; KL VI, 300-9; Johnes I, 284-9. Luce (VI, xi, n. 7) has indicated
    that Froissart's text of the ratification is that found in AN J 639, no. 15,
    the copy destined for the French king.
20 V, 180; KL VI, 182-7; Johnes I, 263. See also Le Bel II, 288-9.
21 Delachenal 1909b: 77-82 discusses the treaty in detail and refers to Froissart's
    'customary inexactitude'. Charles the Bad had never been eager for John's
    release, since it would free the French king to settle scores with him. This
    particular treaty would, in addition, have placed him under English
    suzerainty.
22 V, 181, Johnes I, 263; KL VI, 186. It is significant that the remarks at-
    tributed to John II were not part of Jean le Bel's account.
23 Cazelles 1974: passim. For the famous description of 'King John's Panic',

see Perroy 1951: 125-31.

24 Prou 1888, a work that includes many published documents, is the main source for the crusading plans, but see KL VII, 80-2, and sources cited in Henneman 1976: 173-205.

25 VI, 93-4, 285; KL VI, 387-8. On the princely hostages, see also KL VI, 376-8, 506-8.

26 On the diversion of ransom funds, see Henneman 1976 chapters V and VI, especially p.171. On the probable revenues of the indirect taxes, see *ibid*. 293-5.

27 On John's choice of advisers, see Cazelles 1974: 12-13; Delachenal 1909a: 254-5.

28 See Cazelles 1958: 81-4, 134-54; Cazelles 1960: 845-65; Henneman 1978: 954-5.

29 On the *routiers* in Languedoc in the 1360s under Audrehem's and Anjou's lieutenancies, see Henneman 1976: 161-205, 255-65. It is clear that *routiers* played a significant role in the royal armies under Anjou in the southwest after the resumption of Anglo-French hostilities in 1369. See KL VII, 324-6, 337-8, 361-7; and Contamine 1971: 151-81, especially 167.

30 Henneman 1976: 31, 67; Cazelles 1960: 846-7.

31 Villaines is mentioned in 1358 as marshal of Normandy and a defender of the dauphin's family in the market of Meaux against the *Jacquerie* (KL VI, 55-66, 465). Froissart mentions his presence on numerous campaigns during the reign of Charles V: KL VII, 7, 90, 198, 210, 237-9, 261-9, 274. One of the Marmousets under Charles VI, he survived their disgrace. Military pay records indicate service between 1360 and 1405: BN Pièces Originales 3001, doss. 66602, nos. 4-6, 10-21, 23, 26-8, 31, 32; Coll. Clairambault 113, nos. 44-51.

32 While still dauphin, Charles made peace with the count of Harcourt, who married a Bourbon princess in 1359 (V, 163; Johnes I, 259-60) and served the Valois monarchy thereafter (BN Nouv. Acq. Françaises 7414, fos. 175r, 225v; MS Fr. 32510, fos. 239v, 268r, 292v, 308r). Coucy, who had been a hostage in England, had married the daughter of Edward III and remained neutral when the Anglo-French war resumed (KL VII, 419-20; Johnes I, 438). By the later 1370s, however, he had become one of the most important commanders under Charles V. For a popular history based on his career, see Tuchman 1978. For his military career under Charles V and Charles VI, see Contamine 1971: 573-4; BN Coll. Clairambault 35, nos. 75-83, 89, 92, 99, 100, 102, 104, 106-8; Pièces Originales 875, doss. 19660, nos. 3-6, 10-16.

33 Cazelles 1958: 142-54; Lefranc 1898: *pièce justificative* 2.

34 On the battle of Auray, where Clisson lost an eye, see VI, 155-69, 329-42; KL VII, 28-60; Johnes I, 328-35.

35 VI, 181-2; KL VII, 78; Johnes I, 338. More accurately, perhaps, Froissart identifies Clisson as one of the chief men of Charles V's council when the war resumed: KL VII, 415.

36 KL V, 445-6, for the Poitevin lords serving with John II in 1356. For their service under the Black Prince and his lieutenants in 1369-72, see KL VII, 301, 353-4, 387-8, 450-60; VIII, 29-32, 63-75, 86-90.

37 VI, 57-9, 254-6; KL VI, 324-6; Johnes I, 292 (on the reluctance of the Gascon lords to transfer homage to the Plantagenets). For their presence on the Spanish expedition, see Johnes I, 361. For a dispute between the Prince and the lord of Albret over the size of the latter's contingent, see VI, 228-34, 380-2; KL VII, 143-6; Johnes I, 355-6.

38 VII 66-9, 87-99, 305-11; KL VII, 253-61, 274-87, 291-5, 533-5; Johnes I,

380-4, 390-6. For a recent survey of the Gascon appeals from the political and fiscal point of view, based on other sources, see Henneman 1976: 247-55.
39 See the discussion and citations in Henneman 1976: 299-300.
40 Henneman 1976: 299-301; Mirot 1905: 20-40.
41 Palmer 1972: 18-22; Lehoux 1966: 13-61; Henneman 1978: 958; Mirot 1905: 39-169.
42 IX, 50-4, 143-54; Johnes I, 536-8.
43 IX, 70, 132, 231-2, 289; Johnes I, 591-2, 601, 612, 618, 625-6, 629-30; KL IX, 308-10, 331-2.
44 Charles V had regulated the succession in 1374, giving a principal role to Louis of Anjou (*Ord*. VI, 26-32). It was Burgundy who, with the duke of Berry's help, forced this arrangement to be cancelled. Their side of the story, which obviously capitalised on the public fear of Anjou's greed and played down Burgundy's own ambitions, clearly influenced Froissart's treatment of the succession of 1380. See IX, 279-84, 288; Johnes I, 615-18.
45 Nordberg 1964 has used financial accounts and other official documents to provide a valuable corrective to the pro-Burgundian chroniclers and the modern historians who have relied on them.
46 IX, 32-3, 68, Johnes I, 737-8, 746, 749-50.
47 For a few such references, see VII, 249-54; Johnes I, 396, 432-6, 452-4, 499, 608; KL VII, 215-17, VIII, 40-3.
48 At Cocherel (see n.14 above), Du Guesclin's tactics led Jean Jouel and his men to abandon a superior position. The captal de Buch, who saw through the manoeuvre, could not dissuade Jouel but felt obliged to support his advancing troops. As a result, the battle was lost.
49 VII, 166, 185, 246; and Johnes I, 422, 429, 452, 610 give examples either of explicit orders from Charles V to avoid battle or advice to that effect from Clisson. Contrary to the widespread tendency to link Du Guesclin with this policy, Froissart leads one to think that Clisson, more than anyone else, advocated caution. See also KL VII, 415.
50 Keen 1965 (an indispensable book for anyone wishing to understand Froissart or study the problem of the *routiers*), especially 19-57, 65, 72-4, 86-9, 93-110.
51 See above, n.48, and the famous case of the rejected advice of Audrehem before Nájera: VII, 26; KL VII, 180-3; Johnes I, 367. We lack a modern analysis of how leaders debated tactical questions on the eve of a battle (as portrayed by the chroniclers), but see Johnes I, 329-30, for the difficulty encountered by Chandos in getting Calverley to command the rearguard at Auray.

IV Charles VI and Richard II

1 See chapter 9 below for a detailed analysis of Froissart's journey to Béarn in 1388.
2 Barber 1978: 245-6; but cf. chapter 2 above, where it is argued that the 'later' version of Crécy is, in fact, Froissart's first description of the battle.
3 See below, chapter 5, p.68 for a long quote from Froissart about his enormous labour, pains and expense 'to establish my account on as truthful a basis as I could' (II, 265-6).

4   The best modern accounts are, for England, Tout 1928a and Tuck 1973, and for France, Delachenal 1916.
5   There is a good account by Kingsford in the *Dictionary of National Biography* of Alice Perrers.
6   Tuck 1973 is the best account of the development of the council during the minority.
7   Russell 1955, chapter 11. Fortunately for England, the allied fleet broke up after the death of Charles V.
8   Ordonnances VI, 45-9; cf. Lehoux 1966: 345-6.
9   Lehoux 1966: 9-16 for the events which followed the death of Charles V.
10 Tuck 1973: 92-6 for Gaunt, and 96-7 for the Scottish campaign.
11 P.R.O., E/101/40/9; E.364/20m.71.
12 Lehoux 1966: 185-6 has a detailed analysis of Berry's movements.

V   The Breton Civil War

1   Morice 1742: 1421-4, 1608-13.
2   There is no modern study of the various fragmentary, composite and inter-dependent Breton chronicles like the *Chronicon Brittanicum* and *Les Chroniques Annaulx*, of their place of origin and date, nor of their relationship with the *Chronicon Briocense* or the work of Pierre le Baud (cf. Morice 1742: 1-117).
3   Cf. Meignen 1886: ix; Argentré 1618: 340-474, although the great jurist was the first to exploit the legal records of 1341 seriously (Jones 1972a: 2).
4   Galbraith 1927; Pocquet 1928; Bock 1931; Le Patourel 1954, 1958; Jones 1970.
5   Diller 1002-10 for a concordance; cf. SHF II, 86ff, and Le Bel I, 246ff.
6   Le Bel I, 248, 262, 271 etc.
7   SHF II, 91, 108, 147.
8   SHF II, 99 (La Roche Periou 'seant sus un hault tertre qui s'estent droit sus la mer'. Cf. Le Bel I, 256). The countess of Montfort would have been endowed both with remarkable eyesight to spot ships at sea from the walls of Hennebont (II, 150) and stamina to undertake a journey from there to Brest overnight (II, 145). In this latter case modern opinion favours identification with Brech as the most likely local site (II, xlvii, n.2 and La Borderie 1899: 452-3). For Dinan and Guémené see Le Bel I, 312; SHF II, 148 and La Borderie 1899: 460, n.3. For Goy-la-Forest see Déserts 1970.
9   Plaine 1871: 15-18; SHF II, xxxixff.
10 Le Bel II, xvi-ii, 9, 246, 271 and SHF III, 5. For the chronicler's relations with the Despensers see KL I, i, 143-50.
11 There is one manuscript of the 'first' redaction (A 17) which may well have been possessed by a member of the Du Guesclin family and to which the copyist, Raoul Tanguy, a Breton, added local details (SHF VI, lvii, n.1).
12 III, 8-9, 208-9 — if only for the reason that she never went personally to England for aid (below, p.70).
13 For Mauron the main accounts are Molinier 1882: 105-6 and Thompson 1889a: 189-91, where Bentley's letter announcing his victory is the major text. Froissart briefly alludes to it in the second redaction (SHF IV, 128) and in some manuscripts of the first redaction there is a brief passage based

on the *Grandes chroniques* added to his text (SHF IV, 399, 402). For Crokart and the later stages of the war, see IV, 69-70, 110-15, 302-3, 339-41; cf. Le Bel II, 175-6. For Raoul de Caours, another adventurer, see Viard 1937: 296, 326; Fowler 1969: 89-92 and Le Bel II, 355-6.

14 Viard 1937: 255-6, 260-9, 296-309; Lemoine 1896: 67-70, 77-81 for the campaigns in the Trégorrois and Finistère in 1345-7; Molinier 1882 mentions several small actions in north east Brittany in the early 1350s; Lemoine 1896: 96 has an account of the capture of Nantes by the English in February 1355 and its immediate recapture by the French (see also Delachenal 1910: 50).

15 Plaine 1921 (canonisation). In later sections of the *Chronicles* whenever the name of Blois was mentioned, he was styled 'saint' (Diverres 1953: 16).

16 Delachenal 1931: 236-51; cf. also above, pp. 11-12.

17 Most fully in Book III (SHF XIII, 121-5) which I failed to exploit thoroughly in Jones 1972b.

18 II, 171-3, 404-5 (Louis). The third redaction has the fullest account of the battle of La Roche Derrien (IV, 38-44, 260-9; Diller 810-9).

19 IV, 38-44, 260-9; Le Bel II, 144ff.

20 Déprez 1926, Pocquet 1928a: 301ff.

21 Diller 589-600, 810-19, Cazelles 1958: 151-5 and Cuttler 1978: 91, 123-4 and 194-6 for the traitors.

22 Thompson 1889a: 125-9, 135, 164-8, 177-89, 243, 339-42; Thompson 1889b: 76-7 (1342 expedition with incorrect date of 1345); Lumby 1895: 23-31; Prince 1931: 362-5. PRO C 47/2/33, giving details of a proposed force, which Prince thought referred to the 1340 expedition, is now regarded as dating from the Breton expedition of 1342 (Lewis 1964: 8), the fullest account of which is PRO E 36/204, Wardrobe accounts passim.

23 Diller 499, 504, 592; Le Bel I, 271.

24 Viard 1937: 243; Moranvillé 1893: 207-8; La Borderie 1899: 496. St-André, line 278, records that he was held in prison for more than three years (Lobineau 1707b: 695).

25 Diller 464, 472 for the names of places 'taken' in the 1341 campaign, or, for dates, above n. 9. The reasons for some of the minor changes in the text remain intriguing; Auray, described by Le Bel (I, 311) as built by Arthur, a description borrowed in the first two redactions (SHF II, 146, 364) is now said to have been fortified by Julius Caesar (Diller 472).

26 Le Bel I, xvi-ii; Viard 1905: 540-6.

27 SHF II, 178, 414, 416-17 an alleged truce of the countess of Montfort and Blois in November 1342. The terms of an actual truce between the countess and Philip VI on 1 March 1342 are largely printed in La Borderie 1899: 446, n. 1 from AN J 241, no. 43bis.

28 Thompson 1889a: 126-7, 388, 415-6. Such a newsletter obviously lies behind the account of Dagworth's campaigns in 1346 most fully described in Oxford Bodley MS 462, fos. 31r-32r, extracts from a fuller version of the *Historia Aurea* in a manuscript of c.1420, in all probability compiled under the guidance of Thomas Walsingham (Prince 1931: 365 and Galbraith 1937: introduction) from which it found its way into the *Ypodigma* (Riley 1876: 288-90) in a full but edited form.

29 Viard 1937: iv-vi. The relationship of the *Chronique normande* to the St Denis sources is not at all clear (Gransden 1972: 333, n. 4) but it seems that both the author of that chronicle and the compiler of the *Chronographia* drew on the same sources for the early part of the Breton war, although for the 1350s the *Chronique normande* provides a unique

account of several episodes in the duchy.

30 The lord of Ancenis is present at the capitulation of Nantes in the third redaction (Diller 550; SHF II, 112-14, 322) and another Guillaume d'Ancenis was among prisoners exchanged after the truce of Malestroit (SHF III, 246, 35).

31 Luce 1876: 427. Froissart added his name, together with that of Du Guesclin, to the defenders of Rennes in 1342, in elaborating Le Bel's brief account. There is no other authority for this (SHF III, 31).

32 Jones 1970: 74ff; BN MS Nouv. Acquis. Fr. 20026, no.172, order from Charles V, 10 September 1373, to pay 3,000 francs to ten Breton knights and esquires 'pour entrer en sa foy et homage'.

33 KL I, i, 318; La Borderie 1899: 588, n.4.

34 Cf. the changes in the genealogical table below and the retrospect on the civil war in Book III (SHF XIII, 121-5). The remarks on Breton ducal finances there are remarkably apposite (Jones 1972-4).

35 XI, 104-5; IX, 127-35, an extremely confused account of an alleged journey of John IV to Flanders in 1379; and for events in 1388, XV passim and Jones 1970: 108-11.

36 Thompson 1889a: 339; cf. Viard 1937: 217-20; Lemoine 1896: 54-5; Newhall 1953: 35-6, 159-62.

37 The uncle of Hervé de Léon who was allegedly bishop of St Pol de Léon has never been identified (SHF II, xlix, n.2). A bishop of St Pol testified at the hearing of the succession dispute in August 1341 (BN MS Fr. 22338, fo.125r).

38 Géraud 1843b: 144-5; cf. La Borderie 1899: 403-4, Cazelles 1958: 140.

39 Rymer 1821: 929; *CPR 1334-8*, 191, 245, 412; La Borderie 1899: 405-8.

40 Rymer 1821: 965, 1129; cf. *CPR 1338-40*, 29, 30, 110, 207, 423.

41 Cazelles 1958: 140-2 marshals most of the evidence; AN J 241B, no. 35 (1340), BN MS Fr. 16654, fos. 210-11 and Cazelles 1962: no.118 for Breton money; La Borderie 1899: 40.

42 SHF II, xxxii-iii; La Borderie 1899: 423-32; Lemoine 1896: 55, n.1; Le Patourel 1958: 187, n.57. Viard and Déprez were still inclined to accept the story (Le Bel I, 259, n.1).

43 Morice 1750: plate between 244-5; Le Patourel 1958: 187.

44 PRO E 30/63 = Morice 1742: 1413-15 and Rymer 1821: 1164. The presence at Nantes of quantities of coin from Limoges indicated in this document and remitted in the normal course of events by the vicecomital receiver may be at the base of the chronicler's story about the seizure of treasure which first appears in Le Bel, is followed by Froissart, and is also found in the *Chronique normande* and the *Chronographia*. Fragmentary accounts showing John III appointing joint-moneyers for Nantes and Limoges, and Charles of Blois drawing on their revenues survive, together with a document of 13 August 1341 which shows Joan, dowager duchess of Brittany, exercising her rights in Limoges (AD Basses-Pyrenées E 624, nos. 1, 2, 5, 13, 14). For the separate issue of the succession to Limoges see Spinosi 1961.

45 Geslin de Bourgogne 1864: 384; BN MS Fr. 22338, fos. 117-55, interrogation of witnesses by a commission headed by the bishops of Laon and Noyon, 27 August - 4 September 1341.

46 There was a break in the work of the commission between 1 and 4 September and on this last day only witnesses for Blois were heard (BN MS Fr. 22338, fos. 134v, 152r). For the campaign of the duke of Normandy in the autumn see SHF II, xxxix-xliii; Viard 1937: 220ff.

47 Le Patourel 1958: 187-8. At the end of 1343 it was particularly these

regions which Edward III was anxious to hold (Rymer 1821: 1242).

48 PRO E 101/23/18, 22, 35 E 101/24/10; E 36/204 passim.

49 SHF V, 85-7, 304-8; Fowler 1969: 161-5 for the most recent serious treatment of the siege.

50 Molinier 1882: 117; Lemoine 1896: 110-11; Delachenal 1910a: 110-11; Charrière 1838b: 1053-2029; La Borderie 1899: 551-9.

51 SHF VI, 148-74, 322-52; La Borderie 1899: 582-97; Jones 1970: 19.

52 I would like to thank Antonia Gransden, John Palmer and Malcolm and Juliet Vale for helpful criticisms of this paper even though I have not adopted all of their suggestions.

VI The War in Spain and Portugal

1 Perroy 1933a: 242, n.2. All the topics mentioned in the present essay are fully discussed in Russell 1955 to which the reader who requires further information is referred.

2 I omit in this essay any discussion of what Froissart has to say about the all-important naval consequences of the Franco-Castilian alliance.

3 When giving — mostly correctly — the names of important personages in the Lancastrian army who were killed or died of illness in Spain, Froissart names one of his informants: 'Et oy pour certain recorder ung chevalier d'Angleterre à qui j'en parlay sus son retour qu'il fist parmy France, qui s'appelloit messire Thomas Quimebery' (XIV, 112).

4 Froissart usually refers to Castile as 'Espaigne' and to Castilians as 'Espaignolz'. This usage was common in fourteenth-century Europe; English exchequer records frequently use the term 'Rex Ispannie' to denote the king of Castile.

5 The *Chronicles*, nevertheless, never accord Fogaça his title and always insist on calling him a squire. He had been head of the royal chancery since 1378 and held the post until c.1398. He must have learnt his French during his long stay as ambassador in England.

6 This confusion, apparently acoustic in origin, is further proof of Froissart's reliance on his ear alone. Documents issued by the Black Prince in Gascony after 1366 describe him without difficulty as 'Seigneur de Biscaie et de Castre d'Ordials' (Russell 1955: 113).

7 Froissart could have found the locations of the main cities etc. of the Iberian Peninsula, as well as those of the ports, on some of the portulan charts routinely available for the use of mariners and others. Much more detailed geographical descriptions were available on the much scarcer world maps, like the Catalan Atlas of 1375 in the possession of Charles V of France. Even an approach to merchants or pilgrims who knew the Peninsula would have resolved most of the chronicler's topographical problems.

8 See KL I, i, 460. As far as Peninsular affairs are concerned KL's judgement is, of course, far too optimistic.

9 The detailed evidence will be found in Pope and Lodge 1910: lx-lxii.

10 Froissart does, however, note that the subsequent marriage of the Infanta Isabel to Edmund of Cambridge was decided upon by the council (VIII, 285).

11 Rosell 1953b: 33-4. The *Crónica de Garcí López de Roncesvalles*, written

c.1404 by the then royal treasurer of Navarre, is now available in print but does not add much to information already available (Orcastegui Gros 1977: 86-95).

12 For the biography of this important but mysterious person, a relative of Gaston III of Foix, see Tucoo-Chala 1960: passim.

13 The affairs of Spanish Navarre get little attention from Froissart after 1379 though the passage quoted appears to look to the future.

14 Sir William Willoughby, according to Froissart, who also refers to the presence at Foix of various English knights 'lesquelz estoient de l'ostel au duc de Lancastre, qui pour ce temps se tenoit a Bourdiaux' (XII, 95) -- after, of course, his return from Spain and Portugal.

15 An attempt to account for the presence of this distinguished Portuguese knight in Middelburg in 1390, supposedly on his way to go crusading in Prussia, will be found in Dias Arnaut 1947: 129-59, who suggests that, as there is no mention of such a reason for any journey in contemporary Portuguese sources, the visit may have been connected with the ransom of the Portuguese ambassadors to the pope who had recently been captured in Germany. I do not see any real reason to doubt Froissart's explanation. Pacheco rebelled against John I of Portugal and supported the claims of his half-brother, the Infante D. Dinis, to the throne (c.1397). In view of this it is understandable that Fernão Lopes should not have chosen to refer to any of his exploits in the decade of his treason.

16 Froissart claims that not all the English knights and squires returned to England from Portugal by sea; some, he says, with French knights released from the Castilian army, went to serve the king of Granada for three months (X, 199). If the chronicler got his facts from one of these, he could well not have received information about the way the rest of the army was conveyed to England.

17 Braamcamp 1973; Entwistle 1968. Lopes, like Ayala, had been brought up to believe that the evidence of eye-witnesses was a prime requisite for securing historical truth. Required to chronicle the reigns of Ferdinand I and John I, for which period few eye-witnesses survived, he turned to the documents and registers in his charge in the royal archives and realised from these that the evidence of chroniclers who wrote about events in the life-time of the kings concerned was far from reliable − a discovery which led him to make archival sources his base material as a chronicler (Russell 1941).

18 The king, for example, leaves the battlefield one day and reaches Lisbon, a distance of some sixty miles, the next day. In fact he did not go to Lisbon at all at this time.

19 Froissart supplies a detailed list of the names of some of the 300 knights and squires of Béarn killed at Aljubarrota (XII, 162-3). He also recounts as evidence of the count of Foix's supernatural powers the fact that he knew of the Castilian defeat the day after it happened (XII, 170-2).

20 The chronicler is unaware here of the regency of John I and declares that the Infante D. Dinis was immediately elected king (XII, 8-9). He has, of course, managed to confuse the name of John, master of the order of *Avis*, with that of his half-brother *Dinis*.

21 I have not been able to identify these three squires from surviving English records which list the names of the troops sent from England to reinforce the Portuguese. The chronicler is incorrect when he says no English knights accompanied this force, but there were few of them (Russell 1955: 372 and 396, n.3).

22 The Castilian king's own letter describing the battle, dated 29 August,

clearly states that 'most of the knights who were with us and had experience of other battles advised that the encounter should not take place that day ... but all the rest had such a desire to fight that they attacked without our authority' (Cascales 1775: 195). The king's version of events is amply confirmed by Ayala who, in *D. Juan*, quotes at length the advice of Jean de Rye (and himself) recommending a postponement (Rosell 1953b: 103-4).

23 Nevertheless Froissart still calls Edmund of Cambridge's son Edward, 'John' — as he had done when telling of his betrothal in 1381 in Lisbon to the Infanta Beatriz of Portugal — and still describes chancellor Fogaça as a squire.

24 One example among dozens: Froissart describes the port of Betanzos, on the north coast of Galicia near La Coruña, as 'la derraine bonne ville au lez vers le royaulme de Portingal et ou droit chemin du port de Conumbres' (XIII, 164).

25 Tucoo-Chala 1960: 21: 'C'est que Froissart ne cherche nullement à faire oeuvre d'historien, mais oeuvre de moraliste'. Froissart himself, of course, would not have understood such a distinction.

VII The War in the Low Countries

1 I would like to thank Dr J. L. Price, who translated the original Dutch text; Professor H. P. H. Jansen for his stimulating critical remarks, and Dr J. J. N. Palmer for his friendly support in producing the final draft.

2 Buchon III, 446, 453; Diller, 280: Flemings and Brabantines require English wool. Hugenholtz (1973: 84) calls the first phase of the Hundred Years War 'The Wool Phase'. Cf. Kerling 1954: 15-22, 59, 60; Munro 1977: 229-38; and, in general, Nicholas 1976.

3 III, 453, 457-9, 471; Diller, 260-2, 273, 280ff. Cf. Van Vessem 1966: 49-54; Lucas 1929: 240-83, 339-52, 358-67.

4 At the instigation of James van Artevelde, according to Froissart: I, 85-6; Diller, 341-3. On the Flemings in France: I, 104; Diller, 401.

5 Froissart on Van Artevelde: De Pauw 1920; cf. Van Werveke 1963: 88, 97-8.

6 Cf. Lucas 1929: 204-33, 265-6. On the *poorterie*, Nicholas 1976: 15-16 and the literature cited there, Rogghé 1941a: 21-2; Rogghé 1944; Van Werveke 1963: 10. Such divisions were not unusual: Fourquin 1978: 63ff, 73-4 (Van Artevelde no 'well-to-do fuller'!); Heers 1977: 241-2. See also chap. 1 above.

7 Cf. Pirenne 1908: 122-3: only three towns involved. On the position of the three towns: Nicholas 1968; 1971a, b; 1976; Van Uytven and Blockmans 1969: 400, 414-15.

8 Rogghé 1941b: 14; recognition of the Quarter of Ghent in 1343: Nicholas 1971b: 103.

9 In general, Rogghé 1968; Nicholas 1971; Godding 1973.

10 Diller, 633-9. Cf. De Pauw 1905; Rogghé 1941a: 45-8; 1941b: 30-5; Van Werveke 1963: 83-94; Lucas 1929: 520-7.

11 De Pauw 1920: 239-40, 243, 621-62: Van Artevelde in correspondence with England. Cf. Rogghé 1941b: 25; Van Werveke 1963: 11-12. See also

Fryde 1962, 1967.

12 I, 206-7; Diller, 636-41. The Flemings wished to participate actively in the siege of Calais, but were sent elsewhere by Edward III: I, 264; Diller, 827; cf. Lucas 1929: 553-4, 567-8.

13 I, 257-9, 283-4; Diller, 797-809, 822-3, 878-9; here, too, there are differences between the two versions. Cf. Lucas 1929: 559-65, 569, 571-2, 576-8.

14 He mentions the Flemish refusal to accept Louis of Male as their count in 1347: Diller, 822-3.

15 E.g. I, 58, 61-2, 69, 73-4, 75; Diller, 254-8, 292-3, 297, 308-12, 316-18. See Lucas 1929: 664, index s.v. John III, and chapter 10 below.

16 Diller, 319-20: William IV leaves Edward III; 326-30: William joins Philip VI; 354-5: William against Philip VI (cf. I, 77, 80, 90); Lucas 1929: 334, 384-5. After the truce of Esplechin and the peace negotiations of Arras (1340) from which he was absent, William IV is not mentioned by Froissart before his siege of Utrecht and expedition to Friesland in 1345: I, 124-7, 207-8; Diller 454-7, 460-1, 642-6. Cf. Lucas 1929: 421 (William IV at Esplechin).

17 The main source for this episode is the Dutch version of Froissart's *Chronicles*, translated about 1430 by Gerrit Potter van der Loo, and partly edited by De Pauw 1898: only the account of Flemish affairs has been published. The manuscript of the Dutch version (a copy written about 1470 according to an annotation of the *scriptor* Jan Heynrich Paedssenz) is preserved in the University Library of Leyden, BPL 3[I, II]; only two volumes are still available (of probably 5: the *scriptor* noted at the end of the second volume (f. 263r) that at that moment (26 Jan. 1470) he had finished copying the fourth volume of the Dutch translation by Gerrit Potter van der Loo; another manuscript of this Dutch version (Book III only) is preserved in the Royal Library at the Hague, 130B 21). The first volume contains Book II, the second Book III (of which De Pauw has edited fos. 98v-9v), so the Dutch translation of the first and fourth books of Froissart's *Chronicles* has been lost. Comparison of the Dutch text with the French of Buchon shows that the Dutch version is more extensive. Froissart originally wrote till c.1386 a *Chronique de Flandre*, totally devoted to the events between 1378 and 1385 (with a short addition about the death of Francis Ackerman in 1386 and the arrival of the duke and duchess of Burgundy in Bruges in November of the same year), which as a whole is preserved at Paris (BN Fr. 5004) and of which large fragments are to be found in the town library of Cambrai (MSS 677, 700). Later on, Froissart made corrections in this first draft and inserted it in his second book in an abbreviated form. The Dutch text of Gerrit Potter van der Loo is not just a translation of the final version of Book II; he probably translated a manuscript of Book II including a larger version of the original *Chronique de Flandre* than that normally inserted in Book II. Comparison of the Leyden MS with the BN 5004 version of the *Chronique de Flandre* as well as one or more of the manuscripts of Froissart's Book II or of all books of his *Chronicles* (e.g. BN Fr. 5006; Leyde UB, Vossius fol. gall. 9[II]) might solve this problem. Compare also Froissart's story with for example Pirenne 1902 and De Pauw 1909. There exists no modern comprehensive analysis of the events in Flanders between 1379 and 1385; cf. Quicke 1947: 291-411.

18 Mollat and Wolff 1973: 138-210, esp. 162-78; cf. Fourquin 1978: 155-8; Vaughan 1979: 16-38. On Ghent: Demuynck 1951; Wynant 1972; Van Oost 1973. Bruges: De Smet 1947, 1958; Van Oost 1978. Cf. also De Cuyper 1961.

19 Van Werveke 1968; Nicholas 1976; Blockmans 1979.

20 II, 83; *Cronyke*, 59: the *small trades* had brought Bruges to Ghent's side in 1379. Cf. II, 92; *Cronyke*, 84-7: controversies in Ypres and Bruges; Nicholas 1976. Occupation analysis of populations: e.g. Prevenier 1975; Nicholas 1978 (Ghent, Bruges).

21 II, 66-74, 78, 88, 143, 174, 340; *Cronyke*, 4-6, 8-11, 14-15, 18, 21-7, 32, 42, 68-70, 121, 143-4, 517 (the feud); Van Herwaarden 1978: 7-13, 48-52, 62-3 and literature cited there. Cf. Heers 1977: 205ff; Fourquin 1978: 60-2, 116ff.

22 II, 143, 145, 174; *Cronyke*, 121, 127, 144. Cf. Diller, 270: in his last version of Book I Froissart denominates the forces of James van Artevelde as '*Blans Caperons*'; cf. De Pauw and Vuylsteke 1874: 242, 350-1 (1338); 1880: 424 (1345).

23 Heers 1977: 286, 1970: 113. It is rather ironical to see that the shipmen's guild in 1385 was considered by the French king, Charles VI, as one of the most conciliatory guilds in Ghent, Vuylsteke 1893: 487, n.1.

24 II, 81-3; *Cronyke*, 53-9. Blockmans and Van Uytven (1969: 416-8) considered this reconciliation as 'a constitutional text' which never has been put in action.

25 Johnes I, 695; II, 197; *Cronyke*, 152. Quicke 1947: 307, 311-12, cf. 386-94.

26 II, 91; *Cronyke*, 79. Devillers 1883: 288-91 (nos. DLXXX, DLXXXI).

27 Holland, Zeeland: II, 91-2; *Cronyke*, 81-3 (Hainault knights against Ghent); II, 173, 197, 304; *Cronyke*, 140, 150, 458-9. Liège towns: II, 136, 172, 197; *Cronyke*, 97, 139, 151, 193. Brabant towns: II, 136, 197-8; *Cronyke*, 97, 150-6, 194. Neither Brabant, Hainault, Zeeland nor Holland against Ghent: II, 170; *Cronyke*, 132-3. Also rejoicings in Louvain and other Brabant towns after the victory of Ghent near Bruges in May 1382; the duchess and duke were aware of it 'but it behoved them to shut their eyes and ears, for it was not the moment to notice them' (Johnes I, 707; II, 210; *Cronyke*, 194).

28 E.g. II, 199-200, 201-3; *Cronyke*, 140-1, 145, 154-5, 157; 161, 165 (differences between both versions). Cf. Vuylsteke 1893: 271-3: August 1381, negotiations at Oedelem; October 1381 at Harelbeke; 274-6: messengers to Brabant (end of 1381); 303-7: messengers to Brabant, Hainault, Liège (spring 1382).

29 Vuylsteke 1893: passim. A summary in Quicke 1947: 314; the expedition of Ackerman to Brabant and Liège: *ibid.* 316-17, cf. II, 197-8; *Cronyke*, 151-6. Reactions of the count: De Pauw 1900: passim.

30 *Cronyke*, 132 (not in Buchon). Froissart deplored in the last version of Book I that Van Artevelde's murder was not avenged: Diller, 639.

31 Johnes I, 582 (translation adapted); II, 73; *Cronyke*, 29. Rural land investment: Nicholas 1971a: 267ff.

32 II, 143-4; *Cronyke*, 121-2; cf. II, 339-40; *Cronyke*, 515. Also for example II, 78; *Cronyke*, 42: the death of Jan Hyoens pleased the Mayhuus-clan, the deans of the lesser trades and the supporters of the count.

33 II, 81-2, 85-8; *Cronyke*, 55-70. See also Vuylsteke 1893: 441 (1379), 447 (new magistracy), 167 (1380), 251 (1381), 313 (1382), 467-8 (1383), 473 (1384). Cf. Rogghé 1950.

34 II, 170; *Cronyke*, 133: there (mistakenly) the dean of the weavers. On 6 July 1381 the dean of the weavers was killed because he had failed to prepare Ghent's defence, De Pauw 1909: 21. De Pauw 1900: 406: Jacob Soyszone, the dean of the butchers killed (in 1385 the butchers, together with the *poorterie*, shipmen, old-clothes men and bakers were considered the most conciliatory guilds by Charles VI, Vuylsteke 1893: 487, n.1).

35   Johnes I, 649; II, 146; *Cronyke*, 131. Confiscations: De Pauw 1900: passim;
     De Smet 1958; Van Oost 1973; cf. Vuylsteke 1893: 272: Philip van Artevelde
     with five others and a clerk administered confiscations during twenty-eight
     days, De Pauw 1920: 346.
36   II, 302, *Cronyke*, 456-7. Cf. De Pauw 1909: 42: the lord of Herzele wished
     Artevelde's surrender (Nov. 1382); *ibid.* 46: he left the army near Roosebeke.
37   II, 174; *Cronyke*, 146-7. Cf. Vuylsteke 1893: 272-3: both were involved in
     the negotiations at Harelbeke (October 1381); De Pauw 1909: 30: Simon
     Bette killed without any indications of the reasons; 32: Ghisebrecht
     de Grutere killed for many reasons (among others the deliverance of Jan
     Perneel, see n.39) and treason. De Pauw 1900: 405: according to the
     bailiff's account of Oudenaarde (13 January - 5 May 1382) Ghisebrecht
     de Grutere, Jan Sleipstaf and two others were killed shortly after Artevelde's
     coming to power. De Pauw 1909: 33: after the death of Ghisebrecht
     de Grutere and Simon Bette three others, among whom Jan Sleipstaf, were
     killed.
38   II, 90, 172, 290, 292; *Cronyke*, 74, 138, 442-3: the count would not make
     friends with Ghent; II, 91, 133, 135; *Cronyke*, 79, 86-7; 95: merciless
     attitude of the count in Ypres (1380), Bruges (1381) and again in Ypres
     (1381).
39   II, 90; *Cronyke*, 77, 79: Jan Perneel sacrificed by the *poorterie* (cf. n.37);
     II, 91, 144, 173; *Cronyke*, 83, 124, 143: a reconciliation would mean
     sacrificing the leaders; II, 199; *Cronyke*, 159-61: all men between 15 and
     60 (except priests and monks) should be surrendered to the mercy of the
     count, II, 143; *Cronyke*, 120: 'It will be better that twenty or thirty should
     suffer than a whole city' (Johnes I, 647).
40   II, 242; *Cronyke*, 298: the Ghentish captain of Ypres and some others
     were killed; II, 243-4; *Cronyke*, 302-3; 305-6. Cf. however, De Pauw
     1900: 244 ff: where these acts are attributed to the count who ordered the
     executions at Ypres. Froissart certainly points to the merciless attitude of
     John of Jumont (a native of Hainault), who as sovereign-bailiff of Flanders
     executed many supporters of Ghent, II, 309-10; *Cronyke*, 473-4
     (cf. De Pauw 1900: 267, 439; Van Rompaey 1967: 614: in office 7 Aug.
     1382 - 27 Jan. 1386). In the bailiffs' accounts about 654 or 655 executions
     in consequence of the war are mentioned, among which about 42 executions
     of Englishmen; 7 people had their ears cut off, 2 were stretched on ladders,
     another lost his tongue and yet another his fist; in the same period there
     were 11 'normal' executions of criminals. See also De Pauw 1900: passim;
     De Smet 1947, cf. Mertens 1974.
41   II, 220; *Cronyke*, 225-7. Froissart mentions as participants for Ghent
     Francis Ackerman, Rase van der Voorde, Louis de Vos, ser Jan Scotelair,
     Martin van den Watere and James die Bruwere; the Urbanistic bishop John
     of West was also a member of the embassy. Froissart confused the summer
     embassy with that of October, in which Rase van der Voorde represented
     Ghent, but de Vos, Scotelair and die Bruwere Bruges (Vuylsteke 1893: 458).
     It seems unlikely that Ackerman was a member of that embassy. As *ruwaard*
     of Sluys (De Pauw 1900: 153) and admiral of the Flemish fleet (*ibid.* 134)
     his attendance was more necessary elsewhere. Ackerman's sojourn at Calais
     in November 1382 as a member of the embassy (II, 256-7; *Cronyke*, 294,
     346-8) is quite uncertain. After the disaster of Roosebeke Ackerman possibly
     went by ship to England; when it became clear that Ghent remained inviolate
     he returned (eventually via Calais) and was chosen as one of the leaders of
     the town (II, 265; *Cronyke*, 354).

42 Cf. Vuylsteke 1893: 270: a clerk of the English king arrived at Ghent (17 November 1381).

43 Artevelde as a friend of the English: II, 216, 218, 222; *Cronyke*, 214, 222, 231 (in each case in the opinion of the French); the blockade: Prevenier 1973.

44 Palmer 1972: 22-3, 227-8, 245-8; De Pauw 1900: 347.

45 Palmer 1972: 23, 44-5, 227.

46 II, 208; *Cronyke*, 186; Quicke 1947: 331.

47 Quicke 1947: 332-4. Vuylsteke 1893: 328: inspection of the fleet; 329: embassy of Ghent on 13 Sept. 1382 to England; 330: Flemish embassy on 17 Oct. 1382 to England; 457-9. De Pauw 1920: 364-5: credentials of the embassy; 368-70: instruction: among other things confirmation of old privileges (as during James van Artevelde, copied shortly before this embassy, Vuylsteke 1893: 344) and the wool-staple at Ghent's disposal (= for three years at Bruges).

48 E.g. De Pauw 1900: 225-6, 229, 230-2, 236-8, 318, 322, 367, 449, 452.

49 *Ibid*. 230-2, 260, 322, 324-6, 420-3, 449, 451, 545.

50 II, 254-5; *Cronyke*, 340-1. The sums of money required in consequence of this kind of treaty had to be paid directly by the magistracy or other authorities; they borrowed the money from merchants and money lenders who had to be repaid with interest by citizens and inhabitants. This could only be done by forced loans and taxation; sometimes — when the necessity could be shown and the count and/or the Members of Flanders agreed — such a taxation could be imposed on a much larger scale than merely on the persons and goods of the city or area concerned. The taxation in question was called *Bertoenengeld* (money for the Bretons): De Pauw 1900: 233, 250, which roused armed resistance in Dunkirk (spring 1383) and perhaps also in St Winoksbergen.

51 He mentions the rejoicing in French communalties such as Paris and Rouen after the victory of Ghent in May 1382 (II, 210; *Cronyke*, 193; cf. Quicke 1947: 322) and the remark of Philip van Artevelde before Roosebeke that the communalties of France and England would applaud a Flemish victory (II, 245; *Cronyke*, 311); cf. Petit-Dutaillis 1970: 160-6.

52 I, 376 (*Jacquerie*); II, 242; *Cronyke*, 300-1; II, 259-65. Cf. Mollat and Wolff 1973: 169-75. Compare for example the actions of Ghent against the comital stronghold Wondelgem and the knightly goods in the surroundings of the city (II, 75, 91; *Cronyke*, 31-4, 80).

53 Palmer 1972: 10; cf. 47: mistakenly, May.

54 A laborious process: II, 259; *Cronyke*, 353-4. Cf. De Pauw 1909: 50; Quicke 1947: 377-9; Van Asseldonk 1955: 68. Louis of Male remained Urbanist until his death: II, 60.

55 II, 292, 294; *Cronyke*, 442-4. On these negotiations: Palmer 1972: 50-4.

56 On the crusade: Skalweit 1898; Wrong 1892; Quicke 1947: 341-52; criticism: Barnie 1974: 124.

57 II, 303-7; *Cronyke*, 457-70; cf. Tóth-Ubbens 1964/5; Palmer 1972: 58.

58 Van Asseldonk 1955: 69, 72-3, 74ff; cf. Palmer 1972: 192.

59 II, 497-8, 500-1, 504 (pillages), 513, 526-7, 530-4 (531: riots in Bruges); Gilliodts van Severen 1875: 89-95, 97-103; Palmer 1972: 72-81, 84-5.

60 II, 349-50, 499-500; *Cronyke*, 551-4. Palmer (1972: 91, 95-6, 231-2) maintains that Ackerman was involved in relations between England and Ghent in 1387. In my opinion, however, Ackerman was dead by this date and it was his son — also named Francis — who was involved. This son is mentioned in 1383, when he assisted his father in the surprise of Oudenaarde

and the pillaging of its suburbs (De Pauw 1909: 63; cf. II, 284-6; *Cronyke*, 422-7). Palmer cites Hanserecesse II, 414 in support of his view; but the reference to the events mentioned there – said to have occurred in July 1383 – is itself confused, and the events in question took place either shortly after May 1382, when Ackerman was Artevelde's *ruwaard* in Sluys (De Pauw 1900: 153) or, more probably, in July 1385, after Ackerman had conquered Damme (cf. II, 209, 321-2; *Cronyke*, 189, 494). But in any case, it is clear that this source does not refer to 1387, so Palmer's belief that Ackerman senior was alive in that year must be wrong.

61 Kerling 1954: passim; Alberts and Jansen 1977: 184-5, 248ff.

62 See for a detailed account of this question: Laurent and Quicke 1939; a short survey especially about the dynastic aspects: Alberts 1966: 67-84.

63 Jansen 1966; Van Foreest 1963-4: 1965-6.

64 Cf. Verwijs 1869. A group of Dutch historians led by Dr D. E. H. de Boer, Drs D. Faber and Prof. H. P. H. Jansen (University of Leyden) is preparing an edition of the comital accounts of 1394-6, in which much will be found about the preparations of the expedition of 1396.

65 Froissart mentions several times the Italian banker Dino Rapondi, who was living in Bruges and who had performed services for Philip of Burgundy since 1369 (III, 279, 294-6; cf. Gilliodts van Severen 1875: 277-93). He died at Bruges in 1414; on him: Mirot 1928. On the *aide* in Flanders: Prevenier 1961a: 75, 197; Vaughan 1979: 72ff; Flemish refusal to pay in 1400: *ibid*. 75; cf. Gilliodts van Severen 1875: 287-9, 394-5, 397-400: Bruges had to pay 18,232 nobles to Dino Rapondi.

66 III, 306; Gilliodts van Severen 1875: 395-6, 397-400.

67 It has to be mentioned here that in his account of events between 1379-85 in Flanders, Froissart sometimes praises Flemish protagonists but only the knightly Raas van Liedekerke, captain of Ghent in 1381, obtains Froissart's praise for his *prowess*, II, 140; *Cronyke*, 109. See also on him: De Liedekerke 1961.

68 Huizinga 1949: 521.

69 See also on the subject Hugenholtz 1967 who came to different conclusions. The analysis of the work of medieval historians as symbolic of the structure of society and as a reflection on that structure has also been atempted by Van Gerven 1979, in discussion with Van der Eerden 1979 (concerning the works of the Brabant poet Jan van Boendale, written between 1316 and c.1350).

VIII   Froissart dans le Midi Pyrénéen

1 Dans les archives départementales des Pyrénées-Atlantiques (E. 374) se trouvent encore tous les traités signés par Fébus avec les villes de Bigorre, puis avec les Compagnons de Lourdes pour le partage de ce pactole. Les pièces essentielles ont été publiés dans ma thèse (1960: 297ff). Sur la répétition de cette manoeuvre dans la région de Casteljaloux, voir notre étude 'Une bande de Routiers' (1971: 8-37).

2 Cette affaire de Cazères se place dans le cadre de la guerre de Comminges entreprise par Fébus pour faire valoir les droits qu'il aurait eu sur ce comté en lignée maternelle. Nous avons longuement analysé dans notre thèse

(1960: 309ff), toutes les données du problème; deux documents des archives départementales des Pyrénées-Atlantiques nous apprenent que des seigneurs béarnais et du Marsan avaient perdu leurs titres de famille concernant leur fief d'Ognoas à l'occasion du siège de Cazères; or, ce fief d'Ognoas est aux portes de Cazères de Marsan.

3 Notre but ayant été de concentrer notre attention sur les pages du livre III consacrées au voyage de Béarn, nous nous contentons de signaler la contradiction entre le récit de Froissart (qui place la mort subite de Fébus à l'Hôpital d'Orion) et un document d'archives (E 1596, f. 35) ou un notaire consigna simplement 'L'an 1391, mardi, le Ier jour du mois d'août, à Sauveterre, mourut le trés puissant seigneur monseigneur le comte de Foix. Et le lendemain, mercredi, fut porté et enseveli au couvent des Frères prêcheurs d'Orthez.' Sur tout cela également nous nous sommes longuement expliqués dans notre thèse (1960: 337ff). On peut formuler une hypothèse sur l'informateur de Froissart relatif à la mort de Fébus. Espan du Lion fit partie de la délégation béarnaise chargée de négocier avec le roi de France le renoncement au traité de Toulouse qui faisait de Charles VI l'héritier de Fébus; à cette occasion, il eut l'occasion de reprendre contact avec Froissart.

IX Froissart: Art militaire, pratique et conception de la guerre

1 I, 3. Voir aussi XII, 3: 'Exemplier les bons qui se desirent à avanchier par armes'.

2 Tous les deux cités par Kervyn de Lettenhove 1857b: 101, 105.

3 C'est ce dont l'a convaincu, sans peine, Gaston Fébus: 'Me disoit bien que l'istoire que je avoie fait et poursieuvoie seroit ou temps advenir plus recommandée que nulle autre' (XII, 3).

4 Telle est l'hypothèse vraisemblable avancée récemment par Grévy-Pons et Ornato 1976: 85-102.

5 Voir, en particulier, Chazaud 1876: xix-xxv.

6 On se reportera ici aux annotations copieuses de Siméon Luce dans son édition pour la SHF. Dans le même esprit, Bertrandy 1870; Plaine 1871; Manyon 1926; Artonne 1952.

7 Delachenal 1909a: 189ff; Burne 1938: 21-52; Galbraith 1939: 473-75; Burne 1955; SHF V, 22, 252.

8 Luce 1876: 442 penche pour la rive droite de l'Eure; Mathieu 1964: 91-8 pour la rive gauche.

9 'Cil dou roy dan Piètre estoient si grant fuison, que bien six contre un' (VII, 76).

10 Voir aussi XII, 271: 'Une fois gaignoient nos gens et l'autre fois perdoient, ensi que les parchons d'armes aviennent'.

11 Cris de guerre: XI, 18, 22, 23. Fracas des armures: 'Là estoit li cliquetis sur ces bachinès si grans et si haus d'espées et de haces, de plommées et de maillés de fier, que on n'i ooit goute pour la noise; et oï dire que, se tout li hiaumier de Paris et de Brouxelles fussent ensemble, leur mestier faissant, il n'euissent point fait si grant noise comme li combatant et li freant sus ces bachinès faissoient' (XI, 55). Instruments de musique, qui ne servent pas simplement à divertir mais aussi à transmettre les ordres: 'Sonnerent les tronpetes des mareschaus tantos apriés mienuit. Toutes manieres de gens,

au son des tronpetes, sallirent sus et se resvillierent et armerent; au secont son des tronpetes, on toursa et apparilla, et se missent toutes gens en ordenances des batailles, ensi que il devoient estre et aler. Au tier son, tout monterent a ceval et se departirent' (Diller 707). 'Là estoient muses, calemelles, naquaires, trompes et trompettes, qui menoient grant bruit et grant tintin' (II, 202). Froissart fait aussi allusion aux cors et aux grands tambours utilisés par les Écossais, si bruyants qu'on les entend à quatre lieues anglaises de distance le jour et à six la nuit : 'et est un grand esbaudissement entre eux et un grand effroi et esbahissement entre leurs ennemis' (Kervyn de Lettenhove 1857b : 124).

12 Le mot est de Perroy 1945 : 173 : 'Froissart, tout entier tourné vers le passé, et qui rédige alors ses abondantes chroniques, en une langue diffuse et patoisante, riches de plus d'enseignements sur les sentiments de la société chevaleresque que d'exactitude historique'. Sur le décor héraldique dans Froissart, Prinet 1916. Sur l'idéologie chevaleresque aux quatorzième et quinzième siècles, Keen 1976 et Keen 1977.

13 KL XV, 311 : 'Tout son ost estoit en elles, en maniere de une herche'. On reconnaîtra ici le dispositif déjà signalé par Froissart à Poitiers du côté des Anglo-Gascons (V, 22) et à Crécy du côté anglais (III, 416).

14 KL XI, 48 ; Bellaguet 1839 : 210.

15 *Idem*, 223. De même, Froissart, comme ordre de grandeur, n'est pas nécessairement faux en matière de dépenses : pour le 'voyage de la mer' de 1386, il écrit qu'il coûta 'en tailles et assises ou royaume de France' trois millions de francs (XIII, 100). Chiffre exagéré, certes : remarquons cependant que le montant des quatre tailles pour le 'passage de la mer' (19 octobre 1384, 3 mai 1385, 24 avril 1386 et fin juillet 1386) s'éleva vraisemblablement à 2,750,000 livres tournois (Rey 1965a : 404). Froissart ne s'écarte pas sensiblement de la vérité pour les effectifs des expéditions anglaises entre 1359 et 1380. Pour 1375 comme pour 1380, il parle de 6,000 combattants (VIII, 194, 236), alors que les chiffres officiels sont respectivement de 4,000 et de 5,200 (Sherborne 1964 : 718-46). Pour le support logistique des armées anglaises, Hewitt 1966.

16 Sur les effets de panique dans les armées médiévales, Verbruggen 1977 : 47-50.

17 À suivre Froissart, les Anglais, le 24 août, devaient se trouver devant Troyes, en ordre de bataille, offrant le combat au duc de Bourgogne, qui, de fait, séjourna à Troyes du 23 au 25 août 1380 (IX, civ, n. 11).

18 KL XIV, 236 ; SHF XIII, 96-7.

19 XIII, 2, 3, 5-6, 85, 100.

20 XIII, 84. Froissart note fort bien (85) la différence de situation économique entre les chevaliers et les écuyers retenus par un grand seigneur, et les autres.

21 V, 200 ; XI, 5 ; XV, 107, 116 (où l'on parle de 3,000 ouvriers).

22 X, 248, 272 ; XII, 193 ; XIII, 154.

23 IX, 74, 85. Pour l'état réel de l'artillerie anglaise à cette époque, se reporter à Tout 1911 : 666-702.

24 X, 248. L'accroissement du calibre des pièces est signalée à la même époque dans les Pays-Bas par Gaier 1973.

25 XI, 54, 120. En 1385, un noble, le sire de Clari, était maître des canons du seigneur de Coucy : il fut tué d'un coup de canon au siège de Damme (XI, 239).

26 Mise à torture des prisonniers pour élever le chiffre de leur rançon.

X Froissart: Patrons and Texts

1 I am indebted to the American Council of Learned Societies whose Fellowship made possible readings and research required for this essay.

2 SHF, I, xx-xxv, li-lvii; also Fourrier (1975: 31) '. . . À cette époque [1373] le patron de Froissart était le duc Wenceslas de Brabant . . .'. Fourrier also recalls (32) the 'curieuse omission' of Robert of Namur's name from the extensive list of benefactors given by Froissart in this poetical work composed in 1373.

3 See my study: Robert d'Artois et l'historicité des *Chroniques* de Froissart, *Le Moyen âge* 1980.

4 Trip to Scotland: I, 349; XIV, 4; XV, 141, 171, 172; KL XIV, 5; Diller, 127-8, 779-80. 1395 trip to England: KL XV, 140-67; XVI, 234.

5 Paris and Jeanroy 1927: 184; Shears 190-1.

6 For example: XII, 70, 74-5, 76, 94, 96, 98, 101, 115, 116, 239, 270-1; XIII, 47, 81; XIV, 171, 188-9; XV, 28, 239; KL XV, 181.

7 XII, 70, 74-5, 227; XIII, 222, 223-4; XIV, 9 . . . .

8 See Fourrier 1972: 35-6: '. . . [Froissart] était nourri de toutes les oeuvres importantes en vers et en prose qui avaient paru avant son temps ou à son époque même.' Among others, he knew the following authors and works: Ovid, the *Roman d'Alexandre*, the *Roman de la Rose*, Adenet-le-Roi (*Cléomadès*), Mathieu le Poirier, the *Bailli d'Amour*, Jacques de Longuyon, the *Voeux du Paon*, *Tristan*, the prose *Lancelot*.

9 Exceptions: V, 100; XV, 90. These may be formulaic usages. Both examples are found in highly dramatic scenes: the Jacquerie and the battle of Baesweiler (1371: Wenceslas was taken prisoner). Nothing, of course, prevented the chronicler from being his own penman on occasion.

10 Froissart does refer in general terms to Jean le Bel. See Amiens, fos. 46b, 52b, for example.

11 This despite Shear's solid defence of Froissart the historian and to which should be added Lucien Foulet's strong praise (1948: 127): 'Qui donc, en dehors de Froissart, a jamais réussi à faire avec une telle intensité, soixante-quinze ans de la vie agitée et tumultueuse de deux grandes nations? Quel historien, en aucun pays a présenté d'événements aussi dispersés et aussi complexes un tableau aussi large, aussi puissant et d'un coloris aussi juste? Il faudra, chez nous, aller jusqu'à Saint-Simon pour retrouver une vision aussi directe et pénétrante du spectacle humain'. See also, Artonne (1952: 82-107).

Recent critics, however, have generally renewed August Molinier's severe judgement that as an historian, Froissart is '. . . peu sûr, léger, sujet à des erreurs et à des confessions regrettables, sa chronologie est souvent fautive, il se trompe sur les noms propres et il rapporte aveuglément ce qu'on lui a raconté, sans même avoir idée de soupçonner la véracité de ses informateurs . . .' (1904: 12-13). The following are a few authors who have since viewed Froissart very dimly as a historian: (1) Pauphilet 1952: 373-4; (2) Brandt 1966; and (3) Archambault 1974: 59-72.

12 See also Cazelles 1958: 209-12.

13 Knighton and Baker also record the duke of Brabant's duplicity during this period. See Lucas 1929: 417.

14 According to I, 181-2 and Amiens, fos. 35d-36a, the French retreated first in great discord; Le Bel I, 163-4, describes a mutual withdrawal.

15 This type of collective direct discourse often seems to translate Froissart's personal judgement. It is curious to note that in the Rome text alone

do we read that John III served Edward at his own costs during the siege of Tournai (Rome, 449).

16 For the expression 'abusions', see Picoche who describes this term as (1976: 156-7): '... La surprise désagréable qu'on éprouve en constatant que les espoirs qu'on avait conçus ne se réalisent pas'.

LIST OF WORKS CITED

All works are listed under the name of their editor or author. Unless otherwise stated, works in English are published in London, and those in French in Paris.

ALBERTS, W. J. 1966. *Geschiedenis van Gelderland van de vroegste tijd tot het einde der middeleeuwen*. The Hague.

ALBERTS, W. J. and JANSEN, H. P. H. 1977. *Welwaart in wording. Sociaal-economische geschiedenis van Nederland van de vroegste tijden tot het einde van de middeleeuwen*. 2nd edn. The Hague.

ALLMAND, C. T. (ed.) 1976. *War, Literature and Politics in the Late Middle Ages*. Liverpool.

ARCHAMBAULT, P. 1974. *Seven French Chronicles, Witnesses to History*. Syracuse.

ARGENTRÉ, B. DE. 1618. *Histoire de Bretagne*. 3rd edn.

ARMITAGE-SMITH, S. 1904. *John of Gaunt*.

ARTONNE, A. 1952. Froissart historien. Le siège et la prise de la Roche-Vendeix. *BEC* 110: 89-107.

ASSELDONK, G. A. VAN. 1955. *De Nederlanden en het Westers Schisma (tot 1398)*. Utrecht.

ASTON, M. 1965. The Impeachment of Bishop Despenser. *BIHR* 38: 127-48.

AVOUT, J. D'. 1943. *La querelle des Armagnacs et des Bourguignons*.

———— 1960. Le meutre d'Étienne Marcel.

BAIN, J. (ed.) 1888. *Calendar of Documents relating to Scotland, 1357-1509, 4*. Edinburgh.

BALDWIN, J. F. 1913. *The King's Council in England during the Middle Ages*. Oxford.

BARBER, R. 1978. *Edward, Prince of Wales and Aquitaine*.

BARNIE, J. 1974. *War in Medieval Society. Social Values and the Hundred Years War, 1337-1399*.

BELLAGUET, L. (ed.) 1839, 1840. *Chronique du Religieux de Saint-Denis, 1, 2*.

BERTRANDY, M. 1870. *Étude sur les chroniques de Froissart. Guerre de Guienne, 1345-1346*. Bordeaux.

BESTERMAN, T. D. N. 1958. *Voltaire's Correspondence, 33*. Geneva.

BLOCKMANS, F. and W. P. 1979. Devaluation, Coinage and Seignorage under Louis de Nevers and Louis de Male, Counts of Flanders, 1330-1384. In: N. J. Mayhew (ed.), *Coinage in the Low Countries (880-1500)*: 69-94. Oxford.

BOCK, F. 1931. Some New Documents Illustrating the Early Years of the Hundred Years War (1353-1356). *BJRL* 15: 60-99.

BRAAMCAMP FREIRE, A. (ed.) 1973. Fernão Lopes, *Crónica de D. João I (parte primeira)*. Lisbon.

BRACHET, A. 1903. *Pathologie mentale des rois de France*.

BRANDT, W. 1966. *The Shape of Medieval History*. New Haven.

BUNTINX, J. 1949. *De Audientie van de graaf van Vlaanderen. Studie over het centraal grafelijk gerecht (c.1330-c.1409)*. Brussels.

BURNE, A. H. 1938. The Battle of Poitiers. *EHR* 53: 21-52.

———— 1955. *The Crécy War*.

BUSH, H. R. 1911-12, 1912-13. La bataille de trente anglois et de trente bretons. *Modern Philology* 9: 511-44; 10: 82-136.

BYLES, A. T. P. (ed.) 1926. William Caxton, *The Ordre of Chyvalry*. EETS 168.

CALENDAR OF PATENT ROLLS, 1327-1377. 1891-1916. 16 vols. HMSO.

CALMETTE, J. and E. DÉPREZ. 1937. *L'Europe occidentale de la fin du xive siècle aux guerres d'Italie*.

CARTIER, N. R. 1961. The Lost Chronicle. *Speculum* 36: 424-34.

CASTRO, J. R. and F. IDOATE. 1954a and b. *Catálogo del archivo general de Navarra: sección de comptos, 11, 12*. Pamplona.

CAZELLES, R. 1958. *La société politique et la crise de la royauté sous Philippe de Valois*.

————— 1960. Le parti navarrais jusqu'à la mort d'Étienne Marcel. *Bulletin philologique et historique*: 839-69.

————— (ed.) 1962. *Lettres closes 'de par le roy' de Philippe de Valois*.

————— 1962-3. Une exigence de l'opinion depuis Saint Louis: la réformation du royaume. *Annuaire Bulletin de la SHF*: 91-9.

————— 1964. Du Guesclin avant Cocherel. *Actes du colloque international de Cocherel*: 33-40. Caen.

————— 1965. Étienne Marcel au sein de la haute bourgeoisie d'affaires. *Journal des Savants*: 413-27.

————— 1974. Jean II le Bon: quel homme? quel roi? *RH* 251: 5-26.

CHARRIÈRE, E. (ed.) 1839a and b. Jean Cuvelier, *Chronique de Bertrand du Guesclin*. 2 vols.

CHAZAUD, M. A. (ed.) 1876. Jean Cabaret d'Orronville, *La chronique du bon duc Loys de Bourbon*. SHF.

CLARKE, B. 1975. *Mental Disorder in Earlier Britain*. Cardiff.

CONTAMINE, P. 1972. *Guerre, état et société à la fin du Moyen Âge*.

CORRYN, F. 1944. Het schippersambacht te Gent, 1302-1492. *Handelingen van de maatschappij voor geschiedenis en oudheidkunde te Gent* n.s. 1: 165-204.

COULTON, G. G. 1930. *The Chronicler of European Chivalry*.

COOPLAND, G. W. (ed.) 1975. Philippe de Mézières, *Letter to King Richard II*. Liverpool.

————— (ed.) 1969a and b. Philippe de Mézières, *Le Songe du Vieil Pèlerin*. Cambridge.

COVILLE, A. 1894. *Les États de Normandie. Leur origine et leur développement au xive siècle*.

————— 1949. Jean de Venette. *Histoire littéraire de la France* 38: 333-403.

CURRY, K. (ed.) 1965. *New Letters of Robert Southey, 1*.

CUTTLER, S. 1978. *The Law of Treason and Treason Trials in Later Medieval France*. Oxford Ph.D.

CUYPER, J. DE. 1961. De opstand van Gent (1379-1385) en Hulster Ambacht. Aantekeningen van de tiendontvanger Willem Faytop. *Handelingen van het genootschap voor geschiedenis* 98: 137-55.

DARMESTETER, M. 1895. *Froissart*. New York.

DELACHENAL, R. (ed.) 1900. *Journal des états généraux réunis à Paris au mois d'octobre 1356*.

————— 1909a and b, 1916, 1928, 1931. *Histoire de Charles V*. 5 vols.

————— (ed.) 1910, 1916, 1920a and b. *Chronique des règnes de Jean II et de Charles V*. 4 vols. SHF.

DELBRÜCK, H. 1923. *Geschichte der Kriegskunst im Rahmen der politischen Geschichte, 3*. 2nd edn. Berlin.

DEMUYNCK, R. 1951. De Gentsche oorlog (1379-1385). Oorzaken en karakter. *Handelingen der maatschappij voor geschiedenis en oudheidkunde te Gent* n.s. 5: 305-18.

DÉPREZ, E. 1902. *Les préliminaires de la guerre de Cent ans*.

———— 1907. La mort de Robert d'Artois. *RH* 94: 63-6.

———— 1925. La conférence d'Avignon (1344). L'arbitrage pontificale entre la France et l'Angleterre. In: Little and Powicke 1925: 301-20.

———— 1926. La 'Querelle de Bretagne' de la captivité de Charles de Blois à la majorité de Jean IV de Montfort (1347-1362), 1. Pendant la captivité de Charles de Blois (1347-1356). *Mémoires de la société d'histoire et d'archéologie de Bretagne* 7: 25-60.

DÉSERTS, M. C. DES. 1970. Le chateau de Joyeuse-Garde. Compte-rendu des fouillés. *Bulletin de la société archéologique de Finistère* 96: 75-87.

DEVILLERS, L. (ed.) 1883. *Cartulaire des comtes de Hainault de l'avènement de Guillaume II à la mort de Jacqueline de Bavière, 2*. Brussels.

DIAS ARNAUT, S. 1947. Froissart e João Fernandes Pacheco. *Revista portugesa de histórica* 3: 129-59.

DILLER, G. T. 1980. Robert d'Artois et l'historicité des *Chroniques* de Froissart. *Le Moyen Âge* 86: 217-31.

DIVERRES, A. H. (ed.) 1953. Jean Froissart, *Voyage en Béarn*. Manchester.

DOUËT D'ARCQ, L. 1840-1. Acte d'accusation contre Robert le Coq, évêque de Laon. *BEC* 2: 350-87.

———— 1863, 1864. *Choix de pièces inédites relatives au règne de Charles VI*. 2 vols. SHF.

DU BOULAY, F. R. H. and C. M. BARRON (eds.) 1971. *The Reign of Richard II: Essays in Honour of M. McKisack*.

DUPUY, M. 1970. *Le Prince noir*.

DURRIEU, P. 1885. *Les Gascons en Italie. Études historiques*. Auch.

EMERSON, B. 1976. *The Black Prince*.

ENTWISTLE, W. J. (ed.) 1968. Fernão Lopes, *Crónica de D. João I (parte segunda)*. Lisbon.

EERDEN, P. C. VAN DER. 1979. Het maatschappijbeeld van Jan van Boendale. *Tijdschrift voor sociale geschiedenis* 15: 219-39.

FARAL, É. 1945. Robert le Coq et les états généraux de 1356. *Revue historique de droit français et étranger* IVs. 23: 171-214.

FARLEY, S. M. 1969. *French Historiography in the Later Middle Ages with Special Reference to the 'Grandes chroniques de France'*. Edinburgh university Ph.D.

FINÓ, J. F. 1977. *Forteresses de la France mediévale. Construction, attaque, défense*. 3rd edn.

FOREEST, H. A. VAN. 1963-4, 1965-6. Traditie en werkelijkheid. *Bijdragen voor de geschiedenis der Nederlanden* 18: 143-66; 20: 110-46.

FOULET, L. 1948. *Littérature française*. New edn.

FOURQUIN, G. 1978. *The Anatomy of Popular Rebellion in the Middle Ages*. Amsterdam.

FOURRIER, A. (ed.) 1972. Jean Froissart, *L'espinette amoureuse*. 2nd edn.

FOWLER, K. 1969. *The King's Lieutenant. Henry of Grosmont, First Duke of Lancaster, 1310-1361*.

FOX, J. 1974. *A Literary History of France: The Middle Ages*.

FRYDE, E. B. 1962, 1967. The Financial Resources of Edward III in the Netherlands. *Revue belge de philologie et d'histoire* 40: 1168-87; 45: 1142-93.

———— (ed.) 1969. C. Oman, *The Great Revolt of 1381*. Oxford.

GAIER, C. 1968. *Art et organisation militaires dans la principauté de Liège et dans le comté de Looz au Moyen âge*. Brussels.

———— 1973. *L'industrie et le commerce des armes dans les anciennes principautés belges du xiiie à la fin du xve siècle.*

GALBRAITH, V. H. (ed.) 1927. *The Anonimalle Chronicle, 1333 to 1381.* Manchester.

————(ed.) 1937. Thomas Walsingham, *The Saint Albans Chronicle, 1406-1420.* Oxford.

———— 1939. The Battle of Poitiers. *EHR* 54: 473-5.

GALWAY, M. 1959. Froissart in England. *University of Birmingham Historical Journal* 7: 18-35.

GÉRAUD, H. (ed.) 1843. *Chronique latine de Guillaume de Nangis de 1113 à 1300 et de ses continuateurs, 2.* SHF.

GERVEN, J. VAN. 1979. Sociale werkelijkheid en mentale konstructie in het werk van Jan van Boendale (eerste helfte 14de eeuw). *Tijdschrift voor sociale geschiedenis* 13: 47-70; 15: 240-4.

GESLIN DE BOURGOGNE, J. and A. J. B. A. DE BARTHÉLEMY (eds.) 1864. *Anciens évêchés de Bretagne, 4.*

GILLIODTS VAN SEVEREN, L. (ed.) 1875. *Inventaire des archives de la ville de Bruges. Section première: Inventaire des chartes. Première série: 13e-16e siècle, 3.* Bruges.

GODDING, P. 1973. Le pouvoir urbain en Brabant au Moyen âge. In: *Wavre 1222-1972. 750e anniversaire des libertés communales*: 95-122. Brussels.

GOODMAN, A. 1971. *The Loyal Conspiracy.*

GOSSMAN, L. 1968. *Medievalism and the Ideologies of the Enlightenment. The World and Work of La Curne de Sainte-Palaye.* Baltimore.

GRANSDEN, A. 1972. The Alleged Rape by Edward III of the Countess of Salisbury. *EHR* 87: 333-44.

GRÉVY-PONS, N. and E. ORNATO. 1976. Qui est l'auteur de la chronique latine de Charles VI, dite du Religieux de Saint-Denis? *BEC* 134: 85-102.

GRIERSON, H. J. C. (ed.) 1932. *The Letters of Sir Walter Scott, 2.*

GUENÉE, B. and F. LEHOUX. 1968. *Les Entrées royales françaises de 1328 à 1515.*

GUIGUE, G. 1886. *Les Tard-Venus en Lyonnais, Forez et Beaujolais, 1356-1369.* Lyon.

HARVEY, J. H. 1961. The Wilton Dyptych: A Reconsideration. *Archaeologia* 98: 1-28.

———— 1976. *The Black Prince and his Age.*

HAY, D. 1962. History and Historians in France and England during the Fifteenth Century. *BIHR* 35: 111-27.

HEERS, J. 1970. *L'Occident aux xive et xve siècles. Aspects économiques et sociaux.*

HEERS, J. 1977. *Parties and Political Life in the Medieval West.* Amsterdam.

HENNEMAN, J. B. 1971. *Royal Taxation in Fourteenth Century France: The Development of War Financing, 1322-1356.* Princeton.

———— 1976. *Royal Taxation in Fourteenth Century France: The Captivity and Ransom of John II, 1356-1370.* Philadelphia.

———— 1978. The Military Classes and the French Monarchy in the Late Middle Ages. *American Historical Review* 83: 946-65.

HERWAARDEN, J. VAN. 1978. *Opgelegden bedevaarten. Een studie over de praktijk van opleggen van bedevaarten (met name in de stedelijke rechtspraak) in de Nederlanden gedurende de late middeleeuwen (ca 1300-ca 1550).* Assen.

HEWITT, H. J. 1966. *The Organisation of War under Edward III.* Manchester.

HUGENHOLTZ, F. W. N. 1967. Jean Froissart en het beeld van zijn tijd. In: *De muze der geschiedenis*: 36-51. The Hague.

———— 1973. *Ridderkrijg en burgervrede. West Europa aan de vooravond van de Honderdjarige oorlog*. Bussum.

HUIZINGA, J. 1949. La valeur politique et militaire des idées de chevalerie à la fin du moyen âge. *Verzamelde werken 3*: 519-29. Haarlem.

——— 1954. *The Waning of the Middle Ages*. Garden City.

HUNT, R. A., PANTIN, W. A. and R. W. SOUTHERN. 1948. *Studies in Medieval History Presented to F. M. Powicke*. Oxford.

JANSEN, H. P. H. 1966. *Hoekse en Kabeljauwse twisten*. Bussum.

JARRY, E. 1889. *La vie politique de Louis de France, duc d'Orléans (1372-1407)*.

JOHNES, T. 1839. Jean Froissart, *Chronicles*. 2 vols.

——— (ed.) 1849. Enguerrand de Monstrelet, *Chronicles, 1*.

JONES, M. 1970. *Ducal Brittany, 1346-1399*. Oxford.

——— (ed.) 1972a. Some Documents Relating to the Disputed Succession to the Duchy of Brittany, 1341. RHS. *Camden Miscellany 24*: 1-78.

——— 1972b. The Ransom of Jean de Bretagne, Count of Penthièvre: An Aspect of English Foreign Policy, 1386-1388. *BIHR 45*: 7-26.

——— 1972-4. Les finances de Jean IV, duc de Bretagne (1345-1399). *Mémoires de la société d'histoire et d'archéologie de Bretagne 52*: 27-53.

——— 1976. 'Mon Pais et ma Nation': Breton Identity in the Fourteenth Century. In: Allmand 1976: 144-68.

KEEN, M. 1965. *The Laws of War in the Late Middle Ages*.

——— 1976. Chivalry, Nobility and the Man-at-Arms. In: Allmand 1976: 32-45.

——— 1977. Huizinga, Kilgour and the Decline of Chivalry. *Medievalia et Humanistica* n.s. 8: 1-20.

KER, W. P. (ed.) 1901-3. Lord Berners, *The Chronicles of Froissart*. 6 vols. Tudor Translations 27-32.

KERLING, N. J. M. 1954. *Commercial Relations of Holland and Zealand with England from the Late 13th Century to the Close of the Middle Ages*. Leiden.

KERVYN DE LETTENHOVE, Baron J. B. M. C. 1857a and b. *Étude littéraire sur le xive siècle*. 2 vols. Brussels.

——— (ed.) 1867-77. Jean Froissart, *Oeuvres*. 26 vols. Brussels.

KIBLER, W. W. 1976. Self Delusion in Froissart's Espinette amoureuse. *Romania* 97: 77-98.

LA BORDERIE, A. DE. (ed.) 1881. Jean de Saint-Paul, *Chronique*. Nantes.

——— 1885. Froissart et le début de la guerre de Blois et de Montfort en 1341. *Revue de Bretagne et de Vendée* VIs. 8: 337-70.

——— 1888. La guerre de Blois et de Montfort, 1341-1364. *Études historiques bretonnes* IIs. 117-236.

——— 1899. *Histoire de Bretagne, 3*.

——— 1894. Nouveaux documents sur la guerre de Blois et de Montfort. *Association Bretonne, session d'Ancenis 1894*: 191-211.

LACABANE, L. 1840-1. Recherches sur les auteurs des *Grandes chroniques de France*, dites de Saint-Denys. *BEC* 2: 57-74.

LA RONCIÈRE, C. DE. 1909. *Histoire de la marine française, 1*. 3rd edn.

LAURENT, H. and F. QUICKE. 1939. *Les origines de l'état bourguignon. L'accession de la maison de Bourgogne aux duchés de Brabant et de Limbourg (1383-1407), 1*. Brussels.

LEFRANC, A. 1898. *Olivier de Clisson, connétable de France*.

LEHOUX, F. 1966. *Jean de France, duc de Berri: sa vie, son action politique (1340-1416), 2*.

LEGGE, M. D. (ed.) 1941. *Anglo-Norman Letters and Petitions*. Anglo-Norman Text Society 3. Oxford.

LEMOINE, J. 1896. *Chronique de Richard Lescot, religieux de Saint-Denis, 1328-1344, suivie de la continuation de cette chronique, 1344-1364*. SHF.

LE PATOUREL, J. 1954. L'administration ducale dans la Bretagne montfortiste, 1345-1362. *Revue historique de droit française et étranger* IVs. 32: 144-7.

————— 1958. Edward III and the Kingdom of France. *History* 43: 179-89.

LEWIS, N. B. 1964. The Recruitment and Organisation of a Contract Army, May to November 1337. *BIHR* 37: 1-19.

LEWIS, P. S. 1968. *Later Medieval France: The Polity*.

————— 1962. The Failure of the French Medieval Estates. *Past and Present* 23: 3-24.

LEWIS, W. S. (ed.) 1952. *Horace Walpole's Correspondence, 15*.

LIEDERKERKE, R. DE. 1961. *La maison de Gavre et de Liederkerke. Histoire de sa ligne directe depuis l'origine jusqu'à nos jours*. Les Rasse.

LITTLE, A. G. and F. M. POWICKE (eds.) 1925. *Essays in Medieval History Presented to T. F. Tout*. Manchester.

LOBINEAU, DOM G. A. (ed.) 1707a and b. *Histoire de Bretagne*. 2 vols.

LOOMIS, R. S. 1959. *Arthurian Literature in the Middle Ages*. Oxford.

LORAY, T. DE. 1877. *Jean de Vienne, amiral de France, 1341-1396*.

LOT, F. 1946. *L'art militaire et les armées au Moyen âge en Europe et dans le Proche-Orient, 2*.

LUCAS, H. S. 1929. *The Low Countries and the Hundred Years War, 1326-1347*. Ann Arbor.

————— 1933. The Sources and Literature on Jacob van Artevelde. *Speculum* 8: 125-49.

LUCE, S. 1876. *Histoire de Bertrand du Guesclin et de son époque: la jeunesse de Bertrand*.

————— (ed.) 1862. *Chronique des quatre premiers Valois (1327-1393)*. SHF.

————— 1890. *La France pendant la guerre de Cent ans, 1*.

—————, G. RAYNAUD, L. and A. MIROT. 1869-. Jean Froissart, *Chroniques*. 15 vols. (in progress). SHF.

LUMBY, J. R. (ed.) 1886. Ranulph Higden, *Polychronicon, 9*. RS.

————— (ed.) 1895. Henry Knighton, *Chronicon, 2*. RS.

MACHI, G. (ed.) 1975. Fernão Lopes, *Crónica de D. Fernando*. Lisbon.

McKISACK, M. (ed.) 1926. Thomas Favent, *Historia mirabilis parliamenti*. RHS. Camden Miscellany 14.

————— 1948. London and the Succession to the Crown in the Middle Ages. In: Hunt, Pantin and Southern 1948: 76-89.

————— 1971. *Medieval History in the Tudor Age*. Oxford.

MANYON, L. 1926. An Examination of the Historical Reliability of Froissart's Account of the Campaign and Battle of Crécy. *Papers of the Michigan Academy of Science, Arts and Letters* 7: 207-24.

MATHEW, G. 1948. Ideals of Knighthood in Late Fourteenth Century England. In: Hunt, Pantin and Southern 1948: 354-62.

MATHIEU, R. 1964. Les sources de l'histoire de la bataille. *Actes du colloque international de Cocherel*: 91-8. Caen.

MEIGNEN, H. LE. (ed.) 1886. Alain Bouchard, *Les grandes chroniques de Bretaigne*. Nantes.

MERTENS, J. 1974. De beschuldiging tegen Pieter Huerel, opstandig Brugs hotelier. *Album Albert Schouteet*: 111-16. Bruges.

MICHELET, J. 1876. *Histoire de France, 9*. New edn.

MIROT, L. 1904, 1905. Isabelle de France, reine d'Angleterre, comtesse d'Angoulême, duchesse d'Orléans, 1389-1409. *Revue d'histoire diplomatique* 18: 544-73; 19: 60-95, 161-91, 481-522.

MIROT, L. 1905. *Les insurrections urbaines au début du règne de Charles VI (1380-1383)*.
————— 1915. Une tentative d'invasion en Angleterre pendant la guerre de Cent ans, 1385-1386. *Revue des Études historiques* 81: 249-87, 417-66.
————— 1928. La société des Raponde: Dino Raponde. *BEC* 89: 299-389.
————— and E. DÉPREZ (eds.) 1898, 1899, 1900. Les ambassades anglaises pendant la guerre de Cent ans. *BEC* 59: 550-77; 60: 177-214; 61: 20-58.
MISKIMIN, H. 1963. The Last Act of Charles V. *Speculum* 38: 433-42.
————— 1975. *The Economy of Early Renaissance Europe, 1300-1460*. Cambridge.
————— (ed.) 1977. *The Medieval City*.
MOLINIER, A. 1904. *Les sources de l'histoire de France, 4: Les Valois, 1328-1461*.
————— and E. (eds.) 1882. *Chronique normande du xive siècle*. SHF.
MOLLAT, M. and P. WOLFF. 1973. *The Popular Revolutions of the Late Middle Ages*.
MORAND, F. (ed.) 1876. Jean le Fèvre, *Chronique, 1408-35, 1*. SHF.
MORANVILLÉ, H. (ed.) 1887. Jean le Fèvre, *Journal*.
————— 1889. Conférences entre la France et l'Angleterre, 1388-1393. *BEC* 50: 355-80.
————— (ed.) 1893, 1897. *Chronographia regum Francorum, 2, 3*. SHF.
MORICE, DOM P. H. (ed.) 1742. *Mémoires pour servir de preuves à l'histoire ecclésiastique et civile de Bretagne, 1*.
————— 1750, 1756. *Histoire ecclésiastique et civile de Bretagne*. 2 vols.
MUNRO, J. H. 1977. Industrial Protectionism in Medieval Flanders: Urban or National? In: Miskimin 1977: 229-68.
NEWHALL, R. A. (ed.) 1953. Jean de Venette, *Chronicle*. New York.
NICHOLAS, D. M. 1968. Town and Countryside: Social and Political Tensions in Fourteenth Century Flanders. *Comparative Studies in Society and History* 10: 458-85.
————— 1971a. *Town and Countryside. Social, Economic and Political Tensions in Fourteenth Century Flanders*. Bruges.
————— 1971b. *Stad en platteland in de middeleeuwen*. Bussum.
————— 1976. Economic Reorganisation and Social Change in Fourteenth Century Flanders. *Past and Present* 70: 3-29.
————— 1978. Structures du peuplement, fonctions urbaines et formation du capital dans la Flandre médiévale. *Annales E. S. C.* 33: 501-27.
NORDBERG, M. 1964. *Les ducs et la royauté. Études sur la rivalité des ducs d'Orléans et de Bourgogne, 1392-1407*. Uppsala.
OOST, A. VAN. 1973. Sociale stratificatie van de Gentse opstand 1379-1385. Kritische benadering van confiscatiedocumenten. *Bulletin Oud-studenten in de geschiedenis aan de Rijksuniversiteit te Gent* 23:
————— 1978. Sociale stratifikatie van de Brugse opstandelingen en van de opstandige ingezetenen van de kleine kasselrijsteden en van de kasselrijdorpen in Vlaanderen van 1379-1385. *Revue belge de philologie et d'histoire* 56: 830-77.
ORCASTEGUI GROS, C. (ed.) 1977. Garci López de Roncevalles, *Crónica*. Pamplona.
PALMER, J. J. N. 1966a. The Anglo-French Peace Negotiations, 1390-1396. *TRHS* Vs. 16: 81-94.
————— 1966b. Articles for a Final Peace between England and France, 16 June 1393. *BIHR* 39: 180-5.
————— 1971. English Foreign Policy, 1388-1399. In: Du Boulay and Barron

1971: 75-107.

PALMER, J. J. N. 1971a. The Background to Richard II's Marriage to Isabel of France, 1396. *BIHR* 44: 1-17.

————— 1971b. The Parliament of 1385 and the Constitutional Crisis of 1386. *Speculum* 46: 477-90.

————— 1972. *England, France and Christendom, 1377-1399*.

————— 1978. The Authorship, Date and Historical Value of the French Chronicles on the Lancastrian Revolution. *BJRL* 61: 145-81.

————— 1981. La *Vie du Prince noir* par Chandos Herald. *Le Moyen Âge* 87 (forthcoming).

PARIS, A. P. (ed.) 1836-8. *Les grandes chroniques de France*. 6 vols.

PARIS, G. and A. JEANROY. (eds.) 1927. *Extraits des chroniqueurs français*. 12th edn.

PAUPHILET, A. 1952. *Historiens et chroniqueurs du Moyen âge*. New edn.

PAUW, N. DE. (ed.) 1898. *Jehan Froissart's cronyke van Vlaenderen, getranslateert uuten Franssoyse in Duytschen tale bij Gerijt Potter van der Loo in de xvᵉ eeuw, 1*. Ghent.

————— (ed.) 1900. *Rekeningen der baljuwen van Vlaanderen* (= Jean Froissart's *Cronyke*, 2). Ghent.

————— (ed.) 1905. *L'assassinat d'Artevelde et l'instruction de ce crime*. Ghent.

————— (ed.) 1909. *Vlaamsche kroniek van Vlaanderen* (= Jean Froissart's *Cronyke*, 3). Ghent.

————— (ed.) 1920. *Cartulaire historique et généalogique des Artevelde*. Brussels.

————— and J. VUYLSTEKE. (eds.) 1874. *De rekeningen der stad Gent. Tijdvak van Jacob van Artevelde, 1336-1349, 1*. Ghent.

PERROY, É. 1933a. *L'Angleterre et le grande Schisme d'Occident*.

————— (ed.) 1933b. *Diplomatic Correspondence of Richard II*. RHS. Camden Society IIIs. 48.

————— 1945. *La guerre de Cent ans*.

————— 1951. *The Hundred Years War*.

PETIT, E. (ed.) 1888. *Itinéraires de Philippe le Hardi et de Jean sans Peur, ducs de Bourgogne (1363-1419)*.

————— (ed.) 1893. Séjours de Charles VI. *Bulletin historique et philologique du comité des travaux historiques et scientifiques* 40: 45-92.

PETIT-DUTAILLIS, C. 1970. *Les communes françaises. Caractères et évolution des origines au xviiiᵉ siècle*. 2nd edn.

PHILIPPEAU, P. 1936. Froissart et Jean le Bel. *Revue du Nord* 22: 81-111.

PICOCHE, J. 1976. *Le vocabulaire psychologique dans les Chroniques de Froissart*.

PINCHART, A. J. 1855. *Études sur l'histoire des arts au Moyen âge. La cour de Jeanne et de Wenceslas et les arts en Brabant pendant la seconde moitié du xivᵉ siècle*. Brussels.

PIRENNE, H. (ed.) 1902. *Chronique rimée des troubles de Flandre en 1379-1380*. Ghent.

————— 1908. *Histoire de Belgique, 2*. Brussels.

PLAINE, DOM F. 1871. De l'autorité de Froissard comme historien des guerres de Bretagne au xivᵉ siècle, 1341-1364. *Revue de Bretagne et de Vendée* IIIs. 4: 5-23, 119-36.

————— 1872. Charles de Blois, duc de Bretagne, et ses accusateurs anciens et modernes. *Revue des questions historiques* 11: 41-90.

————— 1875. La journée d'Auray. *Association Bretonne, 17ᵉ session tenue à Vannes 1874*: 85-100.

————— 1876. La journée de Roche Derrien. *Association Bretonne, 18ᵉ session tenue à Guingamp 1875*: 239-59.

PLAINE, DOM F. s.d. (c.1880). *Jeanne de Penthièvre, duchesse de Bretagne, et Jeanne de Flandre, comtesse de Montfort. Étude biographique et critique.* St-Brieuc.

———— 1885-6. La guerre de la succession de Bretagne (1341-1365) d'après des sources inédites. *Revue historique de l'Ouest* 1: 145-63, 299-323, 516-20; 2: 99-122.

———— (ed.) 1921. *Monuments du procès de canonisation du bienheureux Charles de Blois, duc de Bretagne, 1320-1364.* St-Brieuc.

PLAINE, J. 1900. Dom François Plaine, religieux de Silos (Espagne). *Revue de Bretagne, de Vendée et d'Anjou* VIs. 24: 81-9.

POCQUET DU HAUT-JUSSÉ, B. A. 1928a and b. *Les papes et les ducs de Bretagne.* 2 vols.

POIRON, D. 1971. *Littérature française, 2: Le Moyen âge (1300-1480).*

POPE, M. K. and E. C. LODGE (eds.) 1910. Chandos Herald, *Life of the Black Prince.* Oxford.

PREVENIER, W. 1959. Het Brugse Vrije en de Leden van Vlaanderen. *Handelingen van het genootschap voor geschiedenis* 96: 5-63.

———— 1961a. *De Leden en Staten van Vlaanderen (1384-1405).* Brussels.

———— 1961b. Realité et histoire: le quatrième membre de Flandre. *Revue du Nord* 113: 5-14.

———— 1973. Les perturbations dans les relations commerciales anglo-flamandes entre 1379 et 1407. Causes de désaccord et raisons d'une réconciliation. In: *Économies et sociétés au Moyen âge. Mélanges offerts à É. Perroy* 5: 477-97.

———— 1975. Bevolkingscijfers en professionele strukturen der bevolking van Gent en Brugge in de 14e eeuw. *Album Charles Verlinden*: 169-303. Ghent.

QUICKE, F. 1947. *Les Pays-bas à la veille de la période bourguignonne, 1356-1384.* Brussels.

PRINCE, A. E. 1931. The Strength of English Armies in the Reign of Edward III. *EHR* 46: 353-71.

PRINCET, M. 1916. Les usages héraldiques au xive siècle d'après les *Chroniques* de Froissart. *Annuaire-bulletin de la SHF*: 3-16.

PROU, M. 1888. *Étude sur les relations politiques du pape Urbain V avec les rois de France Jean II et Charles V (1362-1370).*

RADDING, C. M. 1972. The Estates of Normandy and the Revolts of the Towns at the Beginning of the Reign of Charles VI. *Speculum* 47: 79-90.

REY, M. 1965a. *Le domaine du roi et les finances extraordinaires sous Charles VI, 1388-1413.*

———— 1965b. *Les finances royales sous Charles VI: les causes du déficit, 1388-1413.*

RIGOLLOT, M. J. 1840. Mémoire sur le manuscrit de Froissart de la bibliothèque de la ville d'Amiens et en particulier sur le récit de la bataille de Crécy. *Mémoires de la société des Antiquaires de la Picardie* 3: 131-84.

RILEY, H. T. 1876. Thomas Walsingham, *Ypodigma Neustriae.* RS.

ROBILLARD DE BEAUREPAIRE, C. DE (ed.) 1870. Pierre Cochon, *Chronique normande, 1108-1430.* Rouen.

ROGGHÉ, P. 1941a and b. *Vlaanderen en het zevenjarig bewind van Jacob van Artevelde (1338-1345).* Brussels.

———— 1944. Het Gentsche stadsbestuur van 1302 tot 1345. En een en ander betreffende het Gentsche stadspatriciaat. *Handelingen der maatschappij van geschied- en oudheidkunde te Gent*, n.s. 1: 135-63.

———— 1950. De samenstelling der Gentsche schepenbanken in de 2e helft der 14e eeuw. En een en ander over de Gentsche poorterie. *Handelingen der maatschappij van geschied- en oudheidkunde te Gent* n.s. 4: 22-31.

ROGGHÉ, P. 1968. Gent in de xive en xve eeuw. De Gentse politiek en politici. Stad en vorst. Gentse koppigheid en fierheid. *Appeltjes van het Meetjesland* 19: 227-304.

ROMPAEY, J. VAN. 1967. *Het grafelijk baljuwsambt in Vlaanderen tijdens de Boergondische periode.* Brussels.

ROSELL, C. (ed.) 1953a and b. *Crónicas de los reyes de Castilla.* Biblioteca de autores españoles 66, 68. Madrid.

RUSSELL, P. E. 1941. *As fontes de Fernão Lopes.* Coimbra.

————— 1955. *English Intervention in Spain and Portugal in the Time of Edward III and Richard II.* Oxford.

RYMER, T. 1821. *Foedera, conventiones, literae (etc), II, ii.* RC.

SAENGER, P. 1975. A Lost MS of Froissart Refound: Newberry Library Manuscript f. 37. *Manuscripta* 19: 15-26.

SCHELER, A. J. U. (ed.) 1870-2. Jean Froissart, *Poésies.* 3 vols. Brussels.

SCOTT, SIR W. 1804-5. Johnes' Translation of Froissart. *Edinburgh Review* 5: 347-62.

SECOUSSE, D. F. *et al.* (eds.) 1723-1849. *Ordonnances des rois de France de la troisième race.* 23 vols.

SHEARS, F. S. 1930. *Froissart, Chronicler and Poet.*

SHERBORNE, J. W. 1964. Indentured Retinues and English Expeditions to France, 1369-1380. *EHR* 79: 718-46.

————— 1967. The English Navy: Shipping and Manpower, 1369-1389. *Past and Present* 37: 163-75.

————— 1977. The Cost of English Warfare in France in the Later Fourteenth Century. *BIHR* 50: 135-50.

SKALWEIT, G. 1898. *Der Kreuzzug des Bischofs Heinrich von Norwich im Jahre 1383.* Königsberg.

SMET, J. DE. 1947. De repressie te Brugge na de slag bij Westrozebeke. *Handelingen van het genootschap voor geschiedenis* 84: 71-118.

————— 1958. De verbeurdverklaringen in het Brugsche Vrije en in de smalle steden aldaar na de slag bij Westrozebeke (1382-1384). *Handelingen van het genootschap voor geschiedenis* 95: 115-36.

SMITH, R. M. 1915. *Froissart and the English Chronicle Play.* Columbia.

SPIEGEL, G. M. 1978. *The Chronicle Tradition of Saint-Denis: A Survey.* Leyden.

SPINOSI, C. 1961. Un règlement pacifique dans la succession de Jean III, duc de Bretagne, à la vicomté de Limoges. *Revue historique du droit français et étranger* IVs. 39: 453-67.

STONEHOUSE, J. H. (ed.) 1935. *Catalogue of the Library of Charles Dickens and William Thackeray.*

STOW, G. B. JNR. (ed.) 1977. *Historia vitae et regni Ricardi secundi.* Pennsylvania.

STOW, J. 1574. *A Summarie of the Chronicles of England.*

STRACHEY, J. *et al.* (eds.) 1767. *Rotuli parliamentorum.* 6 vols.

THIBAULT, M. 1903. *Isabeau de Bavière, reine de France. La jeunesse (1370-1405).*

THOMAS, N. M. 1948. *Froissart in England. A Bibliography of English Translations and Criticisms of the Work of Jean Froissart.* London University Diploma in Librarianship.

THOMPSON, E. M. (ed.) 1889a. Adam of Murimuth and Robert of Avesbury, *Chronica.* RS.

————— (ed.) 1889b. Geoffrey le Baker, *Chronicon.* Oxford.

THOMPSON, P. (ed.) 1966. *Contemporary Chronicles of the Hundred Years War.*

THORNE, C. 1979. Vietnam: Too Soon to Say? *The Listener* 101: 37-8.

193

TÓTH-UBBENS, M. 1964-5. Een dubbel vorstenhuwelijk in het jaar 1385. *Bijdragen voor de geschiedenis der Nederlanden* 19: 101-32.

TOUT, T. F. 1911. Firearms in England in the Fourteenth Century. *EHR* 26: 666-702.

————— 1928a and b. *Chapters in the Administrative History of Medieval England, 3, 4*. Manchester.

TOVEY, D. C. (ed.) 1912. *The Letters of Thomas Gray, 3*.

TUCHMAN, B. 1978. *A Distant Mirror: The Calamitous Fourteenth Century*. New York.

TUCK, A. 1973. *Richard II and the English Nobility*.

TUCOO-CHALA, P. 1960, (rp 1981). *Gaston Fébus et la vicomté de Béarn, 1343-1391*.

————— 1971. Une bande de routiers dans la région de Casteljaloux en 1381-1383. *Casteljaloux et la forêt aquitaine: 23e congrès de la Fédération historique du Sud-Ouest*: 8-37.

TYSON, D. B. (ed.) 1975. Chandos Herald, *La vie du Prince noir*. Tübingen.

UYTVEN, R. VAN and W. BLOCKMANS. 1969. Constitutions and their Application in the Netherlands during the Middle Ages. *Revue belge de philologie et d'histoire* 47: 399-424.

VALE, M. C. A. 1967. *War, Government and Politics in English Gascony, 1399-1453*. Oxford Ph.D.

————— 1970. *English Gascony, 1399-1453*. Oxford.

VALOIS, N. 1888. *Le Conseil du roi aux xive, xve et xvie siècles*.

————— 1896. *La France et le grand Schisme d'Occident, 1*.

VAUGHAN, R. 1973. *Charles the Bold: the Last Valois Duke of Burgundy*.

————— 1979. *Philip the Bold: the Formation of the Burgundian State*. 2nd edn.

VERBRUGGEN, J. F. 1977. *The Art of Warfare in Western Europe*. Amsterdam.

VERWIJS, E. 1869. *De oorlogen van hertog Albrecht van Beieren met de Friezen in de laatste jaren der xive eeuw*. Utrecht.

VESSEM, H. A. VAN. 1966. *De Engelse partij in het koninkrijk Frankrijk gedurende de honderdjarige oorlog*. Assen.

VIARD, J. 1905. La chronique de Jean le Bel et la Chronographia regum Francorum. *BEC* 66: 540-6.

————— (ed.) 1937. *Les Grandes chroniques de France, 9*. SHF.

————— and E. DÉPREZ (eds.) 1904, 1905. *Chronique de Jean le Bel*. 2 vols. SHF.

VUYLSTEKE, J. (ed.) 1893. *De rekeningen der stad Gent. Tijdvak van Philips van Artevelde, 1376-1389*. Ghent.

WEBB, J. (ed.) 1824. J. Creton, French Metrical History on the Deposition of Richard II. *Archaeologia* 20: 1-441.

WERVEKE, H. VAN. 1963. *Jacob van Artevelde*. The Hague.

————— 1968. De economische en sociale gevolgen van de muntpolitiek der graven van Vlaanderen (1337-1433). *Miscellania medievalia*: 243-54. Ghent.

WILLIAMS, B. (ed.) 1846. *Chronicque de la traison et mort de Richard II d'Engleterre*.

WRIGHT, T. (ed.) 1859. *Political Poems and Songs, 1*. RS.

WRONG, G. M. 1892. *The Crusade of 1383, Known as that of the Bishop of Norwich*.

WYNANT, L. 1972. Peiling naar de vermogenstruktuur te Gent op basis van de Staten van Goed, 1380-1389. *Standen en Landen* 57: 47-137.

ZUMTHOR, P. 1972. *Essai de poétique médiévale*.

NOTES ON CONTRIBUTORS

J. J. N. PALMER is senior lecturer in history at the University of Hull. His previous publications include a number of articles on fourteenth-century history, and his book *England, France and Christendom, 1377-99* was published in 1972.

PHILIPPE CONTAMINE is professor of history at the Université de Paris X - Nanterre, and has published a number of books on French society in the late Middle Ages, in particular *Guerre, état et société au Moyen Age* (1972) and *La guerre au Moyen Age* in the Nouvelle Clio series, 1980.

JOHN BELL HENNEMAN is professor of history at the University of Iowa, and held a Guggenheim Fellowship in 1976. His previous books include a two-volume study of French royal taxation from 1322 to 1370, and *The Medieval French Monarchy* (1973).

P. E. RUSSELL is former professor of Spanish studies in the University of Oxford. His book *The English Intervention in Spain and Portugal in the Time of Edward III and Richard II* is the standard work on Spain and the Hundred Years War up to 1400, and a Spanish translation is to appear shortly.

PIERRE TUCOO-CHALA is professor of history at the University of Pau, and has published widely on medieval Gascony and south-western France, including a biography of Gaston Phoebus, count of Foix.

RICHARD BARBER has written a number of books on the literature and history of the Middle Ages, including biographies of Henry II (1963) and Edward the Black Prince (1978), and the *The Knight and Chivalry* (1970), for which he was awarded a Somerset Maugham prize.

GEORGE T. DILLER is associate professor of French at the University of Florida and has edited the Rome manuscript of Froissart, besides publishing a number of articles on Froissart and on courtly romances.

JAN VAN HERWAARDEN is senior lecturer at the Erasmus University in Rotterdam. His previous books have been on pilgrimages during the Middle Ages.

MICHAEL JONES is lecturer in history at the University of Nottingham, and has published *Ducal Brittany 1364-1399* (1970) and a translation of Philippe de Commyre's *Memoirs* for Penguin Classics (1972).

JAMES SHERBORNE is reader in history at the University of Bristol and has published a number of important articles on the late fourteenth century, in particular on various aspects of the war between England and France.

INDEX

197

201